THE QUIET REVOLUTION

The Quiet Revolution

SOCIAL CHANGE IN
A SUSSEX VILLAGE 1871–1971

By

PETER AMBROSE

PUBLISHED FOR
SUSSEX UNIVERSITY PRESS
BY
CHATTO & WINDUS
1974

Ambrose, Peter J.

The quiet revolution

Published for
Sussex University Press
by
Chatto & Windus Ltd
42 William IV Street
London WC2N 4DF

*

Clarke, Irwin & Co. Ltd.
Toronto

ISBN 0 85621 034 X

Printed in Great Britain by
Richard Clay (The Chaucer Press) Ltd.
Bungay, Suffolk

For the Homeless

Contents

PART IV · REFLECTIONS

Illustrations

Acknowledgments

I should like to acknowledge my debt to the following (none of whom should be associated in any way with the book's shortcomings): to colleagues at the University of Sussex including John Dearlove, John Myerscough, Jenny Platt, Tom Bottomore, John Jacobs, John Farrant, Hal Summers and perhaps mostly to David Hitchin for his patient help with the statistical analyses; to Margaret Bacon, Margaret Burrows, Margaret Kroto, Edna McConnell and Kate Ripley for such careful and professional interviewing; to Chris Hadfield, Michael Clark, Michael Ambrose, Angela Snelgar and Val Packer for acting as research assistants; to Judith Brent and her colleagues at the East Sussex County Record Office for much fetching and carrying; to Audrey Harvey, Viv Walters and Eric Woods of *Shelter* for giving information concerning the housing situation; to the University of Sussex, R. Green (Brighton) Ltd., The Frederick Soddy Trust, the International Geographical Congress Fund of the Royal Society, Wates, and Clifford Dann and Partners for collectively providing the funds; to various employers and club officials in the village for providing information; to other people in the village including Michael Rice, the doctor, the Rev. Philip Hayllar, the vicar, Derek Denyer, the Primary School headmaster, Mr. King of R.B.W. Construction Ltd., Viv Stamp, the District Nurse, Miss Parker, the Health Visitor, John Payne and Bob Peters; to Michael Parker, Derek Mumford and Peter Yates of the East Sussex County Planning Department, and to Roy Borley of the county's Social Services Department; to Mr. P. Kent, the Chailey Rural District Housing Manager; to Mrs. Havord of the Census Office, Somerset House; to people who talked to me about the village between the wars, including Mr. A. J. Miller, Mr. C. E. Carey, the Misses Paris, Miss W. Martin, Mr. G. Self, Mr. M. Fenner, Mrs. K. M. Rice, Mr. F. Russell, Mr. and Mrs. B. Robson, Mrs. E. Courage, Mrs. A. Clarke, Mr. and Mrs. C. Tritton, Mr. R. Elphick, Mr. N. Pitts, Mr. G. Kent, Mr. H. Turner and Mrs. D. Woods; to Do Hamer, Val Hennessy and Beryl Pollard who somehow deciphered my handwriting and typed the manuscript; to Jean and Chris Mulvey for friendship and proof-reading; to Bob Colenutt who sees the world more clearly than most of us; and to Liz for helping in all sorts of ways and putting up with it all.

Preface

Somebody once said that the various social sciences, as they carried out their study of man, were like groups of people in a darkened room with an elephant. Each group could feel very interesting components but nobody could quite visualise how they fitted together. This book has an unusual, some would say foolhardy, aim. It tries to describe the elephant, in this case man's changing situation in a Sussex village over the past century, not from any particular disciplinary viewpoint but using ideas and evidence from a number of disciplines. It tries to depict the reality not in any particular way but just to depict it. To do this it has to use certain key social science concepts (like 'status' and 'power') in a lay, rather than a professional, sense. Clearly anyone who does this may be labelled a charlatan but at least he can steer clear of the charge of myopia.

The book is also unusual in that it obstinately refuses to use the word 'class'. The reasons are set out in the final chapter (the second argument) but, briefly, it contends that society is less easily categorisable than most people would have us believe and that individuals vary in infinitely complex ways. The usual attempt to order them into a limited number of categories is analytically imprecise, socially divisive, and has outlived its political usefulness.

Every attempt has been made to use simple language and avoid 'academic' jargon but there will no doubt be occasional lapses. We are all creatures of habit. Some parts of Chapters 8 and 12 may look a little technical for the general reader but one does not have to understand what finer statistical points there are in these chapters to appreciate their main findings. And the network ideas in Chapter 12 can actually be fun.

As for readership, I hope the book may be useful in various social science, planning and history courses in a variety of educational contexts; colleges, polytechnics, universities (including the Open University) and adult education classes. One other sort of reader has been kept in mind; the growing number of people who live in rapidly expanding villages and towns around big cities. Possibly they may find in it something of relevance to their own style of life as they journey daily on the 8.19 a.m. to work or, for the other half of the population, as they contemplate the social opportunities and domestic chores of a more home-centred day.

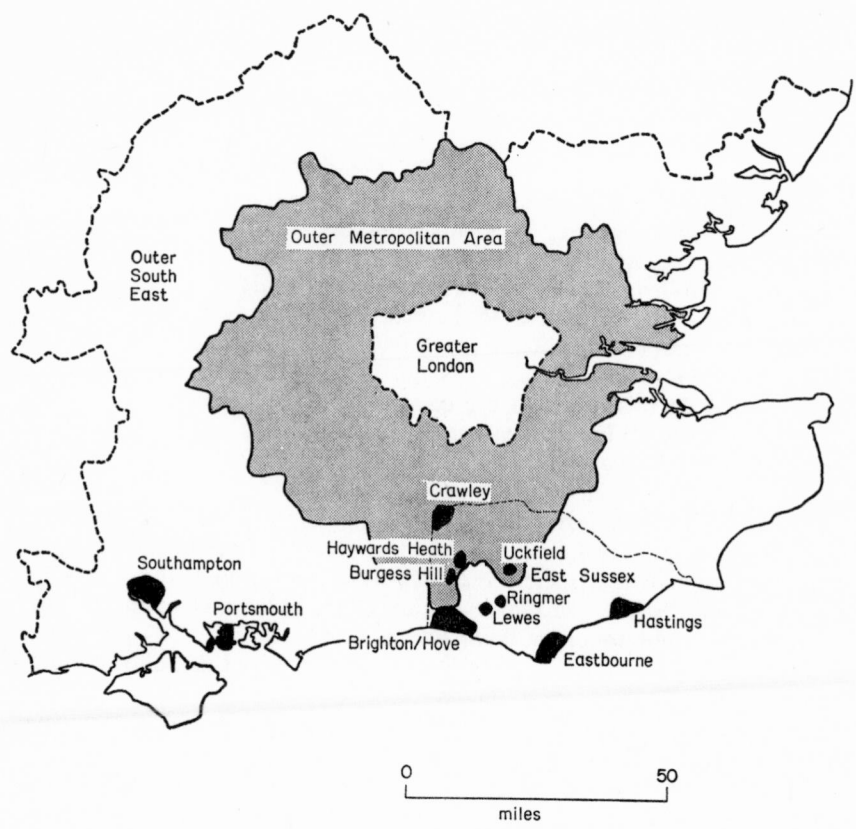

Map 1. The South-East Region.

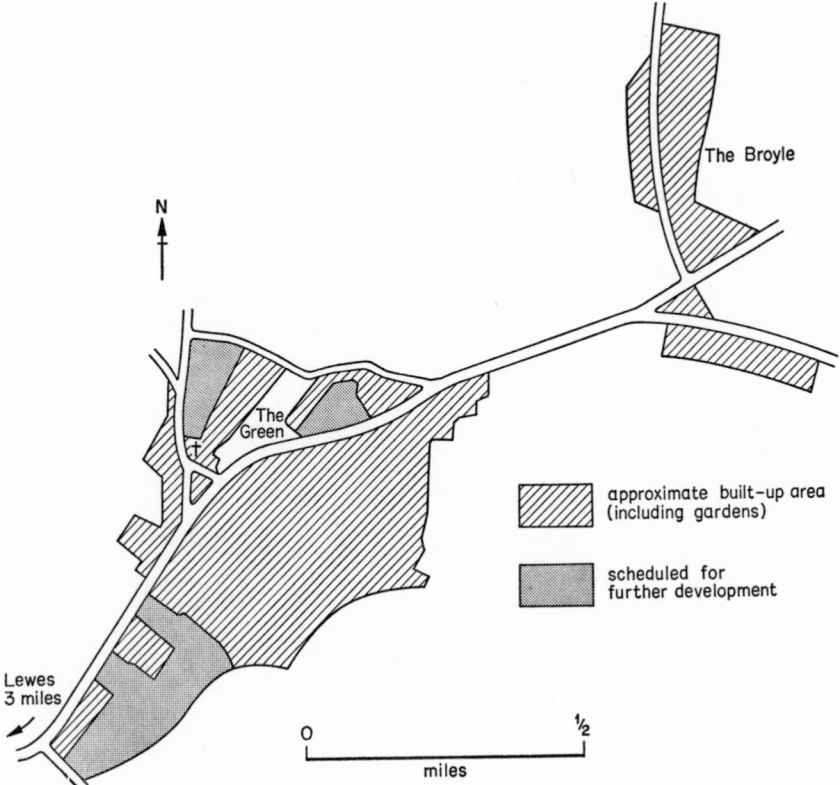

N

The Broyle

The
Green

approximate built-up area
(including gardens)

scheduled for
further development

Lewes
3 miles

0   ½

miles

Map 2. Ringmer 1972.

Prologue · The Problem Defined

To the casual passer-by, or at least to such as are familiar with English villages, Ringmer presents an unexceptional sight. A cheerful confusion of houses straggles for nearly a mile along the main road; a gracious Queen Anne house co-exists with recent pretentious neo-Georgian; red-brick Edwardian 'semis' face a small modern terrace development; well-proportioned grey-white Victorian villas lie opposite a post-war council development. Near by, with striking incongruity, stands a large roadhouse hotel which offers a cabaret featuring, from time to time, rising television 'personalities' and setting music-hall stars. Its neon sign is, at the time of writing, the only illumination visible after dark in the village. Its sounds of expense-account entertaining can be heard for a fair way downwind and certainly drown the baying of the Southdown Hunt hounds from the kennels at the eastern end of the village. Recently the 'disco' and 'group' operations in the Village Hall have managed to make more noise than anybody. Thus is symbolised, in the volume of sounds that fall upon the night air, the changing order of things.

Midway along the straggle, and sloping gently up to the Parish Church, lies the village green, with a war memorial for the past at one end, and swings and roundabouts for the future at the other. The village pump, now made obsolete by technological advance, stands nearly opposite *The Anchor* where, by contrast, business flourishes. A few miles to the south, a lovely backcloth to the green, lie the gentle curves of the Downs providing, in their light soils and water-storing capacity, one explanation for the antiquity of settlement in the locality. The green provides the setting for cricket matches which, due to the shortness of the boundary, are enlivened by a proportion of fours and sixes unusual even for village cricket. It has also been the setting for stoolball, a game older than cricket, largely confined to Sussex, and played nowadays mostly by ladies. In all, taking the visual evidence provided by the main road, Ringmer appears to be a village where change is occurring at a supportable rate and where, in terms both of architectural fabric and recreational pursuits, the recent and the distant past are still very much alive and co-exist comfortably with the present.

Looking down on the village from the crest of the Downs, however, a rather different situation is suggested. Large areas of new reddish-brown roofs fan out from the focal point of a three-storeyed shopping parade. The new sports field, home of the celebrated football team, rivals in area the old village green. Newly extended schools constitute the largest buildings in the landscape, and builders' huts and newly excavated earth corroborate the impression of newness and rawness in much of the residential development. Setting aside the surrounding fields and woods, one might well be looking at a suburban estate.

This spread of development, visually alien to the earlier core of the village,

1

is the physical embodiment of the population growth history shown in Figure P.1. The modern phase of rapid growth dates from the early 1960s. In the century from 1861 to 1961 the parish population (the large majority of whom live in the village) grew from 1522 to 2208, an increase of 686.[1] In the succeeding decade to 1971 the increase was of the order of 1500, over twice the growth

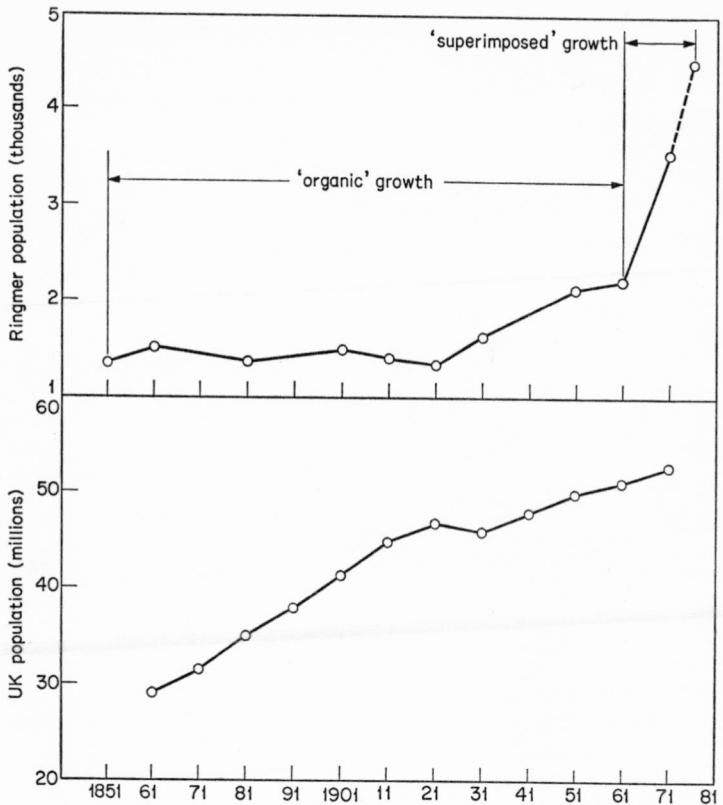

Fig. P.1. Population Growth, Ringmer and U.K., 1851–1976.
Source: various census publications.

of the previous 100 years. And by the mid-1970s it is likely that the parish population will be around 4500 or more,[2] an increase of well over 100% on the 1961 figure. This growth history seems to fall into two clearly defined phases. The first phase is that of slow, steady 'organic' growth. It extends from the mid-Victorian period until well after the 1939–45 war. It is a period when the level of the parish population was a reflection of the capacity of the immediate area to provide a livelihood, whether in agriculture, village crafts, building or such local manufacturing as existed. This situation, the organic, symbiotic relationship between man and land in a small defined area, has been best characterised by Hardy writing of 'Casterbridge', unlike Ringmer a small market town, in the 1840s:[3]

> Thus Casterbridge was in most respects but the pole, focus or nerve-knot of the surrounding country life; differing from the many manufacturing towns which are as foreign bodies set down, like boulders on a plain, in a green world with which they have nothing in common. Casterbridge lived by agriculture at one remove further from the fountain-head than the adjoining villages–no more. The townsfolk understood every fluctuation in the rustic's condition, for it affected their receipts as much as the labourer's; they entered into the troubles and joys which moved the aristocratic families ten miles round–for the same reason. And even at the dinner parties of the professional families the subjects of discussion were corn, cattle-disease, sowing and reaping, fencing and planting; while politics were viewed by them less from their own stand-point of burgesses with rights and privileges than from the standpoint of their county neighbours.

As a settlement one remove closer to the 'fountain-head' mid-nineteenth-century Ringmer no doubt possessed in large measure that intimate functional relationship with the soil and its products and, within the generally accepted status structure, enjoyed the sense of social and economic communality which Hardy describes.

The growth since the early 1960s has differed not just in degree but in kind; not just in its explosive quantity but in its essential quality. It has been conditioned not by the capacity of the soil within the parish to produce wealth but by the growth in employment, nearly all of it totally unconnected with agriculture, in the south-east of England generally and in the area within a 15-mile radius specifically.[4] It derives from fundamental changes that have taken place nationally both in technology and in the social, economic and political organisation of society. And it is conditioned, as it never was in the past, by a complex structure of controls and stimuli exerted on the process of land development by public and private agencies working at district, county or national level.[5] For this reason, because the impetus for change is not generated within the parish but exists as part of a consciously worked-out scheme of events at a broader level, the term 'superimposed growth' has been given to the phase of development in the village since 1961.

How has village life changed over the last 100 years? In what ways has the local social, economic and political organisation been modified by developments at the national scale and by the influx of people into the area in the last decade? To what extent are these 'dormitory' villages, made possible by modern transport technology, the contemporary equivalent of Hardy's manufacturing towns; '. . . foreign bodies set down, like boulders on a plain, in a green world with which they have nothing in common'? What relationships develop between long-standing residents, directly or indirectly involved in agriculture and the social hierarchy that goes with it, and newly arrived ex-urban families whose means of livelihood and social perspectives are quite different? Do the latter, as a result of coming to live in the country, acquire any of the interests or attitudes of the former? As a newcomer of seven years standing I have to confess that no dinner party I have yet attended in the village has discussed '. . . corn, cattle-disease, sowing and reaping, fencing and planting . . .'. And finally, from the point of view of planning policy, how well is the growth being managed, how do people feel about it, and is the rate at which it is occurring compatible with the preservation of 'village community feeling', if so elusive a quality can be sufficiently clearly defined?

This book seeks to examine these, and a large number of related, questions. It attempts to analyse the social, economic and political evolution of a village, not simply to observe the changing way of life in this particular village but also because Ringmer can serve as a case study to exemplify, document and bring alive trends which, inevitably, are normally stated at a more generalised level. The extent to which this specific village represents the national experience, and therefore the extent to which one can generalise from the results is, of course, a matter for further research and discussion. Whether or not it turns out to be a good subject for a case study will be largely a matter of luck, for it was chosen for no more valid a reason than that the author happened to be living in it when he became interested in these questions.

The organisation of the book flows naturally from what has been said about its aims, and about the growth history of the village. In a work that sets out to be a case study, the relevant general trends in the organisation of society must be set out. Ringmer, in both its 'organic' and 'superimposed' phases of growth formed part of a nation, and a world, which underwent unprecedented change in almost all respects in the period 1871–1971. It follows that any analysis and explanation of the evolution of the village during the 100-year period must be couched in the context of concomitant changes in the organisation of British society generally. Chapter 1 consists of a brief sketch of a century of change in Britain. The sketch is highly selective and concentrates solely on those social and technological aspects that are directly, although not exclusively, relevant to the evolution of small rural communities. It sets out trends which can be exemplified at the local level and which, in a very real way, have constrained and influenced local change. In short, it specifies the conditions that were necessary, but not sufficient, to account for the observed changes in Ringmer from 1871 to 1971. In addition, the review provides some sort of 'data bank' to which reference will frequently be made during the course of the work when discussing the relationship between a local and a national trend. Finally, and in self-defence, it must be confessed that Chapter 1 is a short essay in social and economic history written by a layman for laymen. Professionals in that field may, following a cursory glance, feel that it is a chapter they need not spend time on.

Parts II and III of the book (Chapters 2–10) focus down upon the subject village. Part II (Chapters 2–5) deals with changes in population structure, employment and the economy, property ownership, local government and social administration, social structure and activities, and domestic economy over the 100-year period. The analysis in each case is not chronologically continuous but concentrates on three brief periods, 1865/75, 1925/35 and the present. The data for the mid-Victorian period is derived primarily from documentary sources, for example the 1871 Census, parish records, school, church and estate records, and other contemporary sources. The analysis of life between the two world wars is built upon similar sources plus the invaluable addition of anecdotal and other evidence from living memory. A large number of present residents lived through this period in the village and contact has been made with as many of them as possible. Data for the present day have been derived from published documents plus surveys carried out for this specific purpose.

Because of the superimposed nature of the change during the last decade (1961–71) this period has been subjected to an intensive study which forms Part III of the book. This deals with the planning context in which growth is occurring (see map 1 on page xiv), the socio-economic structure of the incoming population, the processes by which they join in the life of the village, the degree to which they enjoy village life and a variety of similar topics. The evidence presented was derived from a sample survey of over 150 households in the village. The survey was carried out by professional interviewers and achieved a response rate of about 86%. In addition, various subsidiary surveys were conducted on such topics as the number of jobs available in the village and the play and friendship patterns of village children.

In Part IV of the book, Chapters 11 and 12 examine the relationship of the Ringmer data to concepts of local social systems and networks. In relation to the latter it also seeks to explore the possible relationships between village design and social interaction. Chapter 13 presents a set of reasoned criticisms of the developments of the last decade and questions the basis upon which they have been carried out, and Chapter 14 goes on to offer a critique of the housing system generally. The book concludes with a brief Epilogue which aims to justify the title.

PART ONE

THE NATIONAL CONTEXT

1 · A Selective Review of Trends 1871-1971

CHANGES IN THE STRUCTURE OF THE LABOUR FORCE

Table 1.1 shows the distribution of the labour force between the primary, secondary and tertiary sectors for the 100-year period. Definitional problems always arise in analyses of this type, especially when a long historical series is involved. But the broad trends are obvious enough. The labour force doubled over the period, but the number engaged in agriculture fell from 1·8 million (15·2% of the total) to 0·8 million (3·5%). This shift is clearly fundamental to any analysis of change in a rural community. The manufacturing sector grew considerably in absolute terms. However, there are now signs of contraction and it occupies a declining percentage of the total. The tertiary sector, broadly defined as those occupations dealing with clerical, professional and service tasks, increased by well over 400%. The section of society that sells, writes, teaches, administers or offers some kind of service now outnumbers the section that is involved in actually producing artifacts. The impact of developing technology on the manufacturing process has been to increase the productivity of labour. Its impact on the tertiary sector seems to have been to produce more and more pieces of paper to record, store or transmit information. This is because many formerly simple operations, for example paying over a sum of money for a product, now involve fairly elaborate apparatus such as computers and credit cards.

The developments in employment trends for women are shown in Table 1.2. These reflect certain fundamental changes in the role of women in society. In 1871, 1·7 million women were employed in domestic and personal service and 1·3 million in the textile and clothing industries. Taken together this represents over 84% of the female labour force. The textile and clothing industries show a decline to 0·6 million workers in 1966, while domestic and personal service, which reached a maximum for women in 1911, has declined dramatically since as a source of employment. Because of the reclassifications in 1931 and 1961, the decline in domestic and personal service can best be seen from Table 1.3. Certain other groups show very large increases. 'Commercial occupations' show a remarkable rise from 5000 to over 2 million workers, while the number of women involved in the professions has risen from 152,000 to 887,000. Women have thus not simply gained a more important proportional role in the national economy (the total of women employed rose faster in percentage terms than the total of men), they have also achieved a very significant expansion in the range of work carried out. Whereas 100

7

Table 1.1 Sectoral Employment Trends in Great Britain, 1871–1966 (000s)

	1871	1881	1891	1901	1911	1921	1931	1951	1961	1966
Primary										
Agriculture, horticulture, forestry and fishing	1,817	1,694	1,556	1,457	1,549	1,481	1,393	1,245	950	844
Mining, etc.	528	612	758	937	1,210	1,249	1,087	677	505	358
Secondary										
Manufacturing	6,813	7,493	8,667	9,975	10,931	11,597	10,981	12,288	11,140	11,050
Tertiary										
Services	2,594	2,932	3,518	3,911	4,596	5,027	7,594	8,400	10,415	11,666
TOTAL	11,752	12,731	14,499	16,280	18,286	19,354	21,055	22,610	23,010	23,918

Source: *British Labour Statistics Historical Abstract 1886–1968*, H.M.S.O., 1971, Tables 102 and 103

Table 1.2 Employment Structure for Women, Great Britain (Selected Occupations), 1871–1966 (000s)

	1871	1881	1891	1901	1911	1921	1931	1951	1961	1966
Commercial occupations	5	11	26	76	157	587	1,349	2,265	1,945	2,246
Professional occupations	152	203	264	326	383	441	443	588	775	887
Domestic/personal service*	1,678	1,756	2,036	2,003	2,127	1,845	2,129	1,610	1,635	2,068
Textiles manuf.	726	745	795	795	870	701⎱	1,207	887	288	236
Clothing manuf.	594	667	759	792	825	602⎰			382	373
Total occupied	3,570	3,887	4,489	4,732	5,356	5,684	6,265	6,961	7,578	8,582
Total unoccupied	6,535	7,567	8,572	10,247	11,432	11,983	12,055	13,084		

Source: *British Labour Statistics. Historical Abstract, 1886–1968*, H.M.S.O., 1971, Tables 102 and 103

* Largely personal service up to 1931; includes service, sport and recreation workers from 1961

years ago it was the accepted norm for a young girl to go into service there now exists a very wide range of occupational choice. These developments are, of course, intimately bound up with developments in education which will be reviewed later.

Table 1.3 Percentage of population engaged in 'Domestic and Personal Service'

1871	15.3	1911	13.9
1881	15·4	1921	6·9
1891	15·8	1931	7·7
1901	14·1	1951	2·2

Source: P. Deane and W. A. Cole, *British Economic Growth 1866–1959*, Cambridge U.P., 1962, Table 50

CHANGES IN WAGE RATES AND THE GROWTH OF LEISURE TIME

The century was a period of improvement in the monetary and real wages of the great majority of the British people.[1] Although in the 1860s it seems clear that Britain had the highest *per capita* income figure in the world (followed by France and Germany),[2] it was equally true that the majority of people received wages which, in real terms, would be regarded as very low by modern standards. Table 1.4 gives some outline details of wage rates and hours

Table 1.4 Wage Rates and Hours of Work

	Engineering (London)		Agriculture (England and Wales)	
	Weekly Wages	*Hours*	*Weekly Wages*	*Hours*
1871	36s.	58½	12s. 1d.	n.k.
1900	38s.	54	14s. 10d.	n.k.
1930	62s. 11d.	47	31s. 8d.	50½
1950	111s. 7d.	44	94s.	47
1968	257s. 8d.	40	225s. 10d.	44

Source: *British Labour Statistics Historical Abstract 1886–1968*, D.E.P. H.M.S.O., 1971, Tables 1 and 7

of work in 'engineering' (manual industrial work) and agriculture. Wages in the early stages of a banking career seem to have been similar to those in engineering, since Best quotes an estimate that, at about 1870, junior bank clerks of age 18–20 were earning £70–£80 per year.[3]

Concomitant with the growth in real incomes has been a growth in the availability of leisure time.[4] In mid-Victorian Britain the concept of an annual holiday with pay, or of a week at the seaside, was virtually unheard of. Works outings and Sunday School treats provided the main means of release from the grind of work for the vast majority of the people. The Bank Holiday Acts of 1871 and 1875, which provided for four days of statutory holiday per year, were the first signs of a trend towards mass holidays. Holidays with pay, unknown for manual workers until the 1880s, began to be granted by more enlightened employers. People in clerical occupations had, of course, begun to take holidays away from home before the 1880s. In fact in 1878 Thomas Cook, first in a long and continuing line of entrepreneurs who have made a large business out of the reduction of working hours, took 75,000 people to the Paris International Exhibition.[5] Nevertheless, Best estimates that in mid-Victorian Britain virtually no family with children and with an income below £100 ever went for more than a day's excursion to the seaside. This threshold figure would obviously exclude not just those involved in manual work in industry and agriculture (see Table 1.4) but also many in junior clerical positions. The difference between the situation 100 years ago and the current, virtually universal, two- or three-week holidays with pay and mass travel to the Costa Brava, is too evident to require comment.

One other change of great significance has been the gradual shift from a six-day to a five-day week. The textile industry worked a 60-hour, six-day week prior to 1874. At this date it was reduced to a $56\frac{1}{2}$-hour week; 10 hours daily from Monday to Friday and $6\frac{1}{2}$ hours on Saturday.[6] This immediately made it possible for workers to participate in a much wider range of spare-time pursuits, for example to play football. The Football Association had already been formed but it administered a game which tended to be played by those of higher status. The F.A. Cup was still won, throughout the 1870s, by ' "gentlemen's clubs" of the home counties and the soccer playing "public schools" '.[7] As the Saturday half-holiday became more widespread, soccer players began to come from a much wider spectrum of society. The change was symbolised in 1883 when Blackburn Olympic beat Old Etonians in the Cup Final. Again the contrast with the present day is striking. Old Etonians now have probably less chance than Ringmer F.C. of winning the F.A. Cup.

Despite the various legislative and other arrangements to increase the amount of leisure for the majority of people, it is as well to remember that various sections of society were, and to some extent remain, inadequately protected. Shopworkers, domestic servants, casual workers and self-employed workers all tended to make do with rather less leisure time than those in highly organised and highly unionised occupations. It is therefore clear that the trend towards an increase in the aggregate amount of leisure time is not yet fully run, and already there is serious discussion in many quarters about the possibility of a four-day week.

CHANGES IN THE EDUCATIONAL SYSTEM

The century has been a period of remarkable educational advance. The number and percentage of those receiving full-time education rose rapidly as did the average age of leaving school.[8] Before 1870 no national system of education existed. A relatively small number of public and grammar schools, heavily emphasising 'classical studies', catered for the children of better-off parents while smaller schools were operated by the various educational societies. Forster's Act in 1870 introduced the concept of free universal elementary education. The Act may fairly be viewed in retrospect partly as an act of charity to the lower classes and partly as a means of maintaining Britain's power in the world. The latter idea was explicitly present in Forster's speech as he introduced the Act:[9]

> Upon the speedy provision of elementary education depends our national prosperity . . . if we leave our workfolk any longer unskilled, notwithstanding their strong sinews and determined energy, they will become overmatched in the competition of the world. Upon this speedy provision of education depends our national power.

So naked a statement of the aims of mass education would, hopefully, be beyond any modern Minister of Education, although there seems to be a recent echo of this thinking in the expansion of spending on education in the U.S.A. during the 1960s following the early Russian sputnik launches.

The Education Act of 1902 produced changes in the pattern and philosophy of education above the elementary level. It has been pointed out[10] that the Act was the first overt recognition that 'secondary' education was a fitting object for public expenditure. It followed that it should therefore be more widely available and that it should lead logically on from the education provided in the elementary schools.[11] The 1944 and 1945 Acts provided the next big advance in that free secondary education now became available to all children up to the age of 15. It was believed that three main types of need existed in secondary education and that these should be served by technical, secondary modern and grammar schools respectively. This view, advanced by the Norwood Report of 1943,[12] and the tripartite division which it entailed, has subsequently been challenged by proponents of comprehensive education who do not deny that children have varying propensities and interests but feel that this does not automatically mean they must be passed through different sorts of schools.

Table 1.5 Percentage of People of Various Ages Receiving
Full-Time Education in Great Britain

Age	1870	1902	1938	1962
10	40	100	100	100
14	2	9	38	100
17	1	2	4	15
19	1	1	2	7

Source: *Committee on Higher Education*, H.M.S.O., 1963, Chapter III, Table 1

This bare recital of the evolution of legislation concerning education needs to be complemented with both data and comment. Table 1.5 shows the percentage of children of various ages who were receiving full-time education in Great Britain at various dates between 1870 and 1962. Before the 1871 Act, only 40% were receiving even elementary schooling up to the age of 10. The remaining 60% received rudimentary education, if any at all. By 1962 all children were receiving secondary education up to the age of 15. The aims of the national educational system, as set out by various high-level authorities, have moved strongly away from those incorporated in Forster's quoted statement. Education has come to be seen less as an instrument of national policy and as a means of maintaining a competitive position in the world, and more as a means of allowing each individual to develop to his fullest intellectual potential. This latter view had a pioneer in Fitch, who was a proponent of 'liberal' education which would seek 'to train the man, and not merely the good tradesman or doctor or mechanic'.[13] Nunn in 1922, called for educational efforts which would secure for everyone 'conditions under which individuality is most completely developed'.[14] Similar statements concerning educational aims have multiplied down to the present day, although some may feel that certain aspects of the present system (school uniforms, compulsory games, disciplined classrooms and, in some cases, cadet corps) tend to militate against these aims.

Developments in the university sector have been equally far-reaching. It has been estimated that in 1900–1 there were approximately 20,000 full-time university students, nearly all, no doubt, drawn from richer families. The growth history since 1922–3 is shown in Table 1.6 from which it is clear that

Table 1.6 Number of University Students (Full- and Part-Time) in Great Britain

	Total	Women		Total	Women
1900–1	20,000	n.a.	1954–5	98,000	23,000
1922–3	59,000	16,000	1957–8	112,000	26,000
1930–1	62,000	16,000	1960–1	126,000	29,000
1936–7	62,000	14,000	1964–5	157,000	41,000
1950–1	102,000	23,000	1967–8	218,000	58,000

Source: Committee on Higher Education, *Higher Education*, H.M.S.O., 1963, Appendix 1, Annex EE

the most striking growth has been in the past decade.[15] While a disproportionately high proportion of students still come from the public schools (13·5% in 1969)[16] much progress has been made in widening the social base from which students are drawn. The admissions policies of most universities, the grants system and the increasing numbers from all types of backgrounds working on the A-level syllabus have all been contributory factors in the achievement of this broadening of the university population. Since this is the population from which most of the senior decision makers in government and industry are drawn, the change is gradually having the effect of replacing an aristocratic with a meritocratic élite in the social and economic management of the nation. Developments have been particularly striking in relation to the university education of women. In *Princess Ida* W. S. Gilbert commented 'A women's college! Maddest folly going'; in 1967–8, 58,000 of the 218,000 full-time university students in Britain were women and the proportion appears to be rising.

CHANGES IN THE ELECTORATE AND PARLIAMENTARY REPRESENTATION

Concomitant with the increase in the availability of education, and the increase in literacy which this has brought about, there has been an enormous increase in the electorate over the period.[17] The size of the electorate, and the percentage this represents of total population, is shown in Table 1.7. Even

Table 1.7 The British Electorate, 1900–65

	Electorate	Percentage of adult population
1900	6,731,000	27
1910	7,695,000	28
1919	21,756,000	78
1929	28,851,000	90
1939	32,404,000	97
1949	34,270,000	98
1965	36,128,000	98

Source: D. Butler and J. Freeman, *British Political Facts, 1900–1967*, Macmillan, 1968

after the 1884 Act, which nearly doubled the electorate, only about a quarter of the adult population was eligible to vote. By the eve of the second world war, virtually universal adult suffrage had been achieved while right at the end of the period the redefinition of 'adult' to mean people over 18 enfranchised the 18- to 21-year-olds.

Simultaneously the trades union movement grew as shown in Table 1.8. Whereas at the end of the nineteenth century something like 1 in 7 occupied males belonged to a trade union the figure is now approaching 1 in 2. Closely

Table 1.8 Trades Union Membership in the United Kingdom

1896	1,608,000
1906	2,210,000
1920	3,348,000
1930	4,842,000
1941	7,165,000
1951	9,531,000
1961	9,883,000

Source: D. C. Marsh, *The Changing Social Structure of England, Wales, 1871–1961*, Routledge, revised edn. 1965

connected with this growth, and benefiting from the sponsorship it provided, the Labour Party representation in terms of seats in the House of Commons rose from 29 seats in 1906 to a high of 394 in 1945, and a total of just under 300 now.[18] Over the same period the Liberal Party declined from 401 seats in Parliament to a representation that would fill one taxi, or occasionally two.

CHANGES IN THE DISSEMINATION OF INFORMATION

One of the most striking social changes of the century has been the enormous increase in the effectiveness with which 'news', however defined,[19] can be disseminated. The chief means of transmitting information are television, radio, newspapers, periodicals and books. The past 100 years has seen the invention of two of these and an enormous increase in the circulation of the other three.

In 1871, of our current daily and Sunday newspapers, *The Times* (founded in 1785), the *Observer* (1791), the *News of the World* (1843) and the *Daily Telegraph* (1855) were already well established. Various other dailies and weeklies, now non-existent, were also flourishing. By 1850 Williams estimates that total daily circulation was 60,000 and total Sunday circulation 275,000.[20] These figures exclude the range of literary and sporting weeklies and 'penny dreadfuls'. Mid-Victorian readership of 'serious' dailies was severely limited to the more wealthy groups in society, since the price was at least 4d. per copy. Sunday papers were, however, more widely read, especially since they were frequently taken by coffee houses and other establishments where many non-purchasers could read them.

By 1871 the *Daily Telegraph* had reached a daily circulation of over 200,000 and was, surprisingly to modern readers, leading in the race to achieve circulation among a new, less affluent, reading public. But the move towards really cheap daily newspapers and mass circulation among the newly literate sections of society occurred in the last few years of the nineteenth century, with the founding of Lord Northcliffe's *Daily Mail* (1896). Using new types of presses and a system of financing based heavily on revenue from advertisements, the paper achieved by 1900 a circulation of nearly one million. In the

Table 1.9 Daily Newspaper Circulation, 1850–1957

1850	60,000
1871	500,000 ⎫ Estimates
1900	1,500,000 ⎭
1920	5,430,000
1930	8,567,000
1937	9,903,000
1947	15,449,000
1957	17,000,000

Source: R. Williams, *The Long Revolution*, Chatto & Windus, 1961

circumstances the insult that it was 'a paper written by office boys for office boys' could be lived with. The *Morning Herald* (later the *Daily Express*) was founded in 1900 and the *Daily Mirror* in 1903. The era of mass circulation and readership had arrived. Table 1.9 shows the evolution of total national daily newspaper circulation. By about 1960 there were 609 copies of daily newspapers for every 1000 people in Britain. This is the highest penetration figure in the world and, in Williams' view, the current circulation figures must be near the maximum possible. Allowing a readership of three people per copy, 88% of the adult population read a daily paper and 93% a Sunday paper.

The increase in book publication has been less striking than that of the popular press but is nevertheless significant. The annual publication of new titles rose as shown in Table 1.10.

Table 1.10 Number of New Titles Published, 1850s to 1971

1850s	c. 2,600	
1901	6,044	
1913	12,379	
1924	12,690	(including 3,190 reprints)
1937	17,137	(including 6,347 reprints)
1950	17,072	(including 5,334 reprints)
1958	22,143	(including 5,971 reprints)
1964	26,154	(including 5,260 reprints)
1970	33,489	(including 9,977 reprints)

Source: R. Williams, *The Long Revolution*, Chatto & Windus, 1961, and *The Bookseller*, January 2nd, 1971

Taking the issues from public libraries into account (currently over 460 million annually) it is estimated that the book readership is something like 15 books per person per year.

While the growth in reading since 1871 may have represented an unprecedented expansion in the use of an old-established form of communication, the growth in information diffusion by means of radio and television

Table 1.11 Percentage of homes in the United Kingdom with a Television

1947	0.2	1956	49.4
1948	0·7	1957	58·4
1949	1·8	1958	65·0
1950	4·3	1959	74·4
1951	8·7	1960	81·8
1952	14·0	1961	84·2
1953	21·8	1962	87·4
1954	30·6	1963	88·8
1955	39·8	1964	90·8

Source: W. A. Belson, *The Impact of Television*, Crosby Lockwood, 1967, Chapter 20, Table 1

probably transcends it in a number of ways, particularly in its impact on social behaviour and in its vulnerability to commercial pressures. Table 1.11 shows the rise in the percentage of homes in the United Kingdom which have a television. In fewer than 20 years the medium has changed from one which reached a tiny proportion of affluent homes to one which has achieved virtually complete coverage. It took newspapers well over 100 years to achieve as much.

Apart from television's obvious significance in the simultaneous diffusion of information about events over the whole nation, it has had a number of other far-reaching consequences. Belson[21] has reviewed some of the hypotheses, tested and untested, concerning the effect of television on social life. There appear to have been effects on book loans from libraries, on the trade of seaside holiday resorts, on cinema attendances (admissions have fallen from 1,365,000 in 1951 to 237,000 in 1968),[22] on the sale of draught beer (but with positive effects for the sale of bottled beer) and on attendances at adult education classes. A study carried out in Greater London demonstrates that, in that area, television tends to have an adverse effect on the pursuit of leisure activities such as reading, card playing and attending theatre and ballet. There also seems little doubt that the provision of 'fireside entertainment' leads in many cases to the nuclear family spending more time as a unit and the television has been seen by Fletcher[23] and others as a device that strengthens family life.

CHANGES IN LOCATIONAL MOBILITY

The advancements in technology which have enabled us to transmit information quickly and on a large scale have been matched by those which have enormously facilitated the movement of people. The ability of almost everyone to buy movement, either in public or private transport, has fundamentally affected the spatial distribution of jobs, and of people in relation to them. It has also brought about new forms of social relationships in types of settlement not previously known, for example in 'dormitory' suburbs and villages. Each advance in the battle to overcome distance and to reduce its frictional effect, results in extensions in the patterns of journeys to work, to shop, to recreate and to visit. The 'action space' of almost everybody, that area which we know well because our activities regularly cause us to traverse it, has enlarged enormously since 1871. The impact of these developments on 'community feeling' in any given urban or rural area must surely have been profound since a small, intensely used, action space which is co-terminous with the action space of one's neighbours, must be one of the main foundations of 'community' in its most commonly used sense. The sense of shared territory is a powerful link between people. The railway, the bus and the car have done much to weaken this link.

By 1871, the railway network of Britain was already very densely developed. Table 1.12 overleaf shows the route mileage for various selected years and the aggregate amount of movement measured in millions of passenger/miles. The significance of these figures in social terms rests less in the structure of the network than in the growth of total flow along it. Between 1875 and 1905 the network length increased by 35% while the passenger/miles figure increased by 245%. This growth in movement seems to have stemmed largely from the widening of the social background of that section of the population using the railways. During the early decades of growth the railway companies seemed to look for their revenue to the middle and upper income groups. Subsequently it began to be pointed out that greater profits might ensue from serving the needs of the much more numerous lower income groups.[24] There were obvious social difficulties, in the context of Victorian Britain, in mixing income groups in the physically confined space of a railway compartment, or

Table 1.12 Railways in Great Britain

	Route mileage	Passenger/miles (millions)
1825	27	n.a.
1835	338	n.a.
1844	2,236	n.a.
1855	7,293	36.9
1865	11,451	65·8
1875	14,510	95·4
1885	16,594	138·4
1895	18,001	174·8
1905	19,535	233·1
1913	20,266	260·7
1925	20,400	261·8
1935	20,152	272·9

Source: B. R. Mitchell and P. Dean, Abstract of British Historical Statistics, C.U.P., 1962, pp. 226–7

even of a railway station. But gradually, in the 1860s and 1870s various of the companies began to offer not only separate accommodation but also cheap rates for specified periods of the day. For passengers on the Great Northern line, for example, a typical return fare to central London from a northern suburb in the 1890s was 1s. to 1s. 2d. if arriving after 8 a.m., 5d. to 7d. if arriving between 6 a.m. and 8 a.m., and approximately half of that on trains arriving before 6 a.m.[25] The 'profile' of the travelling public, on the suburban routes at any rate, was clearly very different from that of the 1850s and 1860s, although the 'cheap fares' policy, regarded suspiciously by shareholders, managers and first-class passengers alike, was not as effective in bringing about mobility for the masses as some commentators have implied. Kellett estimates that, by 1900, there were only about 250,000 rail commuters in London out of a population of about 6½ million.[26] Subsequently the growth in commuting by railway (including underground railway), has been considerable and has led to a vast spread of suburbs around the larger cities.[27]

Just as the first half of the century under review had, from a transport point of view, been dominated by the growth of the railways, the second half has been dominated by the growth in ownership and use of the car. Table 1.13 sets out the number of private motor-cars taxed since the beginning of the century. The present figure represents something like 0·2 cars per head of population. If Buchanan's estimates are accepted,[28] and for the present purposes the trend they show is clear enough, it seems likely that the growth curve will not level off until 0·4 cars per head is achieved. This may come soon after the turn of the century and will entail a total of about 30 million cars. We are, in fact, in the middle of the most explosive phase of private vehicle growth but already its social ramifications are enormous. The effect of the car on settlement patterns has been to fill in the interstices between railway routes in the suburbs and to allow residential development in areas

Table 1.13 Motor Vehicles Taxed in Great Britain

1904	8,000	1938	1,944,000
1910	53,000	1952	2,508,000
1920	187,000	1961	5,979,000
1930	1,056,000	1968	10,816,000

Sources: British Road Federation, Basic Road Statistics and various Annual Abstracts of Statistics

comparatively remote from both employment opportunities and railway routes, a crucial point for Ringmer. In social terms the car has been instrumental in increasing the amount of weekly 'one-stop' shopping and of fundamentally affecting holiday and recreational patterns. It has also, as most of us are painfully aware, risen to a high place in the hierarchy of categories upon which we spend our household income.[29] In fact it is evident that during the past 100 years expenditure on movement, broadly defined, has risen at a much greater percentage rate than expenditure on the more fundamental necessities of life such as food and shelter.

The trend towards greater mobility has no doubt also been a contributory factor in the growth of migration around the country during the past 100 years. Table 1.14 gives some rough idea of this trend for England and Wales. The

Table 1.14 Inter-county Migration, England and Wales, 1901–51

Percentage of population born in county in which enumerated	Number of counties		
	1901	1931	1951
30–60	3	12	24
60–70	17	15	13
70–80	23	19	13
over 80	10	7	3

Source: D. C. Marsh, The Changing Social Structure of England and Wales, Routledge, revised edn 1965, pp. 90–1

increase in migratory movement no doubt stems fundamentally from such factors as the differentials between regions in the growth rate in employment, the increase in the number of retired people, and the growth of large employing organisations whose policy is to shift employees around the country. But the improvements in transportation have no doubt facilitated, or made possible, work-seeking movements to new areas for many families, especially those with low incomes.[30]

CHANGES IN HEALTH AND WELFARE

By comparison with most phenomena reviewed in this chapter, change in the distribution of income, and especially in the incidence of poverty, has been depressingly limited over the period.[31] The amount of poverty before the 1890s is not known in exact terms. There is no doubt that living conditions in the 1870s and 1880s represented, for most people, a considerable advance over the Dickensian state of the middle decades of the century. Public health acts and housing by-laws, the founding of charitable institutions like the Peabody Trust, and the development of water technology, all served to improve the environmental conditions of the lower paid.[32] Nevertheless, following a survey carried out in east London and extrapolated to the rest of the United Kingdom, Booth estimated in 1890 that the army of the destitute, the 'submerged tenth', numbered about 3 million.[33] These included the paupers, the homeless, the starving and those receiving less than about 50s. per week, plus their dependants. Seventy years later, research findings indicated that in 1960 14·2% of the United Kingdom (7·5 million people) were still living below or not far above a defined 'national assistance' level.[34] In the nature of the problem, no precise definition of 'poverty' can be offered, and certainly no definition could achieve exact comparability over a 70-year period. Nevertheless it is clear that the poor are still with us and there seems little evidence to suggest that the situation is likely to change in the short term.

According to Barker *et al.*,[35] however, the diet of the British people has undergone considerable change. In 1862 an analysis of the diet of the 'poorer labouring population' found that farm workers averaged 12½ lb. of bread per week and only 1 lb. of meat (including bacon). Of the families surveyed 30% ate no fresh meat at all. During the 1870s and 1880s, the arrival of chilled beef from overseas led to a fall in prices and an extension of the meat-eating public. In 1881 it was reported that 9·5d. was spent per head per day on food in the following proportions:

1·9d. on meat
1·4d. on bread
0·8d. on milk and eggs
0·7d. on butter and cheese
over 2·0d. on beer and spirits

Although not listed, fish, especially herrings, had always been purchased by even the poorest families especially following the development of rail services from the coast. Consumption was strongly stimulated also by one of the more important advances of the century – the invention of 'fish and chips' (variously attributed, but thought to have been first popularised by John Rouse (Oldham) Ltd in 1880). Fruit, before the 1870s, had always been a rare luxury item but from this date reductions in the cost of transportation, and the development of jam-making, increased the fruit intake of all income groups. Changes in *per capita* consumption of some of the more important foods from 1880 to 1962 can be seen in Table 1.15.

Table 1.15 United Kingdom Food Consumption

| | Pounds per head per year | | |
	1880	1934–8	1962
Milk solids	n.a.	38	56
Liquid milk	213	217	325
Cheese	8	9	10
Meat (inc. bacon and ham)	91	129	142
Poultry and game	n.a.	9	15
Fish	18	26	21
Eggs	11	28	34
Butter	12	25	20
Margarine	—	9	11
Other fats	n.a.	19	24
Sugar	64	96	111
Potatoes	296	190	214
Other vegetables and tomatoes	n.a.	127	127
Fruits and nuts	n.a.	104	108
Wheat flour	280	195	161
Other cereals	n.a.	16	16

n.a. = not available
Source: T. C. Barker *et al.*, *Our Changing Fare*,
    MacGibbon & Kee, 1966

Dietary and public health developments, plus the evolution of a fairly comprehensive system of social security (largely between 1906 and 1950) led to drastic changes in various vital rates. Table 1.16 gives birth and death rates per 1000 population in various selected periods and years (England and

Table 1.16 Birth and Death Rates, England and Wales

	Births (per 1000)	Deaths (per 1000)
1871–5	35·5	22·0
1901–5	28·2	16·0
1921	22·4	12·1
1931	15·8	12·3
1951	15·5	12·5
1961	17·6	12·0

Source: D. C. Marsh, *The Changing Social Structure of
    England and Wales 1871–1961*, Routledge, revised edn. 1965

Wales). The reduction in death rates has been achieved despite the increase in the percentage of people over 65 shown in Table 1.17.

Table 1.17 Percentage of Population of England and Wales aged over 65

1871	5
1901	5
1931	7
1951	11
1961	12

Source: D. C. Marsh, *ibid.*

Infant mortality has declined steadily over the period as shown in Table 1.18.

Table 1.18 Infant Mortality, England and Wales

Deaths of infants under 1 year per 1000 live births			
1861	153	1921	83
1871	158	1931	66
1881	130	1941	60
1891	149	1951	30
1901	151	1961	21
1911	130	1968	18

Source: B. R. Mitchell and P. Deane, *Abstract of British Historical Statistics*, C.U.P., 1962, Ch. 1, Table 12

Table 1.19 shows a comparison between 1860 and 1925 in family size.

Table 1.19 Number of Children Born per Marriage

Number of children	Marriages occurring c. 1860 (England and Wales), percentage	Marriages occurring c. 1925 (Great Britain), percentage
0	9	17
1	5	25
2	6	25
3	8	13
4	9	8
5	10	5
6	10	3
7	10	2
8	9	1
9	8	} 1
10	6	
Over 10	10	

Source: D. C. Marsh, *ibid.*

MID-VICTORIAN RURAL LIFE-STYLE

From the evidence presented, we now have some expectations concerning the situation and daily life of ordinary rural families in the mid-Victorian era. They are expectations broadly in line with accounts of rural life by novelists and other eye-witnesses of the period. We might consider a hypothetical average household in Ringmer in the 1870s. The father would be employed as an agricultural labourer, working six days a week for perhaps 12–14 hours a day. He would earn perhaps £25 per year, and would have no paid holidays except for the newly instituted four days of bank holiday per year. He would have received little or no formal education and stood perhaps an even chance of being able to read. If he could read he might occasionally have seen a much-thumbed copy of a local, or possibly a national, newspaper. His lack of information concerning national events would not have mattered very much since he had no vote, nor did he belong to any organisation aimed at bettering work conditions. In any case membership of such an organisation might add to the sense of insecurity already inherent in his situation as a tenant in a 'tied' cottage.

The labourer's wife would have been employed 'in service' before her marriage. Her main task now would be to produce five, six or seven children, several of whom would die, either from complications following birth or from one of the common childhood diseases, before the age of one. She would be heavily engaged in a variety of domestic tasks; fetching water from the village pump, baking bread, making wine, beer, cheese and butter, and mending clothes. She would be helped by her daughters until they were of an age to go into service, perhaps with one of the local 'gentry' or else in a distant town. The sons would probably follow their father into some agricultural pursuit although with the recent developments in the educational system there was a chance that some of them might rise to a skilled manual, or even a clerical, position.

The life of the family would be strongly based upon the immediate locality into which they had all been born. They would rarely travel away from the village and would never have seen the sea, just a few miles down the Ouse valley. Their movement pattern would be almost entirely confined to the parish itself, with occasional journeys on foot to Lewes, three miles away. They would be aware of the existence of the railway linking Lewes with the other towns of Britain, but they would have had neither the means nor the need to use it. All the immediate necessities of life–work, social activities, shops, artifacts–were available within the parish.

The family were, before all else, poor. They were members of the 'submerged tenth' Booth was to identify a generation later.[36] Their poverty transcended material considerations of inadequate housing, restricted diet and rudimentary medical care. It was a poverty of the spirit and reflected a lack of access to education, travel and information, a lack of equality of opportunity, a lack of incentive and motivation to rise above the inherited circumstances, to change the social and political *status quo*. In these respects and many others, as the next four chapters will try to show in relation to Ringmer, Britain has since become a vastly better place.

PART TWO

CHANGE IN THE VILLAGE, 1871–1971

2 · Mid-Victorian Ringmer

In his classic study of the English village published in 1922, Peake[1] was much concerned with the decline in the quality of community life following the structural changes in agriculture during the first half of the nineteenth century, and specifically with the effects of enclosure:

> Thus with the enclosure of the Common Fields and Waste the community life of the village came to an end. Village society became divided into two camps, often two hostile camps; the squire and the farmers in the one, and often the parson too, while in the other were the farm labourers and perhaps a few smallholders. Thus there were the Haves and Have-nots with no bond of association between them but an ever widening gap; this gap yawned still wider as the parish ceased to count as a civil unit.[2]

This is surely not to deny that there had always been 'haves' and 'have-nots'. Peake's main point was that the open field system necessarily entailed a high degree of communal endeavour and a close, but not necessarily amicable, economic relationship between squire and workers. Enclosure of the land into separate, fenced-off farms concentrated the capital into fewer hands, removed certain operations that had involved most workers jointly, and caused a number of small tenants and proprietors to leave the land altogether. Peake painted a depressing picture of small owners finding their farms uneconomic in the new climate, selling out, and earning their livings as tenant farmers or smallholders. He saw small tenants crowded out as landlords reorganised their estates into larger farms, thus causing the migration of workers to towns where 'their descendants are leaders of Labour movements of all kinds'.[3] He saw that other men made landless had become 'the lower type of agricultural labourer', wandering from farm to farm and known as 'Michaelmassers' since they were hired annually at Michaelmas fairs. Many who could not get work in this way emigrated, or moved to urban slums.

The worst effects of the early nineteenth-century enclosures were perhaps cushioned during the period 1850–75, which were years of generally high corn prices and agricultural prosperity. Peake considered that during this period the more able landowners amassed considerable estates and in many cases rationalised their operations.[4] Certainly many farmhouses were built or enlarged during these years. The boom period ended with the sudden arrival of cheap North American corn in 1875–6, the 1879 epidemic of sheep-rot which caused millions of sheep to be destroyed, and the 1883 foot-and-mouth epidemic. In combination these factors caused numerous farming bankrupt-cies, and many estates were broken up and farmhouses sold off. Thus the decade 1865–75 should, according to Peake, have been a period when villages were experiencing a declining sense of community, compared to the earlier years of the century, but were enjoying considerable agricultural prosperity. Mid-Victorian Ringmer will be examined against these general expectations.

POPULATION STRUCTURE

The parish in 1871 had a population of 1417, 747 male and 670 female.[5] This population figure compares with 897 in 1801.[6] There were 293 separate families or occupiers, giving an average family size of nearly 4·6, and the population lived in a total of 276 houses. The age/sex structure of the popula-tion is shown in Figure 5.1.

Although no published data exists on the rate of infant mortality in the parish, Day[7] quotes a passage which provides some evidence on family size and health in an adjoining rural area:

> I have seen the statement made that mothers of a former generation laid most of their infants to sleep in the Churchyard. So I have been collecting information from my neighbours. In this locality, twenty families had two hundred and six children. Of these, two hundred lived to maturity, and were all brought up on mother's milk.[8]

Day was also much impressed with the longevity of residents in the rural parishes in the vicinity, which tends to be consistent with the fairly high pro-portion of inhabitants aged 65 and over enumerated by the census:

> How different are the people of the Weald to those who live in Brigh-ton! Here the middle-aged are all over seventy and the old folks vary from eighty to ninety years of age. There were a dozen cottages within a radius of a quarter of a mile from my house. I ascertained that fifteen of the men and women living in them were over eighty.[9]

A large proportion of 1871 residents had been born in the parish (756 out of 1417 or 53%). Of those who had migrated in, 93% were born elsewhere in Sussex.[10] Very few marriage movements were made into the parish. Seventy-five couples got married in the parish church in the decade prior to 1866.[11] In 58% of these cases both partners already lived in the parish. The distance distribution of the incoming partner, normally the man, for the remainder of cases is as shown in Table 5.4. The relatively low rates of in- and out-migra-tion evidenced by the birthplace and marriage data would seem to point to a community where social networks and interaction were based, to a larger extent than at present, on the extended family and where a small number of families constituted a relatively large proportion of the total parish population.

EMPLOYMENT AND ECONOMY

It is difficult to make exact comparisons of employment structures through time because of the frequent changes made by the census in the occupational classification system. The employment breakdown for 1871 is given in Table 2.1. Comparisons with 1931 and 1971 will be made in Chapter 5, using 1971 categorisations.

Table 2.1 Occupational Structure in Ringmer, 1871

	Male	Female	Total
Agricultural labourer	236	—	236
Farmer	22	—	22
General servant	1	24	25
Other domestic servants	1	46	47
Gardener	16	—	16
Groom	11	—	11
Brickmaker	8	—	8
Bricklayer	11	—	11
Blacksmith	6	—	6
Carpenter	10	—	10
Miller	5	—	5
Wheelwright	5	—	5
Shoemaker	6	—	6
Dressmaker	—	7	7
Laundry worker	—	16	16
Schoolmistress	—	7	7
Bailiff	5	—	5
Grocer	7	—	7
Innkeeper	7	—	7
Butcher	3	—	3
Brewer	4	—	4
Other	46	3	49
	410	103	513

Source: 1871 Census Enumerators' Returns

Some evidence is available on local wage rates for certain of these occupations. Day was informed that an agricultural labourer's wages in the 1850s were £5 from Lady-tide to Michaelmas, and £4 from Michaelmas to Lady-tide – a total of £9 per year. In addition the labourer might live in and eat well with the farmer's family – even possibly sitting down at the same table.

As I have said, we all sat down together to farmhouse dinner, and what good dinners they gave us. What a help pork was! When pigs were killed the hams and shoulders were cut off, and in the process of time hung up in the chimney to be smoked and dried, while all the rest of the meat was left in the tub, ready to be taken out and boiled whenever it was wanted.

Sometimes we had beef puddings, sometimes pork for our dinner, a good bit of meat and with it plenty of home grown vegetables; then fruit pie or some pudding to finish with. At six o-clock we came in again to supper, when everyone had a good basin of milk to drink and as much bread and cheese as he cared to eat. If the home-made cheese had got dry, then it was warmed in the oven, and we enjoyed it.[12]

From the evidence to be set out subsequently concerning the average size of households and the property valuation list, however, it seems likely that the majority of agricultural labourers lived out. No doubt certain perquisites were available from the farmer, for example faggots, but it is nevertheless clear that farm labourers were the worst-paid section of the community except perhaps for young girls engaged in domestic service.

The employment conditions of one 19-year-old farmhouse servant in the 1850s is given in Day's book.[13] The household consisted of the farmer, his wife, three farm workers and the girl. She worked from 5 a.m. till 10 p.m. with a few hours off in the afternoon. There was no mention in the account of any rest days. Her work consisted of baking (kneading the dough was especially hard work), brewing, churning 50–70 lb. of butter per week, washing clothes, cooking for six, cleaning, chopping wood and caring for the chickens and ducklings. The men and the girl ate at a different table from the farmer and his wife but 'I always had an egg with my breakfast and half a pint of ale with my dinner'. In all she considered that she was 'very kindly treated in that place'. Her wages were 3s. 9d. per week. She subsequently married a keeper and brought up nine children. No doubt her experiences in service enabled her to cope with them quite adequately.

Fragmentary evidence exists on other wage rates in the area. John Constable,[14] the vicar of Ringmer from 1812 until his death in 1863, paid his coachman £6 5s. quarterly, a rate of £25 per year, but no doubt such posts were few and far between. Another souce of non-agricultural employment was the constabulary. The rates of pay were £60–£70 per year. At the end of the 1850s, hours of duty appeared to average 65–70 per week[15] and there was no weekly rest day (there was still no weekly day off in 1893).[16] The amount of leave varied from man to man and between divisions. It was noted that in the period 1st January 1861 to 30th September 1863, P.C. Self had only four days off duty. In 1851 leave was given to anyone who wished, and could afford, to go to the Great Exhibition in Hyde Park. The first case of anyone being granted leave to play cricket occurred in 1866. Policemen, however, had access to supplementary means of income. It was apparently normal for constables to go on duty with a large silk scarf folded in their pocket. This could be used for carrying 'presents', fruit, vegetables, animal products and so on, received during the execution of their duties. Such a system was no doubt very efficient since it reduced paperwork on charges, saved the time of the courts, and enabled slightly lower wages to be paid. Conceivably, too, it provided a very direct incentive to apprehend law-breakers. It seems that superintendents were especially sanguine about the benefits of the system; they sometimes went on duty with handcarts.

A sizeable minority of the population of the village were engaged in crafts and trade. A complete list of the shops and services available in 1867 is given in Table 2.2.

Table 2.2 Shops, Services and Tradesmen in Ringmer, 1867

Publicans	4 (one named Tapp)
Boot and shoe makers	4
Carpenters	2 (one named Cosham)
Corn millers	2
Bakers	2
Blacksmiths	2
Maltster	1
Butcher	1
Tailor	1 (named Coates)
Brewer	1
Wheelwright	1
Grocer and draper	1
Grocer, draper, wineseller, P.O. and Insurance agent	1
Builder	1
Brick maker	1
Police constable	1

Source: Kelly's Directory, Sussex, 1867

Thus, making allowance for employees and dependants, probably well over 100 people, perhaps 10% of the parish population, depended upon retail and service activity for their livelihood. Since their market consisted very largely of those engaged locally in agriculture (passing trade was probably negligible) it is easy to imagine the effects of agricultural depression and low wages on this group as well as upon the group directly dependent on agriculture.

The spread of services available was, even by present standards, extremely comprehensive. All the immediate necessities of life, food, drink, clothes, footwear and the means of house and vehicle construction and repair, were offered in the village. There was even a daily collection of mail at 6.25 p.m., later than it is at present. It is difficult to imagine that anyone, save the very wealthy and sophisticated, should have travelled far afield to shop. Even the vicar, one of the richest and most mobile of village residents, normally shopped within the village, as a subsequent quotation from his diary will show. Unfortunately no records can be traced that would indicate the extent of extra-parochial journeys. The case for the gradual increase in such movement over time, which is one of the themes of this book, is based upon less direct evidence.

One final source of employment remained if jobs in other sectors of the village economy became scarce. One could join the colours. Recruiting sergeants were no doubt a familiar sight. For example in November 1869 the Lewes Volunteers paid a visit to the village,[17] accompanied by a band playing suitably stirring music. They halted for half an hour at the *Anchor Inn*, then marched back to Lewes again, perhaps with a few more recruits to the Queen's Army. In times of national crisis, especially if these coincided with a period of agricultural depression, they were probably very successful.

PROPERTY AND FARM OWNERSHIP

Land and property ownership was, predictably, concentrated into relatively few hands, although the 1873 land-ownership survey of Sussex[18] shows that of those owning 5000 or more acres in the country, none lived in the parish. The largest nearby landowner was W. L. Christie, of Glynde, who owned 4114 acres. The 1867 Ringmer Valuation List shows that of approximately 280 households, only 30 were owner-occupiers. In nearly all other cases the occupiers were tenants of private landlords. In all, only 15 Ringmer residents owned an acre or more of land. Despite this, no one or two landowners had anything approaching a monopoly of property ownership and the first five owners accounted for just over 25% of the total of properties. The data for 1934 given in the next chapter shows a rather different pattern.

The social structure of the time, which will be discussed more fully later, is well reflected in the distribution of rateable values of properties in the parish shown in Figure 5.3. Of the 263 properties, 213 had a value of less than £10 and thus fell in the bottom 4% of the rateable value range. These were occupied largely by agricultural labourers, other unskilled workers, and widows on out-relief. The 12 properties in the village with a value of over £80 constituted, roughly, the 'big house' element. Between these extremes existed a spread of properties, more numerous towards the lower end of the scale, which housed the tradesmen, craftsmen and the smaller farmers, both owners and tenants (see Plates 1 and 2a). These generalisations can be verified by comparing the 1867 Valuation List, which names occupiers, with the 1871 Census enumerators' returns which sets out names and occupations.

The 1867 list shows 15 farms of more than 50 acres extent. These accounted for nearly 3000 of the 5378 acres[20] in the parish. Two large holdings of woodland accounted for a further 500 acres and the rest was spread between smaller agricultural holdings and built-up areas. Only two of the smaller farms, totalling about 300 acres, were owner-occupied. Of the tenanted farms, four were in the possession of titled owners. Duplication of ownership existed to the extent that the 15 farms and two woodland holdings were in the hands of only 11 separate owners, while three of these (Christie, Gage and de la Warr) owned a total of 2100 acres between them. Clearly these three, if they chose to act jointly, could determine policy on a wide range of matters concerning the terms and conditions of service on farm work. Nevertheless, the parish was far from being a 'closed' one, with the ownership heavily concentrated into the hands of a single family, although examples of such parishes did, and do, occur to the south of Ringmer.

LOCAL GOVERNMENT AND SOCIAL ADMINISTRATION

Before the passing of the Local Government Acts of 1888 and 1894, which established the county councils and the county districts, rural local government was largely in the hands of parish authorities.[21] The vestry meeting, which consisted of local householders gathered together in the vestry under the leadership of the clergy, tended to oversee Church property, to supervise the relief for the poor raised in voluntary poor rates on property, and to provide such general welfare care as existed. However, as Bracey remarks, '. . . it became clear that the parish as a principal unit in local government was too small for an emerging industrial society'.[22] Various *ad hoc* bodies appeared during the nineteenth century to fill specific gaps in administration.[23] The 1834 Poor Law Amendment Act created unions of several parishes, run by Boards of Guardians, to administer the workhouses and the other aspects of relief.[24] Under the education acts of the early 1870s, School Boards were set up in each parish to administer the new universal pattern of primary education. And a succession of Highway Acts from 1838 to 1878 removed control over the roads from local turnpike trusts to Highway Boards. Thus, in the mid-Victorian period, Ringmer was 'administered', if that is not too strong a word for the very limited range of collectively organised functions, by a mixture of archaic and specialised authorities dominated either by the Church, the minor landed aristocracy of the area, or by both.[25] One of these, the vestry meeting, was to lose most of its residual powers by the operation of the 1868 Act abolishing Church Rates. These formal administrative structures were, as will be seen, supplemented by a rich and complex range of less formal means of aiding the sick, the old, the poor and those in various other categories of need.

It appears that the 1834 Poor Law Amendment Act, which created the Chailey Union of three parishes, including Ringmer, had the effect of causing the Ringmer workhouse to specialise in the care of female paupers and children. R. A. Durrant, the Chailey Union's rate collector in Ringmer parish, made monthly payments to the overseers. These totalled about £450 for the year 1862.[26] The Union's expenditure breakdown between the three parishes depended on the amount of help each required. The total expenditure of the Union for the six months to March 1866 (at which time the Ringmer workhouse had 23 inmates) totalled £2875 17s. 10d.[27] The proportion attributable to the Ringmer poor and the manner in which it was spent, is shown in Table 2.3 overleaf.

It seems that the general relationship between the amounts spent on in-relief, out-relief, maintenance of lunatics and administration costs are fairly consistent with the national average figures quoted by Best.[28] In both the local and national figures, out-relief is far more significant than in-relief. Best argues that much of this out-relief was '. . . to the able-bodied unemployed. It was used in effect as a dole to keep both the wholly and the partially unemployed alive and available until the return of fulltime work'.[29] Guardians persisted in this policy in the face of Whitehall's displeasure since it was clearly cheaper to provide out-relief than in-relief and it was also in many cases more humane, since it kept families intact in their homes. The vestry meeting was still active as an agency of welfare and was responsible, or partially responsible, for a variety of rates made for specific purposes. For example a Church Rate was levied in 1865 and a voluntary rate of ½d. in the £ was made in 1866. A cheque for the proceeds of the latter, £12 18s. 9d.,

Table 2.3 Expenditure on Ringmer Poor–Six Months to
March 1866

	£	s.	d.
In maintenance	47	15	8
Out-relief	238	19	2½
Medical fees	8	2	6
Vaccination fees		17	6
Registration fees	1	10	6
County and Police Rates	106	19	1
Funerals	1	16	0
General common charges	73	8	6
Relief to irremovable poor	66	8	0½
Maintenance of lunatics	17	5	5
	563	2	5

Source: Board of Guardian Minutes, March 1866

was sent to the Sussex County Hospital.[30] Further voluntary rates were levied in February 1874.[31] One at 2d. in the £ towards the cost of the school raised £69 5s. 11½d. and another at ½d. in the £ raised £17 7s. 4½d. for the hospital. The first one was paid by 54 of the 100 or so owners of property and the second by 69. Hospitals seemed to represent a more worthy cause than schools to the property owners of the time.

The village asylum was closed in 1855 under the provisions of the 1853 Act which made the care of pauper lunatics a county concern and which led to the development of St. Francis Hospital at Haywards Heath. It seems well worth while to set out various details relating to the care of the mentally ill, although these details do refer to a period 10 years earlier than the decade under review.[32] The Visitors noted, in 1853, that one young lady suffering an 'attack of despondency' was locked up in a disused room from which she could not look out and where she heard the filthy and disgusting language of a neighbouring patient'; conditions 'calculated rather to confirm than to relieve her melancholy'. The Visitors also felt that Mrs. Ivory, the proprietress, was humane and intelligent but that 'her bodily infirmities led her to entrust supervision to others' who, by implication, were less humane. The buildings, too, needed considerable attention while there were few amusements and 'no endeavour to make the place cheerful and social'. On the brighter side, it had been noted in 1851 that '. . . lately the amount of restraint in use appears to

1a *Vicar.* 'Middleham' the home of John Constable, vicar of the parish from 1812 to 1863. In 1861 the household included eleven servants. From here the vicar and 'Cousin Lucy' dispensed charitable good works (see Chapter 2).

1b *Farmer.* The substantial home of a tenant farmer in 1867. The building has clearly been added to from time to time. Note the interesting range of window types. The attic room was probably for a domestic servant.

1c *Tradesman.* Four houses near the village centre, one of them is also a butcher's shop built partly of salt-fired bricks. The boy on the fine flintstone wall is the butcher's roundsman; he carried the meat on the four-handled board.

2a *Labourer.* A one-storey, weather-board cottage, probably formerly the home of a farm labourer.

2b The 'board' school, built in 1876 following the 1870 act which made education compulsory to the age of eleven: a measure seen by some of the squirearchy as a device to deprive them of servants. Taken about 1905–10, the photograph also shows the headmaster's house and a pole for swinging in the playground.

2c The first pedalled bicycle ride in Britain began at these gates and proceeded uncertainly away down the road. The date was 1868 and the machine was made by W. F. Martin, who lived here. Note the tile hung and weather-boarded walls – both local features.

have been much diminished'. The reasons for admission provide an insight into the nature of mental breakdown at the time.[33] There were, in the early 1850s, six inmates, all women aged 30 to 60. Reasons for committal included the following:

'. . . is insane on religious subjects . . .'

'. . . dreadfully depressed and fancies herself possessed by an evil spirit . . .'

'. . . believes there is a design on the part of her friends to poison her . . .'

'. . . fancies that large sums of money that have been left to her have been destroyed . . .'

'. . . fears that evil spirits are about her . . .'

'. . . fancying policemen are continually under the bed . . .'

Professionally competent analysts of mental ill-health could no doubt draw out a great deal from these reasons but it appears to a lay observer that fear of religious and other authority of one sort or another is uppermost in the largely paranoid states of mind revealed by the committal orders. Clearly little or no actual treatment was available and the level of diagnosis of conditions is betrayed by the committal forms on which people coming in were categorised as 'lunatic' or 'idiot' or 'person of unsound mind'.

The Church provided considerable relief to those in need, and John Constable, vicar of Ringmer from 1812 to his death in 1863, made frequent reference to welfare activities in his diary. It is not clear from the diary whether the help he dispensed was paid for by rates levied by the vestry meeting or whether it was from his own pocket. A combination of the two is the most likely answer. Certainly he was not a poor man. Back in 1825 he had 'bought £1200 of the new 4 per cents' while in 1828 he recieved 'two years interest for the Burwash and Wadhurst Turnpike'. In fact so numerous were his financial involvements that in 1825 'I put the management of all my Sussex property into his [an accountant's] management to receive the rents of land and tithe for me which he agreed to do for 25 guineas per annum'.[34] The diary is not complete but some quotations from 1851 will give an idea of the vicar's role in the welfare of the parish:

'I walked to the back Green and promised the Tivals, a family of nine, some mutton broth.'

'I walked up the Broyle and called on old Clarke and the Russels and Mrs. Tasker and found her ill in bed and on Mrs. Bridger and promised them broth.'

'I walked to Ashton Green with Cousin Lucy and called at 5 or 6 cottages and promised them broth.'[35]

The aristocracy too, were active in providing welfare. In the neighbouring parish of Glynde '. . . the Rt. Hon. Brand has caused soup to be distributed weekly among the people in general . . .', while '. . . W. L. Christie also has given £5 for the purchase of blankets for distribution'.[36] Such help from the Church and gentry would not, of course, be regarded as a right and no doubt the receiving of it was an occasion for the proper cap-doffings to be carried out.

Small private charities were another feature of the welfare system of the time. Of the three such charities in Ringmer, the Hays Charity can perhaps serve as an example.[37] Miss Henrietta Hay, one of the family who owned the estate of Glyndebourne, died in 1787 leaving £2000 to be invested in public funds. The interest, which was to supplement not replace parish relief, was to be paid to 13 old people of Glynde and Ringmer who were to be '. . . of reputed good character for honesty, industry and sobriety . . .'. Taking the two parishes together, three people over 70 were each to receive £20 p.a., five over 60 were each to receive £10 p.a. and five others over 60 were to receive £5 p.a. In a letter dated 1958, J. Christie (then a trustee of the charity) elaborated on the terms, stressing that 'regard should be had to the character and not the particular poverty' of those to be selected. He made it clear that Miss Hay would have equated 'good character' with 'sound religious principles', which might, perhaps surprisingly, be of an anglican, non-conformist or catholic nature. Payment could be reduced or withdrawn for 'notorious or flagrant illconduct'. No doubt similar terms had applied through the nineteenth century.

Another important feature of the mid-Victorian system of collective security were the benefit societies. Several of these existed in Ringmer, each based on a public house where business was transacted and annual dinners held. Each member of a society paid in a monthly sum and in return received sick pay when unable to work, plus a small allowance in old age. For a variety of reasons the system, while incorporating the enthusiasm inherent in any self-help scheme, had certain drawbacks. One of these was that the enthusiasm was most unbridled at the annual dinner which, according to Day,[38] was sometimes so successful that all the funds paid in during the year were used up. Another problem was that young men in stable employment did not like to join an existing club because all their contributions for the foreseeable future went to the support of others. Young men, therefore, frequently formed new clubs, leaving older established ones to fold up, causing destitution among older members who might have subscribed to the defunct clubs for many years. In addition, elderly retired members could be debarred from benefits if they engaged in such technically defined 'work' as putting sticks on a fire. This might cause them to lose their status of 'unable to work'.

Despite these disadvantages the clubs flourished in the 1860s and 1870s. Dividends were paid, 'the object being to provide for the working classes in time of sickness and to assist the widows and families at death'.[39] In addition, a collection was held for the children of the Union and oranges distributed. At the 1868 *Anchor Inn* Society dinner, attended by most of the important figures in the parish, including the gentry, tribute was paid to the 'upright honest officers' and their 'just and skilful management'.[40] Overtures and operatic selections were performed by the band. At another dinner it was recorded that there had been 'unusually heavy cases of sickness last year' and since the society was 'composed principally of the labouring classes' it 'ought to be well supported by every farmer and landlord'.[41] It therefore seems that in some years more money was distributed than was received in subscriptions and that the societies constituted another mechanism for the voluntary re-distribution of wealth from the richer to the poorer members of the community.

A final element in the welfare system was provided by individual and group initiatives to combat the hardships of the time. For example, Day records[42] that in some years the harvest was very bad and this meant that some farmers were unable to pay their men through the winter. In one such year a vast stockpile of vegetables, flour, rice, oatmeal and meat was amassed for an outlay of £25. From these ingredients, 40 gallons of soup were made every two weeks during the winter and a quart was issued to each member of all needy families twice a week. The children brought cans to collect the soup. If any soup was left over it was sold to 'outsiders' for 1d. per pint. The system provided soup over a 5 month period. A similar spirit is evident from the recollections of an old lady:[43] 'What I particularly remember is the way we used to help one another. There were no village nurses in those days. When a woman was confined a neighbour came in to look after her and her children, and keep things straight and clean.'

Important developments in education came at the end of the decade under review. During this decade, before the implementation of the 1870 Education Act, primary education was provided in the local villages either by a 'National' school run by the National Society or by one of a number of 'dame' schools. Unfortunately no records of the Ringmer National school can be traced. Conditions in the 'dame' schools can, however, be gauged from the following two quotations relating to a near-by village (the first refers to 'Sophy's school'):

> Besides the National School at Hadlow Down there was a dame school in the village, kept by a tall thin woman who lived in a small cottage. The room had a table in the centre, and there were benches for the children to sit on, one being quite low for the tiny tots. In this primitive schoolroom were gathered over twenty boys and girls, representing the families of the farmers and tradespeople.
>
> Mothers used to say 'I send my children to Sophy's School because she allows no rough manners. Then see what good needlework she teaches.'[44]
>
> Questioned about the bringing up of her family, Mrs. Sands said to me 'Well ma'am, I brought up ten children and paid the 1d. a week for their schooling for about two years each. I never sent a girl to service before she was ten years old, could read her book (i.e. the Bible) write a letter, figure out a washing bill, and make a chimmee, and I never had one to disgrace me.'[45]

The education given, if brief, seems to have been eminently practical.

The passing of the Education Act led to fundamental changes. In Ringmer the newly constituted School Board held its first meeting on 6th January 1876.

The vicar acted as chairman and of the other four members, one was a farmer and two were from families engaged in trade. None of the larger landowners was involved. The first problem was to build, or adapt, suitable premises. Earl de la Warr, the owner of the National School, was approached but his terms for allowing the use of the old school, which included the provision that the vicar must have the right to teach religious instruction, were unacceptable to the Board. Instead a ¾-acre site was found, and following a joint expedition to inspect the new school in neighbouring Laughton, a loan of £2150 was raised from the Public Works Loan Commissioners and the new school was built by W. F. Martin, of whom more will be heard subsequently (see Plate 2b).

In July 1879 Mr. Frederick Jones was appointed Schoolmaster at a salary of £120 p.a. plus a free house and garden. Mr. Jones' wife and son were enrolled as Assistant Teachers. The fees in the 'mixed' (senior) school were:

> children of labourers 2d. each per week
> mechanics 4d.
> farmers   4d.
> master
> tradesmen 6d.

In the infants section all children were charged 2d. per week. The new idea of compulsory primary education began to bite locally in January 1881 when an acting Attendance Officer was appointed to visit and serve notices on parents whose children were absent. This provision caused inevitable hardship to those of limited means, and in 1883 the Board set up a precedent by remitting the fees for a widow with four children aged 9 to 3. It is clear from the Board minutes that all decisions except for those of the most trivial nature were made by higher authorities. For example, the decision to change the annual examinations from November to April was specified by Whitehall (1883). No longer, as in the case of Sophy's school, were the curriculum and form of education locally prescribed. The Board minutes contain much other information throwing light on the way of life at the time, ranging from the frequent requests for older boys to be absent to go to work for varying periods, to the periodic closure of the school on account of 'fever' and 'bad weather' (few, if any, of the roads in the parish were surfaced and many were difficult to traverse following heavy rain).

A final aspect of the social administration system of the time was provided by the police force. Lawbreaking in rural areas was rarely sinister in nature. The charge book at Uckfield police station shows that between 1872 and 1875 the most frequent charges were for drunkenness, minor assaults and poaching.[47] Burglaries, housebreaking and sexual offences were all very rare, which reflects perhaps the social control exerted by life in small communities with low rates of migratory movement. Drunkenness alone accounted for 65 out of every 100 charges and it was met, on conviction, by a fine of from 1s. to 5s., depending on the 'character' of the accused, or the alternative of seven days hard labour.[48] Poaching was viewed rather more seriously and in 1872 a labourer at Mayfield, on being convicted of poaching one partridge, received six weeks' hard labour since he could not pay the fine of £2 10s. 0d. plus 1s.

costs. Any form of begging was punished by a sentence of 7 to 14 days' hard labour, while in 1872 an attempted suicide was sentenced to one month's hard labour. Refusal to work in the Lewes workhouse led to a 62-year-old man being sentenced to 14 days' hard labour ('the treadmill, the crank or the breaking of stones').

Although, as noted earlier, policemen were able to augment their earnings by receiving gifts in kind, their lot was not an entirely happy one; in fact on many occasions they must have felt that their hearts were in their boots. In 1858 P.C. Cox recorded in his journal[49] that he did not go to a scheduled meeting in Lewes 'there being so many drunken navvys about the town'. Nor were they quite in the Poirot class as sleuths. Instructions issued in 1858 to constables investigating robberies suggest that: '. . . in comparing footmarks they are not to make comparisons by placing the boot or shoe over the footmark which has been discovered, but by the side of it'.[50] Perhaps it was, on the whole, a wise move to set up a squad of specialist detectives in 1882.

SOCIAL STRUCTURE AND ACTIVITIES

The rural social structure of mid-Victorian England consisted of various well-defined categories: the gentry (normally landowners), the larger farmers, the 'professional' group (the clergy, doctor, schoolmaster, etc.), the smallholders, craftsmen and tradesmen, those 'in service', the agricultural labourers and, finally, paupers and others receiving relief of some kind. Naturally the categories are not mutually exclusive nor internally homogeneous. For example, a rigid status hierarchy existed within the 'in service' category. Nevertheless it is clear from the data presented on property ownership that distinct gulfs existed between certain of these groups. These gulfs were clearly understood and accepted at the time as various newspaper reports show. A Church choir treat in 1868, for example, was reported as being: '. . . one of those delightful reunions in which class distinction for the time was entirely dispensed with, all dancing indiscriminately together as one class'.[51] In the same year a purse containing £7 16s. 0d. was presented to a retiring postman as a reward for his '. . . honesty, sobriety and obliging disposition to all classes'. The money was raised by voluntary contributions from the 'principal inhabitants'.[52] Two years earlier at a Southdown Hunt steeplechase held at Broyle Place Farm, the reporter recorded that it was '. . . refreshing to notice the absence of the lower class of turf frequenters'.[53]

Even in the last decade of the century, 'class' lines were rigidly drawn. The daughter of a prominent builder in the village (W. F. Martin) recalls that when she was very young the family had a limited range of possible friends.[54] The 'hunt' people were above them and similarly they would not expect to dine with the doctor or the vicar. Yet the punishment for playing with the daughter of the publican, clearly lower on the scale, was to be stood in the corner. Career possibilities for such a girl were virtually restricted to teaching or nursing. Work 'in service' would be unthinkable and shop work not acceptable. It was the tradesmen and craftsmen, and their families, who had perhaps the most restricted range of all from which to draw their friends. The gentry and professional group probably had a social network that extended over a much wider geographical area, to include families of similar status elsewhere in the county. For example, in the 1850s the vicar of Ringmer travelled quite frequently to Penton in Hampshire to visit friends.[55] Also, if one wanted to avoid falling foul of the law, it certainly helped to be one of the gentry. The 1872–75 analysis of the Uckfield charge book shows that of the 716 people prosecuted during the period only three were 'gentlemen' and these were charged with the no doubt forgivable crime of assault on trespassers.[56]

Although the status groups were well defined, and social barriers clearly accepted, upward and downward social mobility was not impossible. Day records various recollected accounts of:

> people close by who had, by hard work, frugality and integrity, raised themselves into the position of working farmers, though born in a labourer's cottage.

The recollection continues:

> I find no difficulty in showing you plenty of men who in their own time–or that of their fathers–have risen from the ranks.
> How have they done it? In no case by depending on the produce of a small piece of land. Everyone of them went to work for wages, or fattened fowls, or in some other manner earned extra money. As to myself, my father was a carrier between Hadlow Down and Lewes. He saved a little money and bought ten acres of land which he farmed, continuing his journey to Lewes.[57]

About twenty other cases of such upward mobility are quoted. Other methods by which it was achieved include learning a trade, for example as a carpenter, keeping a cow and selling butter, sowing crops on pieces of rough and unused land, working as a navvy on the railways currently under construction, or by keeping poultry. For several of these, and especially the last, the help of a dutiful and hardworking wife was considered invaluable.

The pattern of social and recreational activities is best understood in the context provided by the village social structure. Many of the activities appear to have been specific to particular status levels. The gentry, for example, indulged in equestrian pursuits. Lower notes in 1870 that 'The Broyle is now a favourite spot for steeple chases, which are held annually'.[58] These were competitive rides on horses from one church steeple to another. The Southdown Hunt met frequently, sometimes as often as four times in a week.[59] As we have seen from a previous quotation, these occasions were very much the province of the upper echelons. John Constable, the vicar until 1863, engaged in hunting and coursing. The less vigorous social activities of the gentry can perhaps best be gauged from Constable's diary. He frequently took tea with visitors, rode to Brighton to visit friends and occasionally went by train to London. On one such occasion he visited Westminster Abbey, the Tower of

London and the 'Diorama', and finished the day with a visit to the theatre. Exceptionally, in the context of the times, he was able to take an annual holiday. On 10th August 1851, 'all business having been set in order and the haymaking completed', he set off with his family for a six weeks stay in St. Leonards. He found the lodgings '. . . comfortable though not quite to our minds . . .'. On the way back he spent five days in Eastbourne.

Moving down the social scale, cricket provided a frequent diversion during the summer months. Ringmer played regular matches, mostly against neighbouring villages but sometimes against teams from Newhaven or Tunbridge Wells. Visiting teams sometimes found, when matches were played on the green, that the combination of bumpy wicket and steeply sloping outfield was too much for them. By checking the names of the team listed in the local paper[60] against the 1867 Valuation List it is clear that the Ringmer club included at least one member of the gentry, several tradesmen and farmers, and a fair proportion of players from properties of very low rateable value. The game seemed to transcend social barriers, although the order in which the team was named in the paper (and conceivably the order in which they batted!) was almost exactly similar to the order of the rateable values of their properties.

Harvest suppers given by the farmers were also big social occasions. Farmer Knight of Norlington Farm (see Plate 1b), for example, gave a supper for about 30 of his tradesmen and labourers at *The Anchor*. There were toasts to the Queen and to the prosperity of Ringmer, and songs continued until a late hour.[61] In 1866, Farmer Page gave a harvest supper and holiday. Over 50 men and boys sat down to 'a bountiful supply of good things' and the men 'with the aid of good Newhaven tipper' sang until the small hours. 'Tipper' was no doubt some form of cheering ale. The weddings of members of the gentry provided social occasions in which all members of the community were involved. The wedding of Major Harwood's daughter in 1865 was one such occasion. 'About 11 a.m. the whole village was astir in anticipation of the pleasing event. On the approach of that lady many a heartfelt "God bless 'em" was uttered.'[63] A large, no doubt carefully selected, party went to the breakfast at 'The Elms' where Major and Mrs. Harwood lived and 150 children of the parish were entertained in a neighbouring field, while nearly 70 of the older inhabitants were given 'a substantial meal' and 'a pecuniary donation' by 'the gallant and hospitable major'.

The lower orders of the community benefited also from various 'treats'. In 1868, for example, the children of Chailey Union were taken to Crystal Palace by train to hear a grand rehearsal for a Handel Festival which, the reporter fervently notes, 'will doubtless form a theme for conversation in after life'[64] (by which he presumably meant later life). On passing the residence of the prodigal Major Harwood each child received a 6d. piece. Twenty other Ringmer people accompanied the group, the veteran of the party being an old soldier in his 79th year. The major paid for the children's rail fare '. . . with that open-hearted liberality for which he is so well known to so many'. In the same year there was a treat for the Church choir in the school room at which 'capital sentimental and comic songs' were sung and dancing continued until after midnight.[65] Punch, ale and wine were drunk, hopefully with decorum since there were several ladies present, as well as the vicar's family. The expenses on this occasion were paid by the vicar, the Reverend Symons. Benefit society anniversaries were other occasions for merrymaking. The 1865 anniversary of the *Anchor Inn* society was an all-day affair.[66] The society met at 10 a.m. and went to Church headed by the Brighton town band. Following the sermon and a visit to the vicarage, the party of over 120 dined in a booth on the village green and engaged in 'the usual sports' until evening rain brought them to a close.

Other social activities were of a more improving kind.[67] There was, during the 1860s, an Improvement Society. Meetings, attended entirely by men, were held to hear learned lecturers on such topics as 'Health' and 'The Planets'. The talks were sometimes illustrated by lantern slides. Musical events also occurred quite frequently. Concerts were held in the National School room, given by musicians from as far afield as Chichester Cathedral. Works by Handel and Mozart seemed to be especially popular. Concerts were no doubt also given by members of the Ringmer Church band, which consisted of a violin, 'cello and flute.[68] It was quite usual for a church to have such a band before it acquired an organ.

One final recreational activity was uniquely appropriate to Ringmer. In 1868 W. F. Martin, then only 19 and later to become a successful builder, built a Penny-farthing bicycle with pedals based on an illustration of a French machine that he had seen in a magazine.[69] It is believed to be the first pedalled bicycle to be built in this country. Having built it he looked around for a slightly sloping piece of road on which to try it out. Nervously he mounted it outside the gate of his house near the centre of the village (see Plate 2c) and rode a few hundred yards eastward down to the fork at the Broyle, where he managed to get off the machine by stopping against a bank of earth. This seems to have been the first pedal bicycle ride in Britain. Later in the year he rode it regularly to Lewes, although the police warned him on his first ride into the town that he would be forbidden if he frightened any horses. He must have made some subsequent machines because the following year under the heading 'Velocipedism' the local paper noted that Captain A. Harwood (whose stamina appeared to match his generosity) and Mr. S. Harwood rode a distance of 60 miles to Portsmouth, leaving at four in the morning.[70] They came back to Lewes, with their velos on a train, the same day. A new sport had been born.

Reviewing this wide range of social events and activities, certain features stand out. Most of the activities involved people drawn from a limited part of the social spectrum. The rich and the poor tended to take their pleasures separately and in different ways. If they were involved together, as at an important wedding or 'treat', then it was clear that the gentry were paying and the event was so planned that social distinctions could be maintained (for example by having the recipients of the largesse in a neighbouring field). Cricket, like most sports, was a potential leveller although it is not possible to gauge to what extent the usual social observances would have been kept up had a prominent farmer dropped a sharp chance at mid-off. A second significant point is that very few of the recorded social activities seem to have involved women. No doubt they remained at home, engaged in domestic chores, while the men hunted, celebrated after a cricket match or harvest supper, or listened to an improving lecture. It is to be hoped that women took their pleasures in other ways, perhaps in the satisfying form of gossiping about their menfolk or about each other.

DOMESTIC ECONOMY

The distribution of household sizes in Ringmer in 1871 is shown in Table 5.1. There were only sixteen one-person households. Elderly people, especially widows, must frequently have lived with younger relations or have been inmates in the Union Workhouse. Families were not as large as might have been predicted from the evidence on a national scale (see Table 1.19).[71] The average size of household was approximately 4·6 and only about 18% of households included more than seven people.

Fewer than 10% of Ringmer households employed domestic servants[72] so in most cases the domestic work was carried out by the housewife, helped no doubt by her daughters. A large amount of food was grown, manufactured or prepared on the premises. The 1867 Valuation List shows that most plots were large enough to grow considerable quantities of fruit and vegetables (a ¼-acre garden was regarded as normal). Many, if not most, cottages, kept a pig. The women made wine and vinegar, hopefully distinguishable, preserved fruit and baked bread. Day[73] notes the recollections of the 1850s and 1860s of one old lady in the area. She was one of a family of six. The mother had died and the family was living on the father's wages. Since he was a farm labourer, earning a wage of 6s. per week, not much food could be purchased. The father therefore grew vegetables, caught wild rabbits, killed and cured a 'yearly pig' and got up at 3 a.m. once a week for the 'weekly bake' of bread. When the informant was old enough, she helped cut wood to make and sell hop poles, and she engaged in haymaking at harvest time to increase their income. She went to school for six months in the year and no doubt spent the other six months supplementing the family budget. The rent of their cottage was 1s. 6d. per week and this included the use of a ¼-acre garden.

A rather later example of nineteenth-century domestic economy is provided by the household of W. F. Martin, builder of houses and inventor of bicycles, in the 1890s.[74] Martin was a prosperous craftsman and built his own handsome double-fronted house. He had a 1-acre garden and a timber yard close by. He kept two or three pigs, two cows, chickens and pigeons. The household grew its own vegetables, fruit, figs, grapes and melons, the latter two in a glasshouse. It produced most of its requirements of meat, jam, eggs, cakes, wine, butter and ointment made from animal fats. Very few foodstuffs were bought apart from bread (surprisingly), sugar, tea and certain rarely eaten fruits such as bananas and oranges. It is perhaps fortunate for the household accounts that Mrs. Martin did not charge for her labour.

Some idea of the prices of foodstuffs in the shops can be gained from the records of the Board of Guardians' meetings. In 1863 the cost of various provisions was as shown in Table 2.4. It is hardly surprising that households on an agricultural labourer's income made their own butter or went without, bought cheaper cuts of meat and kept a pig. Few households, presumably, could afford tea. At the other end of the social scale, John Constable, the

Table 2.4 Cost of Provisions in 1863

	Price per lb
Beef	5*d.*
Shins	2*d.*
Mutton	6*d.*
Suet	5*d.*
Meat (for the officers)	7*d.*
Cheese	5¾*d.*
Butter	10½*d.*
Tea	3*s.* 0*d.*
Sugar	4¼*d.*
Soap	4*d.*
Candles	6*d.*
Rice	2*d.*
Salt	¼*d.*

Source: Board of Guardians Minutes (11th March 1863)

vicar, was doing rather better. His diary shows an entry in 1851 '. . . paid Morris the butcher for the last seven months £47. 1. 2 . . .'.[75] His annual meat bill alone therefore seems to have exceeded by a factor of three or four the total annual income of an agricultural labourer's family. And his position in the community enabled him to pay bills up to seven months in arrears. There seems to be a moral to be drawn from this somewhere.

3 · Ringmer Between the Wars, 1925–1935

In 1912 George Bourne published a book about changes in social and economic life in his native village of Farnham, Surrey, during the period 1890–1910.[1] Although the book relates to a village in a neighbouring county, and deals with a period falling between those analysed in the present work, it provides a valuable context for the study of inter-war Ringmer in the light it sheds on village life around the turn of the century. It also makes a number of general statements which can be corroborated from the later Ringmer evidence. Indeed in some respects it seems that there was surprisingly little change in rural social attitudes between the 1890s and the 1930s.

Bourne looked back nostalgically to the pre-industrial times when the village was self-contained, and the physical embodiment of the 'peasant' system: 'the parish where the peasant people lived was the source of the materials they used, and their well-being depended on their knowledge of its resources', while: '. . . [the system] permitted a man to hope for well-being without seeking to escape from his own class into some other'.[2] He felt that the daily work undertaken demanded a high degree of skill and craftsmanship and was willingly done because the end result, whether a good crop or a well-thatched roof, was visible and rewarding in itself. All this was changed by the re-structuring of agriculture and particularly by the enclosure movement: 'To the enclosure of the common more than any other cause may be traced all the other changes that have subsequently passed over the village. It was like knocking the keystone out of an arch.'[3] Men had to leave the land to take on non-agricultural, unskilled, tasks and their daily work life was greatly impoverished. The honest, stable 'peasant system' was replaced by a commercially dominated one. It is conceded that the cheapening of food resulting partly from a large-scale importation of produce enabled men to work fewer hours in order to stay alive yet few villagers were equipped to put the new-found leisure time to enjoyable use: 'So lightly was it valued that most villagers cut it short by the simple expedient of going to bed at six or seven o'clock.'[4]

In a period of increasing fluidity between the various status groups in society, inter-group relations worsened. There was increasing bitterness between employers and workers as the status hierarchy began to be questioned, while the coming of universal elementary education was seen by some of the gentry to be a device to deprive them of servants. The law and the police were clearly seen to stand for the interests of property and unequal treatment of different status groups was accepted as the norm. Despite the fears of the gentry, mass education did not enable the ordinary village youth to cope with the intricacies of W. S. Gilbert's humour in a local production of *Cox and Box* More seriously, Bourne refers to the severe reading difficulties of even the better-educated labourers which led them, through deprivation of information on wider issues, to be concerned purely with things of the moment

43

and to be unable to grasp the significance of political and social principles or world events. Allied to this was the lack of imagination and general intellectual poverty of children's play. But at least in these respects things were seen to be improving as the popular press increased its circulation, with the consequent widening of people's horizons: '. . . thanks to the cheap press, ideas and information about the whole world are finding their way into the cottages of the valley';[5] Bourne's analysis of changes in his village can be criticised on a number of counts. He seems to have over-romanticised the 'peasant system' (not all labourers were deeply satisfied in their work and happy in their place on the status ladder), and to have under-stressed the significant improvements in real incomes, health and diet which must surely have been felt in the Farnham of 1900 as compared to that of 1850. Nevertheless his deeply thoughtful account of the local impact of social and political change provides useful points of comparison for the study of Ringmer between the wars.

One source of quite fundamental change for Ringmer was provided by the 1914–18 war. Reference to a number of tables in Chapter 1 will demonstrate the great differences between 1910 and 1920, in the employment structure for women (Table 1.2), the number of domestic servants (Table 1.3), the infant mortality rate (Table 1.18), the size of the electorate (Table 1.7) and the total newspaper circulation (Table 1.9). Peake saw the war as one possible source for the rebirth of village community spirit generally:

> During the war all the young men of the villages, and many of those approaching middle life, passed their time amidst thousands of their fellows. The close association with others of their kind in the trenches or the YMCA huts has left a lasting impression on most of them, and in the Village Clubs which are being started all over the country we may see the germ of a new sociability and of the revival of the community spirit.[6]

This levelling experience must have been shared by those who went from Ringmer; '. . . some 150 men had gone from their parish but they still had 30 to 40 men left who were eligible for military service . . .'[7] This quotation shows that about one-quarter of the total male population of the village had gone, or were about to go, to the trenches. The effects of this depletion, part of it tragically permanent, on the demographic structure, on the social and political attitudes and on the place of women in the community were far-reaching during the ensuing years of peace. It will be possible to trace some, but by no means all, of these effects.

POPULATION STRUCTURE

Because of the destruction of most of the unpublished material from the 1931 census in a fire during the second world war, it is not possible to reconstruct the age/sex characteristics of Ringmer for that year. It has therefore been necessary to use the 1921 census to trace the more detailed aspects pf the inter-war demographic structure. This choice of date is clearly not ideal but it will at least illuminate more clearly some of the effects of the 1914–18 war. The total population in 1921 was 1359, of whom 638 were males and 721 female. This compares with 1417 in 1871 and 1398 in 1911 (when males slightly outnumbered females). There were 346 separate families or occupiers (giving an average family size of 3·9) and the population lived in a total of 340 houses.[8] The age/sex structure of the population in 1921 is shown in Figure 5.1. The war seems to have produced certain other effects apart from the imbalance between the total of males and females. The number of children in the youngest five-year cohort was appreciably below that of the next three cohorts. And the imbalance between males and females was most marked between the ages of 20 and 39 (162 men to 203 women). The percentage born within the parish was surprisingly low at 33%.[9] The largest proportion of residents (41%) was born elsewhere in the county. This seems to indicate a very high degree of short-range migration. No information is available on the birthplace of the 355 extra-county in-migrants except that 329 were from the rest of England and Wales, a further 16 from elsewhere in the United Kingdom and 10 were born abroad.

During the period 1926–35, 90 couples were married in the parish church.[10] In 46% of these cases, both partners already lived in the parish. The distance distribution for the incoming partner (normally the man) for the remainder of cases is shown in Table 5.4.

The birthplace evidence provided by the census conflicts with various statements made in interviews with longstanding village residents. Without exception these all stressed the 'closed' nature of the community and especially the near absence of newcomers during the inter-war years:

'. . . no new people moved in; there were the same people here for ages . . .'

'. . . there was some emigration, mostly for work purposes, but few people came in . . .'

If one is part of a network of lifelong friends, and if, as is often the case with country people, one enlarges this network only slowly and with caution it is easy in retrospect to feel that one's circle of friends and aquaintances comprised the entire village. Newcomers to the village were perhaps not remembered because they were socially 'invisible'. In this respect as with endlessly repeated claims that 'everybody knew everybody', subjective impressions of the past do not equate with reality. It is therefore quite possible for informants to exaggerate the extent to which the village functioned as a single community and to deny the extent to which immigration occurred.

Certain demographic information is available for 1931 from the published census material.[11] The population in that year was 1607, of whom 800 were male and 807 female. There were 433 families in the parish and the average family size was therefore 3·7. Apart from this information at the parish level, other contemporary data are available for Chailey Rural District, of which the parish forms a part. The 1933 vital rates for the district were as follows:

Vital Rates–Chailey R.D.C., 1933

Birth rate   12·9 per 1000 (England and Wales 14·4)
Death rate   11·2 per 1000 (England and Wales 12·3)
Death rate (under 1 year)   33·1 per 1000 (England and Wales 64·0)
Source: Annual Report of the Medical Officer of Health, Chailey
    R.D.C., 1934

The 1931 age/sex breakdown of Chailey Rural District[12] shows that in the 30–59 group, those who 12–15 years previously had been most affected by the 1914–18 war, there were only 2477 men to 3128 women (792 men per 1000 women). No doubt this imbalance reflected factors other than the effects of the war but it is, nevertheless, a striking one. It may reasonably be assumed that the 1931 imbalance in Ringmer parish was of similar order.

EMPLOYMENT AND ECONOMY

The analysis of the employment structure and economy of the village between the wars should perhaps begin with a brief reference to the part played by the Christies, a landowning family living just outside the parish, in setting up various non-agricultural enterprises in the early 1930s. John Christie, who as a young man fought in the 1914–18 war, was instrumental in starting a construction works, a motor-servicing works, a sawmill and the celebrated Glyndebourne Festival Opera. Much of the initiative was taken during the worst years of the slump. One long-established resident felt:

> . . . if you take John Christie's enterprises away from the village in your mind there was very little left for craftsmen of the type that were employed by him . . . these people would have had extreme difficulties in finding employment at the time . . . there are a number of people in the village today who owe their whole standard of existence to the start given to them by Christie . . .

This informant considered that while Christie's work for the village may not have been fully appreciated at the time, there was never any feeling of hate for this 'big house' family as there was in neighbouring parishes to the south. Other informants of various political persuasions made similar, if less detailed, comments. It was especially noted that Christie would always 'pass the time of day' with a workman and that he 'made a point of spotting talent and helped people'.

Christie's private motives in creating work in a difficult period may be interpreted in a variety of ways. It is sufficient for our present purposes to note that the action and capital of a member of the landed gentry was of critical importance to the prosperity and employment growth of the village between the wars. In fact, in the recollection of various people, workers were actually commuting into the village from Lewes, Uckfield, Eastbourne and Brighton during the early 1930s.

It is not possible to reconstruct the inter-war employment structure of village residents with any accuracy. However, an examination of the stated occupations of the Ringmer men who married in the parish church between 1926 and 1935 provides the pattern shown in Table 3.1. Although the population subset formed by those marrying in the parish church is biased by age and possibly by social status, the table provides a few useful points. Only about one-third of the total were directly involved in agriculture while a slightly larger proportion were engaged in a variety of jobs in the manufacturing sector of industry. Only seven of the total were engaged in the service sector.

Again, the recollections of several informants who stressed that most men in the village were employed in agriculture is confounded by the facts. It seems likely, from the pattern of employment, that Christie was the largest single employer of men. One informant thought that: '. . . most people were employed in the village or in village-based organisations' (a clear reference to the various Christie enterprises).

Table 3.1 Occupations of the Ringmer Men Marrying in the Parish Church, 1926–35

Farmer	2	Mechanic	2
Farm labourer	5	Wheelwright	1
Gardener	5	Bricklayer	1
Mushroom grower	1	Milkman	1
Cowman	1	Police constable	1
Council worker	3	Hotel porter	1
Motor driver	1	Clerk	1
Lorry driver	2	Chemist	1
Bus driver	3	Haulage contractor	1
Carpenter	2	Seed merchant	1
Builder's labourer	1	Engineer	1
			38

Source: Ringmer Parish Marriage Register

The pattern of work for women was rather simpler. Most young girls, on leaving school, went into service or shop work. In service, a girl would proceed up a status hierarchy that was well defined, from scullerymaid through parlourmaid, under housemaid, second housemaid, upper housemaid and head housemaid to housekeeper at the top. In the case of the largest house in Ringmer, nearly all staff lived in and the only time off was between 2.30 p.m. and 10 p.m. on Sunday. This enabled the staff to attend evening service at the church (the morning service attracted a higher-status congregation). There were clear-cut loyalties and some lower-status families tended to supply domestic servants to the same 'big house' for generations. On marriage, nearly all women would stop working: '. . . very very few married women went out to work, they stayed at home and looked after the family; there were just not the jobs for married women in those days, it was a scandal if a married woman went out to work'. This informant could have added that in the absence of modern domestic appliances there was simply no time left over for women with a family to work outside the home. These are very significant points, both socially, in that women had no chance to form a work-based circle of friends, and economically. Their consequence was that families were entirely dependent on the earnings of the head of the household and unemployment, or cuts in wages, were even more serious matters than they would be now since there were no supplementary earnings to fall back on:

'. . . there wasn't very much in the way of extra coming in if the breadwinner fell out of work; I don't really know where one got one's money from, people were really down on their beam ends'.

Wage rates for manual workers tended to be tied to the very low agricultural rates early in the period but were raised later. A letter dated 2nd June 1919 from Chailey R.D.C. to the Clerk of the Parish Council reads: '. . . the council was unable to adopt the recommendation to pay the man engaged at the sewage outfall works increased wages of 40 shillings per week, but adopted instead a resolution that he be paid according to the standard rate for agricultural labourers'.[13] This standard rate had been considerably improved towards the end of the war by the work of courageous labour leaders: 'a local branch of the farm workers union was formed in 1917–18 and this had a big effect, for wages went up . . . but most workers lived in tied cottages and did not want to speak out'.

Despite this action the average income of farm labourers in the village just after the war was perhaps a little over 20s. per week. '. . . wages were from, say, 22s. 6d. up to 50s. later, it did not vary much from farm to farm'.

Thus it is clear that, just after the 1914 war, wages for non-agricultural workers were being held down to agricultural levels. These, in turn, had been decided largely by the farm-owners. Several factors combined to improve matters. As a result of the Agricultural Wages (Regulation) Act of 1924, average minimum wage rates for male agricultural workers rose to a little over 30s. per week. Unfortunately there was little further improvement during the 1920s and 1930s. It is clear also that hours of work were often considerably in excess of the basic week of 50 hours. One informant recollects that her father worked long hours for seven days a week and had very few Sundays off. The widow of a carpenter recalls that her husband worked on average from 6.30 a.m. to 8 p.m. for a wage of 50s. Shop assistants could expect to work from 8.30 a.m. to 7 p.m. six days weekly (with a half-day on Wednesday) while the council employee referred to in the letter quoted above worked from 7 a.m. to 5 p.m. six days a week. It is evident that most employees, whether agricultural or not, were working something like 60 hours a week, some much more than this. In these circumstances, holidays must have been especially welcome. There were no paid holidays for farm workers and, in the case of the carpenter, no holiday at all until 1929. It was almost unheard of to take a holiday away from home. Bank holidays were regarded as very important events in the year, and people no doubt made certain that they did not waste their Sundays.

One other factor contributed to the rise in local wage levels between the wars. Christie, in his various enterprises, offered wages considerably above the agricultural level. He appears to have been especially generous to craftsmen who were good at their job. One informant recalls that, in 1934, at least half a dozen men in the building works, craftsmen not managers or foremen, were coming to work by car. This provides clear evidence that wages were above agricultural levels as it is unlikely that any farm workers at this level owned cars. Other employers in the area, if they wished to keep their staff, had to improve their wages to match those offered by Christie. Relationships

Out for a walk, or perhaps going home from Church in Sunday best, sometime around 10. Bicycles, horses and small carts are the main traffic. Efforts to take a photograph from the same spot in 1972 were abandoned on grounds of safety.

b Wedding of Farmer Holford's daughter before the first world war. The bridal party travelled in the gaily decorated wagon. The Holfords lived in the farmhouse shown in Plate 1b. Several members of the squirearchy appear to be present. The dog cannot be induced to look at the camera.

4a The collapse of a wall of the Post Office following drain digging, perhaps around 1920. The merchandise from the shelves has been stacked outside. Note the range of commodities and services available (cf. Plate 8b) and the shopkeeper wondering what to do about the draught in his bedroom.

4b Ringmer Cricket Club in about 1920. The clerk to the Parochial Church Council sits with the Postmaster, two 'Gentlemen' and the Vicar, while the Clerk to the Parish Council (second from the right) stands. Caps are de rigeur for most standers; pads are in short supply, playing gear varies, moustaches are magnificent. Presumably the lad with the ball is the demon bowler.

between employers and employees varied a great deal. One informant considers: '. . . farm workers were always afraid of losing their jobs, you had to toe the line very much; you had one Sunday off in seven and it was no use protesting'.

Since, under the 'tied cottage' system, dismissal meant the loss of a home as well as a job, it is easy to see how cautious an employee had to be and how little a farmer who was acting oppressively had to fear. Farmers varied considerably as employers. Several were known to be excellent, and this showed in a low turnover rate of farm workers. Others were unable to keep their workers and tended to employ 'bad' families who went the rounds from parish to parish, never staying long in any one job. There was a clear consensus in the minds of several informants about which farmers were good employers and which were bad. Relationships 'in service' could be very close. One informant who had been in service recalls that: '. . . we were all, you know, pally–they were very friendly and helped you out. If my husband was on the dole [the houseowner] used to give me a chit for some groceries.' No doubt relationships were not always as friendly but the quotation does explain, in part, the loyalties and even affection felt between families at different status levels.

The shops and other services provided in the village in 1927 are shown in Table 3.2. This represents a very full range of services for a population of

Table 3.2 Shops, Services and Tradesmen in Ringmer, 1927

Publicans	5	Builders	2
Boot- and shoemakers	2	Beer retailer	1
Carpenter	1	Insurance agent	1
Corn miller	1	Chimney sweep	1
Bakers	2	Garage	1
Blacksmith	1	Tax collector	1
Butcher	1	Cycle agents	1
Wheelwright	1	Laundry	1
Grocers	3	Undertaker	1

Source: Kelly's Directory for Sussex, 1927

1600 people, especially at a time when consumer demands were less sophisticated than they are today. One informant recalls:

'. . . all the everyday necessities of life were available in the village . . . probably in the early 1930s there was a number of people who never left the village' (see Plate 4a).

This implied a degree of self-sufficiency that is supported by the comment of another informant: '. . . we would never dream of going to Brighton [11 miles distant] to shop'. There was a considerable improvement in the bus service to Lewes during the period under review, the frequency increasing from four a day to a frequency, just before the war, rather better than that today. Many people, however, walked or cycled to Lewes rather than waiting for, and paying for, the bus. As one informant recalls:

'. . . if something was sixpence cheaper in Lewes one walked there rather than buy in Ringmer.'

Presumably if there was one thing that was better then than now it was the shape of one's leg muscles.

PROPERTY AND FARM OWNERSHIP

The 1934 Valuation List for Ringmer classifies over two-thirds of the 499 properties as 'cottages' with an average rateable value of £7–£8 while most of the other residential properties were classified as 'houses' with an average rateable value of £20 or so. The ten 'mansions', most of which had sporting rights, were over three times more valuable, on average, than the 'houses'. The terminology, and the values, suggest a neat three-part division of society. Comparison with the 1867 valuation shows a new category of property, local authority housing, which on the evidence of rateable values was superior to the cottages but averaged only half the value of the private houses. One man, Christie, owned over 25% of properties in the parish. In 1867 the five most important property-owners taken together accounted for a similar percentage. Of the total of approximately 434 households in the village, 105 were owner-occupiers, 273 were tenants of private landlords and 56 were local authority tenants. It therefore appears that about 45% of the private tenants were in properties owned by Christie.

The distribution of rateable values is as shown in Figure 5.3. The pattern is not dissimilar from that of 1867 although the mean value has moved up a little. Two-thirds of the properties fall in the lowest 4% of the total range and over 90% fall in the lowest 12%. The 1934 valuation lists 27 properties designated as farms, although no doubt some of these should more accurately be termed smallholdings. Of the 27, 9 were owned by the farmer, 4 by the East Sussex County Council and 14 by private landlords. Of the latter, 9 were owned by Christie. Taking the acreages of the farms into account, it seems likely that the proportion of the total farmland of the parish owned by this family was probably of the order of 40–50% of the total area, rather more than it had been in 1867. Clearly decisions made by this one landowner concerning terms and conditions of service could have had decisive effects on the standard of living of a large proportion of those employed in agriculture and related occupations.

LOCAL GOVERNMENT AND SOCIAL ADMINISTRATION

Far-reaching changes in local government occurred between the 1870s and the 1920s. In 1884 many rural householders were enfranchised and this resulted, in many cases, in the election to Parliament of a professional man rather than the squire. The establishment of county councils and rural district councils threatened the power of the squirearchy still further. The same act set up the parish councils to supersede the 'vestry meeting' system of parochial administration. Arnold-Baker summarises the effects of these changes for rural areas:

> In 1894, the squire, the parson and sometimes the schoolmaster were the leaders of the village, their influence depended upon their traditional prestige, their superior education and their relative wealth and, in a hierarchical society, upon their social standing. The vestries had followed their lead, taken their advice or bowed to their power. The parish councils were regarded as an intrusion. Most of them began without the co-operation of the influential and had even to face their active opposition. This, in an age when higher education was the privilege of a class, was a serious matter.[14]

Tensions between the landed gentry and the new councils were inherently likely over a number of issues. These included, for example, the effect on rates of increased public spending, the question of public rights of way across estates, and the more general issue of the democratisation of local government decision-making.

Some of these tensions could be exemplified in Ringmer where, for many years, the clerk to the parish council and the biggest landowner were, to quote one recollection 'at daggers drawn'. There were also pressures from farmers on the parish council to keep down the level of parochial expenditure. When sending an apology for absence for a forthcoming meeting to discuss the new village sewage system one farmer member wrote: 'I trust our chairman will do his usual good work in pointing out the fact that the rates of Ringmer are already very heavy, and so make any alterations that must be done as small as possible . . .'[15] To set this request in context, it was believed at the time that the spread of diphtheria was caused by inadequate sewage arrangements and Ringmer had already suffered one bad outbreak of this killer disease earlier in the century. Such concern with the level of the rates was invariably uppermost in the deliberations of the parish council since, between the wars, it was largely composed of farmers and landowners. Elections were infrequent. One respondent recalls: '. . . one has only to think of what a fiasco an election would have been . . . could you have imagined a farm labourer who was living in a tied cottage under the thumb of a farmer failing to put up his hand and vote for his employer?' The same general tendency was evident in general elections: '. . . there was not much political activity in the village . . . when the time came for the cross to be put down it was put down for the Conservative party without much thought'. Thus, either from fear or indifference, many low-income voters failed to support candidates who would have had their interests at heart.

Two quotations sum up the significance of the parish council to the village between the wars:

> '. . . a very small number of people knew of the existence of the council . . . it was not generally known who served on it and there were

no elections because there were never more nominations than vacancies
. . . it made no impact on the village.'

'. . . I'm not sure what the parish council did . . . people did not seek
amenities like street lighting, refuse collection or built-up roads . . . we
just accepted the village as it was.'

The interests of women were particularly poorly represented. There were
virtually no women members at parish or rural district level, and the few who
sat on county councils were members of the 'gentry'. One old lady in the
village commented: '. . . I was just busy doing housework and so on. I don't
remember anything about these details.' It is evident that, with a very few
honourable exceptions, the members of the parish council did not collectively
represent the urgent needs of the great majority of people in the village, and
the council itself did not constitute much of a threat or 'intrusion' to the
power of the gentry. As one authoritative observer put it: '. . . one of the
basic objectives of a local authority in those days was to do nothing and spend
no money, thus saving on the rates'. Ringmer parish council, in fact, spent
only about £25 per year during the period.[16] This is one powerful explanation
of the survival of archaic standards of public health, and thus low standards of
private health and welfare, up until the outbreak of the second world war.

The system of collective social security had broadened considerably since
the 1870s as a result of national legislation. A review of the social reforms of
1905 to 1914 and the even more complex tangle of measures between 1919 and
1939 would be neither helpful nor possible in the present context, especially
since several good one volume works exist on the subject.[17] Major reforms
concerning pensions and unemployment had been passed under the pre-war
Liberal administration and the most thoroughgoing review since 1834 of the
working of the Poor Law was carried out in 1905–9. But the rate of unemployment after 1919 (the national rate never fell below 10% between then and
1939) forced further reforms. As Bruce pointed out: 'What had not been
anticipated was that unemployment insurance and the poor law together
would face, as the years went by and economic stability did not return, a test
of exceptional severity beyond the range of pre-war experience.'[18]

For the village, the main impact of these measures was the change in the
administration of the poor law. The 1929 Local Government Act abolished
the unions of parishes and the Boards of Guardians and transferred most of
their functions to the county councils. The Lewes Union of nineteen parishes,
to which Ringmer belonged up to 1929, ceased to exist and the parish thus
lost all vestiges of its former responsibility for the relief of the poor. Some
details of the operation of the union up to that date may be instructive. In
October 1924, for example, a 2½-year-old illegitimate girl was taken from her
mother, who had been sentenced to three months' imprisonment for felony.
The mother was obliged to forfeit all rights to the child until she was 18:
'having regard to the mode of life of the mother'.[19] In another case out-relief
was stopped to a man because he was living with a woman other than his
wife.[20] One Guardian remembers[21] a lengthy discussion in committee on
whether workhouse inmates should have cake twice, rather than once, per

week. The more liberal course was finally adopted. The 'casual wards', where wayfarers and tramps were allowed to stay one night, were by far the worst. For example, little effort was made to repair the heating and hot-water system of the wards when it broke down. The same Guardian recollects that '. . . the workhouse was shoved far away down a side road where it could be conveniently forgotten . . . in theory the inmates could make any complaint to us but I don't remember any of them ever doing so'. His request to inspect the casual ward was received with astonishment; nobody had made such a request in living memory.

Despite the plethora of national social security measures, many categories of need were still quite inadequately catered for, even by 1939. For example, Bruce[22] points out that nearly 20 million dependants were left unprotected by national health insurance and the unemployment relief was quite insufficient to cope with long-term unemployment. The Poor Law Unions, in fact, dispensed over £150 million in the years following the war,[23] much of it to chronically unemployed men. In 1939, also, some 60,000 of a national total of 206,000 hospital beds were still being maintained under the Poor Law, or, as it had been renamed, 'public assistance'.[24] It should be recorded that the official principles laid down in 1930 included the following: 'The relief provided should be repressive, by making it morally repulsive, and severe in the treatment of the idle, immoral and vicious.'[25]

In the light of the patchy nature of the national collective security system, the level of unemployment, and the well-founded fear of the workhouse, it is easy to see why Ringmer residents, of all political views, should feel retrospectively grateful for the employment produced by the various Christie enterprises in the early 1930s.

The quality of housing in the parish was, by today's standards, extremely poor. The 1934 Annual Report of the Chailey R.D.C. Medical Officer of Health records a total of 3325 houses in the district of which 2101 are classified as 'working-class houses'. These cottages would typically obtain their water from a well, use oil lamps for lighting, have a pail under the sink for drainage and have a pail or earth closet. Pail drainage was in fact recommended by the Ministry of Agriculture to the county council in the 1920s as the appropriate standard for the council smallholdings. Several local Sanitary Inspectors in the 1920s made themselves extremely unpopular with the landed interests by condemning cottages as 'unfit to live in'.[26] This was presumably a new concept to the squirearchy. Fortunately the inspectors had job security protected by legislation independent of the district council, and they could pursue this policy without fear of dismissal. There were, as a result, some memorable rows in the council over the question. The worst cottages in Ringmer were in a terrace known as Kennel Cottages at Rushey Green. They had been used as an isolation hospital for infectious diseases in the Napoleonic Wars and subsequently as kennels for dogs. They had a maximum ceiling height of about six feet at the apex. This did not prevent their being used for human habitation until the mid-1930s.

Housing legislation passed just after the first world war required district councils to provide more local authority housing. This prompted a public enquiry in Chailey Rural District in the mid-1920s.[27] In view of housing conditions, and since the authority had not been active in this sphere since the war, the council was ordered by the Ministry to build some houses. As a result, about 50 houses were built in the late 1920s, 36 of them in Broyle Lane at the eastern end of the village. It is not absolutely clear why the location was chosen, since it has not been possible to trace any reports from the housing committee of the day. It may be significant, however, that the land did not previously belong to the Christies and that the development is hardly visible from the village centre. The houses were built under a 'package deal' arrangement with a developer who subsequently went bankrupt. They were of the poorest possible quality and, in particular, the insulation was poor so that they were always cold. Improvements, including facing the exteriors with brick, had to be carried out in the 1950s. This development had another undesirable feature; it formed the nucleus for later development at this outlying point and led indirectly to the present unfortunate separation of about one-fifth of the village from the main shops and services. This situation will be examined more closely in Part III.

Even by the mid-thirties, mains services were not well developed in the village. Water came largely from wells. A survey of water supplies in 1934 showed that: '. . . the existing supply is both inadequate and unsafe . . . a public supply is definitely needed from all viewpoints and especially from a Public Health viewpoint'.[28] Of 44 water samples taken for analysis, 14 were reported unsafe for drinking. No doubt, too, bathing occurred less frequently in view of the trouble one had to take. One informant recalls that it took half an hour's hard work to raise enough water for a bath from a 150-foot well. Some of the houses owned by Christie used a private supply pumped from Glyndebourne but this, too, was sometimes polluted. Adequate mains water did not reach the village until during the second world war. Electricity began to be available in the village during the 1930s, but very few houses could afford to use it in the pre-war period. Sewers had been laid to the village before the first world war but relatively few houses were connected to them. The idea of refuse collection was unheard of until the late 1920s, and at one public meeting on the subject a loud and very rural voice demanded 'What's wrong with burying rubbish in the garden?' Unfortunately the tremendous increase in the use of food packaging, and especially of tins and bottles, produced more domestic rubbish than most gardens could assimilate and a monthly refuse collection service began in 1931.

Much of the food consumed within the parish was locally produced. Local cattle were taken 'on the hoof' to one of the 18 slaughterhouses in the rural district, and the cutting up and preparation of the meat was done, usually on Monday mornings, by the butcher who was to sell it in his shop later in the week. Milk was fresh from the cows but was unpasteurised and frequently contaminated. It often went sour in less than 24 hours in hot weather, and as a result it was sometimes impossible to give milk to babies late at night. In any case meat and milk formed a much smaller proportion of the total diet than they do now, while bread and potatoes were much more frequently eaten.

These various circumstances were reflected in the pattern of general health, illnesses and death. In 1933, the most frequent infectious diseases notified were respiratory TB, scarlet fever, pneumonia and dysentery.[29] Of the 156 deaths recorded in Chailey R.D.C. in 1933, 28 were due to heart disease, 15 to cerebral haemorrhage, 15 to tuberculosis, 13 to malignant cancer and 11 to pneumonia. The low protein and vitamin B content of many diets led to serious problems of malnutrition and rickets. Fortunately, Ringmer school was one of the pioneers in the development of a school canteen in 1928. This ensured that children had at least one hot meal a day. Very soon a large majority of the children were using the service (at 1s. 3d. per dinner) and this made a great deal of difference to standards of health in many families. Two quotations will convey the general attitude towards health at the time:

'. . . the old people looked after themselves . . . people take tablets and that now but in our day there were no tablets . . . if you had a headache you had to go to work and forget all about it.'

'. . . the standard of health was not as good as it is today but we were tough children–we grew up tough because you had to. I think malnutrition was probably the commonest ailment.'

The vast majority of Ringmer children went to the village school. The roll averaged 180–230 children,[30] compared to the estimated maximum of 15–20 attending the grammar school in Lewes. Attendance at the grammar school entailed the payment of fees:

'. . . some families, if they wanted grammar school education, had to send their children to the school one at a time.'

The village school had an infants' section and seven 'standards'. It is difficult to discern precisely the balance of subjects and the mode of teaching used. An inspector's report in 1928[31] notes that the arithmetic was generally weak, that there was too much note-taking in history and geography, and too much 'reading aloud'. However, the boys were commended for the excellence of their 'practical project'; this had consisted of laying the drains on the sports field recently donated by the Christies. The Women's Institute assisted in the May Day celebrations and the British Legion collaborated in the organisation of Sports Day. Concerts and recitations were given by artists sent by national organisations which specialised in providing culture to villages and country towns.[32] At Christmas, presents were collected for distribution to the schoolchildren. In 1926 over 600 presents were received, enough to provide three for every child. In addition they each received a bag of sweets and an orange from Colonel Craven of the British Legion, an echo of the benevolence of Major Harwood 60 years previously. The relatively poor general state of health in the village is reflected in various other entries in the school log. There were frequent visits from the doctor and the nurse to inspect 'verminous' children and regular outbreaks of whooping cough, mumps, scarlet fever, influenza and chicken pox. Attendances varied seasonally from about 55% of the total roll to about 90%. In January 1933 the incidence of colds and influenza caused the Medical Officer of Health to close the school for 17 days. In the circumstances, the provision of the hot school dinners, which were being taken by 170 of the 230 children by 1931, must have been invaluable.

SOCIAL STRUCTURE AND ACTIVITIES

This section on village social structure in the inter-war years draws heavily on the recollections of at least ten residents who lived through the period. The informants came from a wide range of backgrounds, from near-gentry to the widow of a manual worker. While the selectivity of memory is well known, and perceptions of long-past relationships and events vary widely, there was a clear consensus among the informants, who were interviewed individually, on a number of points. Everyone stressed that the lines between different social groups were much more clearly drawn 40 years ago than they are today. There was near unanimity about which families constituted 'the gentry' and that there were only a small number of families intermediate between this group and the much more numerous 'cottagers'. This is not entirely consistent with the rateable value data which suggest a quite large number of middle-income families.

The gentry were, in the words of one informant, 'all elderly and bridge playing'. They constituted a 'calling circuit'—an incoming family of appropriate status would be called upon (not at a meal time) by various others. They would then perhaps be invited to dine with the callers. One had to be a little careful of the activities one indulged in. The following quotation is representative of many:

> The differences were much greater than they are today. In those days you were always very particular to be polite to the vicar of the parish and the gentry . . . I remember my grandfather was terribly worried when he worked at —— [a big house] . . . he didn't dare to say what his politics were and if you wanted to vote Labour you wouldn't dare to say so otherwise you might be in danger of losing your job . . . we were always very discreet about things like that.

A similar remark was:

> '. . . people knew their place and were happy in their place.'

Another informant, a highly respected old gentleman felt that:

> . . . there was clear class differentiation but no class feeling . . . no animosity . . . perhaps the upper classes were a bit condescending . . . people accepted the social structure, you wouldn't get any spontaneous objection to the system as it was—you got the occasional hothead like me stirring it up. I was the Labour organiser for the constituency when I arrived [in 1927] and I was very much under a cloud.

This informant showed a quite remarkable generosity to old political opponents. Although he had served as a Sunday School teacher for 25 years, some members of the church sought to prevent his becoming a lay reader by means of a petition to the bishop. This was unsuccessful. In view of his known socialist leanings it was also suggested that he should resign as a Parish Councillor and as a school manager.

The church was characterised by at least two informants independently as 'the conservative party at prayer'. There was a sequence of incumbents during the period. One gave up the parish on becoming a lord while another achieved a degree of popularity, especially among the less wealthy, by 'going around giving out halfcrowns'–an echo of the distribution of mutton broth undertaken by his nineteenth-century predecessor.

The Christies, the apex of the village social structure, were regarded by almost all informants as good landlords and interested in their tenants. A surprising number of ordinary people claim to have known them quite well. They held parties to which large numbers were invited, not all gentry by any means, and they gave gifts and Christmas trees at appropriate seasons. Christie's birthday was marked by the distribution of cloaks and jerseys to the children of the village. At various times the family gave land for the school playing fields, space for a car park near the church and a new organ for the church (once opposition to accepting the gift on the part of some parishioners had been overcome). On the other hand it was considered by some that:

'. . . the Christies had very little effect on everyday social life, they were rather aloof from normal village activities',

and

'. . . he did not act as the "great I am" unless you overstepped the mark, then he let you know.'

Most of the recorded observations concerning the social structure relate to the gentry. None of the higher-status people interviewed gave any evaluations of the lower-status families, or offered comments or episodes that would illuminate their place in the village community. This is perhaps an instinctive judgment on the relative social significance of this group as compared to the gentry. It was clear, however, that when the first 30 or so local authority houses were built a half mile to the east of the village centre in the late 1920s they were regarded by some as socially, as well as physically, beyond the pale. The new estate was, in fact, referred to as 'Tiger Bay' and was known, or thought, to be a very rough area.

Despite the many references to social distinctions, all informants stressed that 'the village was a single community' and 'everybody knew everybody'. One further quotation makes this point, and demonstrates the power of informal social sanctions, very clearly. The reply was in answer to the question 'Was it widely socially acceptable to go to a pub?'

I don't think anything was acceptable in those days compared to what is acceptable today. It seemed a very strict regime. It seemed that shame came into this. If anyone did anything that was against the law or which was bucking authority or society, the fear was in the shame which it brought. You were almost pilloried in this way . . . People knew everything about you. You see, you walked everywhere. People did not see you from the chest up through the windscreen of a car, they saw what you were wearing and whether you went to church with dirty shoes or clean shoes.

The review of village social activities 40 years ago must take into account the limited extent to which the village was connected to the outside world. One informant recalls:

'. . . if you went to Brighton it was a real treat . . . you just didn't go anywhere very much.'

While another estimated that in 1934 there were still only about 25 cars in the village. The mass media, too, penetrated strikingly less than today:

'. . . there was no radio or T.V. when we were younger [in the early 1920s] I don't think we took a daily paper so there was no way of keeping in touch with national events as we do now.'

Towards the end of the period, the radio was beginning to have very great effects:

'. . . wireless was beginning to have tremendous effects on people's understanding of national events . . . they became personally involved on Cup Final Day and Boat Race day.'

Around 1930, however, nearly everyone's social activities were village-based and everybody must have talked about, even if they did not partake in, the main social events of the year.

Then, as now, there was a rich array of social institutions and events. For many people the church was at the centre of the social, as well as the spiritual, life of the village. Estimates about the importance of churchgoing varied from '. . . it was voluntary (!) but not very many went' and 'it was not very important', to '. . . so many people went to church it was packed absolutely solid morning and evening'. Various other informants agreed on the decline in churchgoing that had occurred since before the 1914–18 war. A number of social organisations existed. Of these the Women's Institute was perhaps the most energetic. Their activities included musical programmes and plays, performances by conjurers and ventriloquists, the organisation of flower shows, fairs and maypole dancing on the green. They also ran cooking and knitting competitions. Other church-connected clubs and activities included the Sisterhood, the Mothers' Union, the annual church bazaar and the Scouting activities for both sexes. Christie donated the Scout hut and his butler acted as Scoutmaster, as well as performing monologues and recitations in the village hall or 'parish room' as older residents term it. Music played an important part in social life. The church choir was of a high standard, frequent musical evenings were held in a number of homes, and a choral society performed in the parish room. Bonfire night was an eagerly awaited annual event and dances, jumble sales, whist drives and talent competitions attracted wide participation. Also popular were 'Canadian Feasts', a form of social evening in the parish room where everyone brought refreshments and exchanged them with selected partners. For men, specifically, the 'Ringmer Club' met at *The Anchor*.

The Cricket Club was the most important sporting institution, as it had been sixty years previously (see Plate 4b). The Football Club was less well known but stoolball and bowls prospered. An annual stag hunt was held with a stag specially imported from Surrey while, working downwards in size of prey, foxhunting and the annual sparrow shoot attracted a wide following. The annual fête on the village green, organised by the British Legion, often incorporated the 'Caburn Run' when men of the village competed in a 2½-mile run down from the top of a near-by chalk outlier. Point-to-point races on horseback over fences were held, and attracted large numbers of spectators. Indoor organised social activities included whist drives and billiards in the parish room, and cribbage and darts in the pubs. There was a large party at Glyndebourne every Christmas for the young people of the village. Apart from these organised activities, family walks on Sunday were popular, and several landlords had paths and fences built up and placed seats in a number of convenient stopping places. In the words of one informant:

'. . . people were walking everywhere . . . you would often bump into the same family more than once on the same walk' (see Plate 3a).

A day trip farther afield was a real treat:

'. . . we never had any holidays but mother would take two of us at a time down to Seaford or Newhaven for a day.'

Children, as always, devised their own amusements. The lack of traffic meant that they could play and cycle safely in the main road and, such was the rarity of cars, collecting car numbers was a popular pastime. Other reported activities included bird's-nesting, fishing, swimming in a near-by river, skating on the dewponds, looking for meteorites and fossils in the chalkpits (which involved inducing small landslides) and tobogganing on the steep grassy slopes of the downs on homemade toboggans. All these activities, if somewhat hard on limbs and clothes, are typically and specifically 'rural' and make an interesting contrast to the present pattern of children's play described in Chapter 10. Rather more prosaic were the festivities arranged for children by the W.I. for Empire Day each year (24th May). These included maypole dancing in the school playground (see Plate 2b), a tea provided by the dutiful ladies, and prize-giving for various competitions, one of which involved writing a composition on 'Heroes of the Empire'. For some, the hills, fields and streams must have beckoned even more invitingly as that dreary day wore on.

DOMESTIC ECONOMY

In 1921 there was an average of 3·9 people per household. The distribution of household sizes is shown in Table 5.1. There was a total of 1829 habitable rooms, giving an average of 0·73 people per room although the 12 households living in houses with 11 rooms or more had an average of only 0·41 people per room. As might be expected, the larger families had much less space per person. In the households of seven or more people, there was an average of over 1·3 people per room.[33]

Reference has already been made to the general state of housing in this rural district. By today's standards, the sanitation was especially bad. Of the 4818 closets in the district in 1934, only 2246 were flush water closets. Of the rest, 1195 were earth closets, 1124 were cesspools and 253 were middens. Several informants remember the conditions very well:

> '. . . in the tied cottages conditions were terrible, there was no electric light and no mains water . . . despite this the children were usually well dressed and cared for.'

> '. . . only the larger houses had water, I well remember old ladies crossing the green to the village well to carry away water and on some occasions this was labelled "not fit for drinking". There was outside sanitation and oil stoves for heat and light. These were very dangerous, old people often had accidents with them.'

Both these informants, although not experiencing poor conditions at first hand, were very well qualified to comment. Another informant experienced the meaning of the statistics:

> . . . it was terribly cold in the mornings, my mother was always first up very early to light the fire in the kitchen and, often, the fire under the copper in the outhouse. It took 1½ hours to get a copper of boiling water. Bath night occurred twice a week. We all bathed in turn on the kitchen table and all the water had to be heated on the range. There was no electric light till about 1936 and then it was very expensive. We had oil lamps which provided a very poor light and made one's hands smell perpetually of paraffin. Life was very spartan but everybody was living in this way.

There were, however, compensations:

> '. . . there was wonderful bread from the local baker and milk fresh from the cow. Most cottages had a large garden for vegetables and most people owned chickens and possibly a pig. Half the things people buy in the shops now just weren't in existence.'

For one cottager, movement into a local authority house forced a reorganisation of housekeeping arrangements. The minutes of the Chailey Rural District Council meeting of 30th October 1931 record that:

> '. . . the Council regret that the tenant at —— [a recently erected council house] cannot keep a pig'

– it was probably a difficult decision for the tenant to understand.

An informant who lived in an older cottage recalls:

> '. . . every cottage had a bread oven, my mother would never dream of buying bread, cake or jam, it was always homemade.'

Farm labourers also enjoyed certain fringe benefits:

'. . . the cottage was free and we used to get faggots and things like that and so much milk a day, there might also be the occasional rabbit.'

Despite this:

'. . . I was the seventh one of nine and sometimes it was a bit of a squeeze to make do, we didn't often have cake–if you had cake for tea it was quite a luxury.'

Finally, one old lady was convinced that dietary standards have not risen since the 1930s but have fallen:

'. . . the children were more healthy in those days than they are to-day . . . they used to have Irish stews, meat puddings and jam roly-polys and things. They don't have those these days.'

4 · Ringmer in 1971

DEVELOPMENTS FROM THE 1930s TO 1971

The four decades between the early 1930s and the present saw great changes in both national and local life. The festering unemployment problem, fortunately less severe in the Ringmer area than elsewhere, was finally solved by the outbreak of the second world war. Following the war, the Labour administration vastly extended the collective social security services[1] and introduced a system of town and country planning which, with various subsequent modifications, continues to guide the development process.[2] The war itself led to permanent changes in the social and economic structure. The degree of central planning required for a wartime economy provided a useful precedent for the post-war attack on a variety of problems, including those concerning housing and health, while the gravity of the external threat united the nation into a single community more effectively than anything else could have done.

When war broke out in September 1939 it was assumed that invasion, or at least destructive bombing, would follow immediately. Ringmer, in common with other local parishes in the invasion zone, prepared itself for war. A war 'triumvirate' was set up consisting of the civil representative (a prominent farmer), the Home Guard leader (a retired major) and the Police (the village constable).[3] If an invasion occurred the church bells would be rung: '. . . the vicar and the Sexton have access to the ringing chamber and either will undertake the duty at any hour of the day or night.' To avoid false alarms they were to act on word of mouth instructions only. A full range of services, including the Civil Defence, the Police, the Fire Service and the Women's Voluntary Service, were ready for instant action. There was a Water Officer to supervise the use of water and a Billeting Officer to cope with any sudden influx of soldiers or refugees. They could make use of the school, the Church and Chapel, the Scouts' hut and the *outbuildings* of Middleham, the largest house in the village. The parish room was to be the first-aid point and the 'rest centre' where emergency rations were stored. Eight villagers were registered as messengers 'who will distribute messages by cycle'. Emergency transport consisted of a list of horses and carts, and handcarts. Two vans (immobilised at the time for lack of petrol) were designated as ambulances. Furthermore: '. . . if slit trenches are necessary the civil population will be recruited and will provide their own tools.' Various other equipment to be used in emergency included 'a cooking stove (oil) in Mr. Mildmay's attic'. It was presumably not necessary to be more precise about its location. Finally, and fittingly, the vicar was appointed as Burial Officer. Two emergency mortuaries were designated and the field behind the village green was earmarked as a common grave.

Apart from the para-military nature of these various arrangements they had social implications and consequences. If community feeling derives partly from external threat,[4] and to a degree commensurate with the size of the threat,

Ringmer was united as never before or since in the period 1939–45. It is evident from the names of those manning the various services that all status levels were involved in the common effort. All types of people contributed together in the necessary tasks to an extent probably unprecedented since the village was a functioning agricultural system before enclosure. Under the stress of wartime conditions people no doubt made new evaluations, independent of social background, status and sex, of the worth of their fellow-villagers, particularly as recruitment removed the natural leaders and the young men of the village.

The fear that London would be bombed produced another crisis for the village in the form of evacuees. In the first few days of the war, several hundred London schoolchildren ranging in age from 5 to 15 arrived in the school playground.[5] Many of them were frightened and lonely, and few had previously experienced any but an urban environment. They raised a large set of problems, for example billeting, supervision, feeding, welfare and education. There was also the occasional clash of urban and rural life-styles as city children mixed with country families. It was rumoured (probably falsely) that one retired brigadier in the village impressed his values by crisply marching his evacuees to church every Sunday morning. The importance of evacuation as a means of broadening horizons and giving insights into alternative norms and modes of behaviour was recognised by the County Welfare Officer. In the final report on the operation, written as she handed over responsibility for evacuated children to the Public Assistance Committee at the end of the war, she wrote: 'So ceases Evacuation–with all its turmoil and all its strange offshoots. But yet Evacuation has brought about one of the greatest social revolutions of our time for we have learned how the other half of the world lives.'[6] No doubt the returning servicemen had learned about 'other halves' as well, as had those locally who had come into close contact with German and Italian prisoners of war working on the land. The war was clearly a mixer as well as a leveller.

Since there had been no house building or public works during the war years, the end of the war brought another set of problems. There was a shortage of houses and many of those that existed were of an unacceptably low standard. The Medical Officer of Health noted: '. . . pail closets predominate in cottages occupied by farm workers . . . it is becoming increasingly obvious that the neglect of property during the war years is now having serious consequences.'[7] Furthermore, 'in view of the unsatisfactory state of the public well', 80 house-owners were circulated concerning their attitude to possible connection to the mains water supply.[8] Attitudes varied, some were happy with the public well, some had adequate private wells and some simply could not afford the capital outlay involved. As a result, connection took place in a piecemeal fashion over the ensuing decade.

There was an exchange of correspondence early in 1946 between the parish council and the rural district (the housing authority) on the question of more local authority housing for the village.[9] There were local objections to the use of a suitable site near the village centre for such housing, and eventually it was agreed to build some accommodation at a peripheral location even further away than the site used for council housing in the late 1920s. A number of 'prefabs' were built in this location '. . . to be replaced as soon as possible by permanent houses'. They were replaced in 1971. The episode is perhaps indicative of the social values held by local councillors at the time. The fact that Ringmer Parish Council was not even consulted about the number of houses required in the parish is also indicative of the extent to which decision-making about such crucial village issues had moved outside the parish to larger units of administration.

POPULATION STRUCTURE

The 1971 age/sex structure information is taken from an interview survey of 150 households carried out in the summer of 1971, the survey upon which much of Part III of this book is based.[10] The survey achieved an 86% response rate (174 households were identified randomly from the Electoral Roll and 24 were lost to the survey for the usual variety of reasons). The age/sex distribution of the sample is shown in Figure 5.1.

The sample probably under-represents the over-65 category because several old people in a local authority home in the village, although in the original 174, were not interviewed since they appeared to be worried by the idea. The total population of the parish in 1971 was 3720 of whom 1830 were males and 1890 females. There were 1255 separate families or occupiers giving an average household size of 3·0.[11] The sample therefore represents 12·9% of the parish population.

The evidence concerning in-migration indicates a very different situation from those of the previous two periods studied. Only 9% of the sample had been in the village all their lives. 23% had moved from Lewes or Brighton and 39% from elsewhere in Sussex. Moves from London were very infrequent (6%) and only 13% had moved in from outside the south-east region. There is, of course, no balancing information on the destinations of out-migrants from the village over the period, so it is impossible to gauge whether the local figures reflect a net inter-regional flow to the south-east or not. What is clear, however, is that even in the metropolitan south-east, the alleged magnet for migrants from all over the country, this particular study shows a high preponderance of intra-county movement; movement which would not be discerned by migration analyses based on county data. The relationship between previous place of residence and length of time since arrival will be examined in Chapter 7.

In the period 1961–71, 138 couples were married in the parish church.[12] In 25% of these cases, both partners already lived in the parish. The distance distribution of the incoming partner, normally the man, for the remainder of cases is shown in Table 5.4. As in the case of the 1925–35 period, it has not been possible to ascertain vital population rates for the parish. The 1970 rates for Chailey R.D.C., however, are shown in the table opposite.

The rates quoted are crude rates. When adjusted by the Registrar General's correcting factors, which allow for local age/sex structures, the birth rate becomes marginally above the national rate while the death rate becomes markedly lower at 8·2 compared to 11·7. Considerable improvement occurred in the adjusted death rate over the decade 1961–70 since the 1961 figure was 11·9.[13] The 1970 Chailey Rural District figures, while indicative, do not

Vital Rates–Chailey R.D.C., 1970

Birth rate	12·4 per 1000 (England and Wales 16·0)
Death rate	14·7 per 1000 (England and Wales 11·7)
Death rate (under 1 year)	11·0 per 1000 (England and Wales 18·0)

Source: Annual Report of the Medical Officer of Health,
Chailey R.D.C., 1971

accurately reflect the situation in Ringmer parish since it is likely that the inflow of young fertile families here has been proportionately more significant than in the district as a whole.

EMPLOYMENT AND ECONOMY

The occupational structure of the heads of household in the sample survey is set out in Table 4.1, using the Registrar General's seventeen socio-economic groups. Nearly a quarter of the heads of household are employers, managers, or professional workers. Non-manual workers outnumbered manual by more

Table 4.1 Occupations of Head of Household, Ringmer, 1971

1. Employers and managers in large establishments (over 25 employees)	16
2. Employers and managers in small establishments (under 25 employees)	7
3. Professional workers–self-employed	3
4. Professional workers–employees	10
5. Intermediate non-manual workers	24
6. Junior non-manual workers	13
7. Personal service workers	1
8. Foremen and supervisors–manual	1
9. Skilled manual workers	19
10. Semi-skilled manual workers	9
11. Unskilled manual workers	4
12. Own account workers (other than professional)	4
13. Farmers–employers and managers	7
14. Farmers–own account	3
15. Agricultural workers	1
16. Members of Armed Forces	1
17. Occupation inadequately described or retired	27
	150

Source: 1971 Ringmer Survey

than two to one and in both categories it is the intermediate and skilled, rather than the junior and unskilled, that predominate. The agricultural sector constitutes about 8% of the total labour force, and the sample managed to include only one agricultural labourer. The occupational structure is therefore completely different from that of 40 or 100 years earlier, when manual workers, especially farm workers, predominated.

It is popularly believed that many villages in the south-east are 'commuter villages' with a very low ratio of jobs to population and hence a virtually complete daily movement out to work. Ringmer does not entirely fit this pattern as Table 4.2 shows:

Table 4.2 Location of Head of Household's Work, Ringmer, 1971

Location	Percentage of cases
Ringmer	31
Lewes (3 miles)	27
Brighton (11 miles)	16
London (*c.* 50 miles)	4
Other (less than 10 miles)	12
Other (over 10 miles)	10
	100

Source: 1971 Ringmer Survey

Certain features are worth noting; for example nearly a third of heads of household work in the village (although, as we have seen, very few are in agricultural work), very few indeed commute to London, and only 14% of the sample work more than 11 miles from their home. The pattern of work journeys appears to be rather more localised than that found in 1966 in a study of Hampshire villages (where the lower quartile range of journeys to work for rural workers extended up to $3\frac{1}{2}$ miles).[14]

To throw further light on the employment situation a complete survey of jobs in the village was carried out. This revealed the unexpectedly high total of 422 jobs. Table 4.3 shows the distribution between the 17 socio-economic groups. Most of the group 2 workers are employed in the shops and services of the village while a high proportion of groups 9–11 are engaged in the two building works. Other important employing organisations include the two schools (which employ 50–60 people), the Ringmer Hotel (14 people) and the abattoir (16 people).

From the household survey data, the total number employed from the 150 households was as follows:

Full-time workers (over 30 hours per week)   176
Part-time workers (10–30 hours per week)   47
Casual workers   (under 10 hours per week)   8

This gives a full-time equivalent of about 200 workers. If this figure is multiplied by 7·7 (the survey was of a 13% sample) and compared with the total job count (422) it appears that the village is approximately 36% self-sufficient in jobs. This finding is reasonably consistent with the data in Table 4.2, which showed that 31% of heads of households worked in the parish. There are, however, indications of a mismatch between the jobs that exist in the village

Table 4.3 Jobs in Ringmer, 1971

1. Employers and managers in large establishments (over 25 employees)	2
2. Employers and managers in small establishments (under 25 employees)	32
3. Professional workers–self-employed	5
4. Professional workers–employees	2
5. Intermediate non-manual workers	44
6. Junior non-manual workers	69
7. Personal service workers	19
8. Foremen and supervisors–manual	25
9. Skilled manual workers	130
10. Semi-skilled manual workers	14
11. Unskilled manual workers	21
12. Own account workers (other than professional)	11
13. Farmers–employers and managers	10
14. Farmers–own account	6
15. Agricultural workers	32
16. Members of Armed Forces	—
17. Occupations inadequately described or retired	—
	422

Source: 1971 Ringmer Jobs Survey

and the occupational structure of village residents. It seems obvious that many residents in groups 1–5 must work outside the village. On the other hand there might be something approaching self-sufficiency in junior non-manual work and in groups 8–11 (manual work). On the evidence of the sample it seems highly likely that agricultural workers are actually commuting *into* the parish.

It has not been thought worth while to examine wages and conditions of service in any detail. The extent to which these reflect national agreements has increased considerably over time and the approximate details of salary and wage structures for most of the types of work done by Ringmer residents is well known from other sources. Data have been collected, however, on the average length of time that members of the sample households are away from home daily at work or school. These data are socially perhaps even more significant than the hours of work since it might reflect the impact of work absences on family life (for example, whether or not the husband was home from work by the children's bathtime/bedtime). The analysis showed that fewer than 15% of heads of household were away from home for more than 10 hours daily and this is consistent with the pattern of generally short-range journeys to work.

The range of shops and services available in the village was greatly enlarged in 1968–9 when the new 14-shop parade was built in conjunction with one of the private estates (see Plate 5a). The range is shown in Table 4.4.

Table 4.4 Shops and Services in Ringmer, 1971

Public houses	3	Nurseryman	1
Supermarket	1	Electrical goods shop	1
General food stores (including a		Banks (part-time)	2
sub-P.O.)	5	Solicitor	1
Baker	1	Building Society office	
Butcher	1	(part-time)	1
Greengrocer and florist	1	Estate Agents	2
Chemist	1	Garage/service stations	3
Shoe shop	1	Café/teashops	2
Launderette	1	Doctors surgery	1
Ladies' hairdresser	1	Newsagent	1
Clothes and haberdashery shop	1	Hotel/restaurant	1
Children's clothes and toys shop	1	Forge	1
Hardware shops	2	Pet food	1

Source: Field Survey

Although a much more precise analysis would be required to ascertain the extent to which the services existing match the spending pattern of village residents it is clear that, at least for low-order goods, the provision of retail facilities is fairly adequate for a population of 3500–4000. The ratio of retail outlets per head of population has worsened since 1927 (see Table 3.2) but this index means little without knowledge of the turnover of the various outlets.

The extent to which the village is self-contained from a retail/service point of view can be better gauged from an analysis of the extent to which households obtain their basic low-order goods (food, chemist's goods, cleaning materials, etc.) within the village. It was established that 45% of households purchased more than four-fifths of their basic needs within the village. It was also found that a sizeable minority of the population obtain at least half their low-order needs outside the village despite the presence locally of a full range of shops. This may reflect the fact that prices tend to be high in 'spatial monopoly' circumstances. Almost everything can be obtained more cheaply in Lewes or Brighton, and with the increase in car-ownership a large proportion of households now habitually shop outside the village. This price differential is, of course, a serious matter for those without access to private transport.

PROPERTY AND FARM OWNERSHIP

It has not been possible to match completely the data given for 1867 and 1934. The rateable values of properties are accessible but not the names of the owners. It was, however, possible to establish that of the 1263 properties in 1971, 70% (878) were owner-occupied, 18% (233) were rented from the local authority and 12% (152) were rented privately. The distribution of rateable values is shown in Figure 5.3. The marked peak that occurs in the £71–£80 category is explained by the presence of a large proportion of the local authority property in this range. The very significant differences between 1867, 1934 and 1971 will be discussed in Chapter 5.

Of the 27 properties listed as farms in 1934, three were no longer worked as farms in 1971. Of the 24 remaining, 10 are owned by the occupier (who may not in every case be the farmer–one occupier is a well-known politician), 4 are owned by East Sussex County Council and 10 are owned by private landlords. Of the latter, 5 were owned by the Christie family (compared to 9 in 1934) and 3 by another family, who also appear as owner-occupiers of a fourth farm. It seems that there has been relatively little movement towards a pattern of owner-occupancy of farms since 1934 and two landlords still hold a relatively high proportion of the total means of agricultural production.

LOCAL GOVERNMENT AND SOCIAL ADMINISTRATION

The parish council in 1971 consisted of 13 members. Occupations included two housewives, a farmer, a retired farmer, two salesmen, an electrical engineer, a postman, a coal merchant and the vice-principal of a local technical college. The council appears to be fairly representative except that recent arrivals to the village are, perhaps inevitably, under-represented. In striking contrast to the 1870s, very few decisions of any significance are made at parish level. The 1972 Chairman's report[15] dealt with relatively minor matters concerning footpaths and the renovation of the village sign. In fact the Chairman characterised the council's task as follows: '. . . once again our major function has been the collecting, collating and passing on to the appropriate authority many items of varied interest in which we expressed our views which higher authority may not accept unless they so desired.' The relative insignificance of the council to the lives of village residents is reflected by a lack of knowledge concerning local government representatives. In fact the household survey established that only 29% of respondents could name the Chairman of the Parish Council and only 34% a resident serving on Chailey R.D.C. It seems clear that to most village residents the parish council means very little despite the no doubt excellent work of its members on small local tasks. This impression could, unfortunately, only have been strengthened in the minds of impartial observers attending the 1972 annual parish meeting where at least one of the items raised (at some length) from the floor, the relative nuisance value of large versus small dogs in fouling the green, had distinctly comic overtones.

Clearly, decision-making about most of the issues that crucially concern people lies elsewhere than at parish level. Decisions regarding social security, pensions, health insurance, unemployment pay, family allowances, supplementary benefits and so on, are nearly all vested in the central government, although in some cases payment is made in the village through the Post Office. Various other social security services, the district nurse and midwife, school clinics, the health visitor, the home help service and so on, are local government responsibilities but in nearly all cases these are administered by the rural district or county authority rather than by the parish. There are a few welfare organisations administered at the parish level but these tend to be purely voluntary services, for example, the Evergreen Club, and the chiropody clinic run by the local Red Cross Branch. The total picture is of social security services run by agencies outside the parish–a marked contrast to the situation 100 years earlier.

Municipal housing in the parish is the responsibility of Chailey R.D.C. to whom rates are paid. At the time of writing a drastic shortage of houses exists. The 1970 Annual Report of the Medical Officer of Health shows that a total of 340 houses was built in the district in that year. Of these 285 were private and 55 local authority; an imbalance of five to one. This question will be discussed more fully in Chapters 13 and 14. The district council also administers the various schemes of improvement grants for bringing 'low category' houses up to modern standards. Fifty-two houses were improved, by grants of up to £1000, in 1970.[16] This is clearly a substantial incentive to an owner to improve property, provided he has the stamina to come through the requisite dealings with the council's creaking administration. Public health is similarly a district responsibility. This entails the inspection of water supplies, sewage and refuse disposal, slaughterhouses and dairies, hygiene in shops, knackers' yards and so on. The 1970 report of the Public Health Department also notes, under the heading of 'Nuisances', that two Jazz Festivals were held in the rural district in 1970. The report observes of one of them that: '. . . the noise emitted from the site again gave rise to a number of complaints and under certain climatic conditions the music could be heard up to 4 miles away.'[17] The life of a Public Health Inspector is nothing if not varied.

The local authority responsible for education is the East Sussex County Council. The two schools in Ringmer, the county secondary school and the county primary school, are administered by boards of governors and managers respectively. The powers of primary school managers are set out in the Instrument of Management.[18] These powers include the authorisation of small expenditure on premises and some control on the use of premises outside school hours. More importantly, managers comprise one-half of the committee that recommends on the appointment of new headteachers, and they have the power in consultation with the headteacher to appoint assistant staff, subject only to the confirmation of the education authority. The managers can suspend staff for 'misconduct or any other urgent cause'. They can, by resolution, exclude the headteacher from their meetings. These powers are clearly considerable, on paper at any rate, and similar powers rest with the governors of the secondary school.

An assessment of the apparent suitability of boards of governors and managers to carry out these tasks would presumably rest upon a consideration of the extent to which they are professionally competent in the field of education. The appointment of chief executives and staff in business, the services, the universities, the police or any other complex modern organisation is made by those who have, themselves, achieved distinction in the field. Presumably distinction in the field of education can be measured in terms of degrees gained, publication record, teaching experience, or some combination of these.

Seen against this expectation, the professional competence of primary school managers in the area around Lewes (which includes Ringmer) gives rise to considerable disquiet. A 1969 survey by the East Sussex Association for the Advancement of State Education[19] showed that, of 25 managers who stated their occupation, only one was professionally engaged in education. The rationale by which farmers, chartered engineers, antique dealers, stockbrokers and insurance company managers are presumed to be competent to play a decision-making role in the management of so complex and expensive a matter as education is difficult to discern. Presumably the stockbrokers and engineers involved would think it very curious to find their boards of directors manned by people with no professional experience in these fields. The survey also revealed other disturbing aspects. The sampled managers as a group included more people over 70 than under 40, a curious feature of a system that deals with the young, 92% of the sample came from Social Classes I or II, compared to 25% of the total population of the South-east, while roughly 50% of the managers sent their children to non-state schools. Apart from these ascertainable facts, other hearsay evidence suggests that at least one local manager views the management board as some sort of social 'club' at which one can meet the 'right' people.[20] On the face of it the system appears to be an archaic survival.

SOCIAL STRUCTURE AND ACTIVITIES

The percentage distribution of the 150 heads of households in the survey was as follows (using the Registrar-General's Social Class categories):

Table 4.5 Distribution of Survey Households between Registrar-General's Social Classes, Ringmer, 1971

	%
Social Class I (Professional)	9
II (Intermediate)	44
III (Skilled non-manual)	9
III (Skilled manual)	18
IV (Partly skilled)	13
V (Unskilled)	3
Services	1
Unclassifiable	3
	100

Source: 1971 Ringmer Survey

Compared to the national average the village has an over-representation in social classes I and II and an under-representation both in the proportion in classes IV and V, and in the total proportion of manual workers. The bi-modality of the distribution echoes that of the rateable value data shown in Figure 5.3. Both distributions probably reflect, to some extent, the distinction between council tenants and owner-occupiers.

The household survey attempted to gauge the perceived level of social differentiation within the village by asking:

'Do you think that there are signs that the village as a whole is divided up into groups with different social standings?'

The answers were as follows:

	%
'Clear signs'	20
'Some signs'	23
'No signs'	36
'Don't know'	21
	100

Respondents in the first two categories (43% of the total) were then asked 'What groups do you feel exist?' The spread of responses is given in Table 4.6.

Table 4.6 Criteria upon which Recognition of Social
Differentiation was based, 1971

Criterion	Percentage of total responses mentioning this criterion
'Social class' criteria	20
Council/private housing	13
Exclusive 'cliques'	13
Locational criteria (specific to this village)	10
Differences in length of residence	10
Differences in income	7
Other criteria	3
N.B. Some respondents gave several criteria.	

Source: 1971 Ringmer Survey

It is evident that national criteria such as 'class', and whether or not one owns property, are somewhat more frequently mentioned than local criteria such as where one lives in the village and how long one had lived here. It is also worth noting that income appears to be relatively insignificant as a grouping variable in people's minds.

Some clear differences in the perceptions of the social structure became apparent when the responses were analysed by age and 'social class' subsets:

Table 4.7 Analysis of Levels of Perceived Social Differentiation

Age group of head of household	Percentage seeing 'clear signs' or 'some signs'	R.G. social class	Percentage seeing 'clear signs' or 'some signs'
21–30	53	I	69
31–40	65	II	44
41–50	47	III NM	35
51–65	30	III M	39
over 65	37	IV	37
		V	50

Source: 1971 Ringmer Survey

As measured by the percentage perceiving clear signs or some signs, awareness of social differences seems to be much more marked among the under-40s, and to fall off fairly evenly with increasing age. This is perhaps surprising in that it is frequently the 'older generation' who are held to believe in the rigid structuring of society. The Table also shows that there are clear relationships between occupational status and the perception of social distinctions. Class I respondents were not only more positive about the issue, as measured by the lower percentage of 'don't knows', but were also much more strongly conscious of social divisions than all other categories (the class V respondents constitute a tiny and unreliable sample).

Attitudes towards the 'gentry' in the village were gauged by asking the question:

'Fifty years ago, or so, many activities in this village were run by a few leading families known as the "gentry"; do you feel that this group . . .?' (five alternatives offered).

The distribution of responses is shown in Table 4.8. The proportion who consider that the 'gentry' still have some substantial importance, just over a third

Table 4.8 Attitudes to the 'Gentry', 1971

	%
'Is very important in the life of the village'	8
'Is quite important in the life of the village'	29
'Is of minor importance in the life of the village'	22
'Is largely irrelevant to village life'	23
'No longer exists'	13
'Don't know'	5
	100

Source: 1971 Ringmer Survey

of the sample, is perhaps surprising in view of the way the village, and society generally, has changed in recent decades. There is, for example, only a minimal dependence on local landowners for job opportunities (as was evident from the analysis of the employment structure). Those who ascribed some measure of local importance to the 'gentry' were asked the subsidiary question:

'In what ways are the gentry of importance to the life of the village?'

The responses to this open question varied considerably but could be categorised as shown in Table 4.9. Evidently the 'gentry' are seen as important, by

Table 4.9 Reasons Given for the 'Gentry's' Importance, 1971

Reason	Percentage of responses mentioning this reason
'They provide "leadership" '	25
'They provide money for clubs, etc.'	24
'They act as "figureheads" '	12
'They have political importance'	10
'They are important to church affairs'	8
'They are important to the scouts/guides'	6
Other reasons	21
N.B. Some respondents gave more than one reason.	

Source: 1971 Ringmer Survey

those that grant them importance, in terms of the money they provide for local clubs and societies and for such vague qualities as providing 'leadership' and acting as 'figureheads'. 'Political importance' was mentioned much less frequently as a significant function. There is a clear occupational status bias in the degree to which the 'gentry' are judged to be important. The percentage of responses falling in the first two categories ('very' and 'quite' important) was 62% for social class I and 41% for social class II.

The village has an impressive array of clubs and societies. These are shown in Table 4.10. With getting on for 30 organisations it is evident that a wide range of interests is catered for at a very local level. It also seems self-evident that the average urban suburb of 3700 people (assuming this could be meaningfully defined on the ground) does not have anything like this range of formal associations within its boundaries. A large proportion of the total amount of social contact between people in the village occurs in the context of these various organisations, either in the process of working together on committees to run them or in terms of more general and less binding participation in their programmes of events. This is a clear distinguishing characteristic between social life in villages and suburbs. The ratio of social contact in organisations to social contact in less formal contexts is probably higher in villages than in suburbs.

Table 4.10 Clubs and Societies in Ringmer, 1971

Bowls Club
British Legion (Men's Branch and Women's Section)
Conservative Association (Branch of Lewes Division)
Evergreen Social Club for the Not-so-young
Horticultural and Home Produce Society
Leukaemia Research Fund Group
Mothers' and Toddlers' Service
Mothers' Union
Raystede Animal Welfare Centre
Red Cross Centre
Rifle Club
Ringmer Cricket Club
Ringmer Football Club
Ringmer Dramatic Society
Ringmer Scout Group
Ringmer Guide Company
Ringmer Brownie Guide Pack (2 Packs)
Ringmer Road Safety Council
Ringmer Women's Institute (afternoon and evening groups)
Ringmer Infant Welfare Centre
Ringmer Old People's Welfare Committee
Ringmer Sisterhood
Ringmer and District Youth Association
Ringmer Village Hall Committee
St. John's Ambulance Brigade
St. Mary's Ringmer Men's Club
Young Wives' Group

Source: *Ringmer Parish Magazine*, December 1971

The importance of the clubs and societies to the social life of the village can be gauged from Table 4.11 overleaf. Nearly 60% of households had at least one membership in a village club or society and the average of memberships was over 1·6 per household.

There was no very significant occupational status bias in the total level of memberships. Class III non-manual shows less involvement than the other classes for no immediately apparent reason. In all other groups the clear majority of households have at least one club membership and multiple memberships occur with fair frequency in each group. Social class I, however, does provide a disproportionate number of multiple membership households. The 13 households in this group contain 43 memberships, an average of 3·3 memberships per household. The membership of each individual club and society is, of course, likely to be biased by a number of factors such as age, sex, occupational status and so on. It has not been possible to examine this in detail since the sample size of the survey is too small for the purpose and it would not be realistic to seek the necessary information on members from the organisations concerned. The main present purpose is to show that involvement in village clubs and societies as a whole is spread reasonably well between all occupational-status groups.

Table 4.11 Number of Organisational Memberships in Survey Households, 1971

Number of memberships	Number of households	Total number of memberships
0	62	0
1	27	27
2	24	48
3	13	39
4	8	32
5	8	40
6	3	18
7	1	7
8	2	16
9	2	18
	150	245

Source: 1971 Ringmer Survey

The household survey did, however, collect data on the pattern of social activities as measured by the length of time since each household had participated in a set of specified activities. Activities at friends' homes, for example parties, were specifically excluded. This pattern is shown in Table 4.12. The table shows quite clearly that going for a drink, driving and in-

Table 4.12 Social Activities of Survey Households, 1971

Activity	Number of households participating in previous 7 days	Number of households participating in previous month
Pub/licensed club	44	60
Car outing (picnic/drive)	40	64
Sporting event (to play)	23	29
Sporting event (to watch)	21	36
Car outing (to specific attraction)	14	35
Dance/disco	9	15
Theatre/show	8	16
Dinner or dinner/dance	7	15
Cinema	6	26
Bingo	5	7
Other	31	45

Source: 1971 Ringmer Survey

volvement in sport are much more frequent recreational activities than more 'formal' pursuits such as the theatre, the cinema or dining out. All the more commonly carried out activities, with the exception of car outings, tend to occur in the village or, less frequently, in Lewes. The more formal pursuits usually entail a trip into Brighton. Recreational trips to London are extremely rare. In all, the pattern of social activities is much more localised than might have been expected.

Regular churchgoing is confined to a fairly small minority of village residents, as shown in Table 4.13. Attendance at church seems to be selective

Table 4.13 Churchgoing in Ringmer, 1971

Frequency of churchgoing (any member of household)	Percentage of sample households
Regularly (at least three times per month)	18
Sometimes	32
Never (except for weddings, etc.)	50
	100

Source: 1971 Ringmer Survey

N.B. The percentages over-state the proportion of *people* who attend church because even if only one person from a household attended regularly this would count as a 'regular' household.

by occupational status. Of regular households, 68% are in social classes I and II whereas only 50% of non-attending households are in these two classes. A complementary finding was that no class V household members in the survey attended church at all. As suspected there were some differences between churchgoers and non-churchgoers in feelings towards the gentry. Of the regular churchgoers, 50% grant some importance to the gentry and only 2% regard them as irrelevant. The corresponding percentages for the non-churchgoers was 35% and 29%.

DOMESTIC ECONOMY

The average size of the household in the sample survey was 3·2 people. The distribution of household sizes is shown in Table 5.1. The total number of habitable rooms in the 150 households surveyed was just over 700 giving an average of 0·66 persons per room.

The provision of mains water and of adequate domestic sanitation is now virtually complete. In Chailey Rural District as a whole, 12,423 of the 12,601 dwellings (or 98·6%) are served by a public mains water supply.[21] Most of the houses still on a private supply were in Firle, Glynde and Iford (the former two of which are latter day 'estate villages'). During 1970 it had been necessary to warn consumers from some of these private sources to boil the water and as a result these areas, too, will soon be connected to a safe supply. No mention was made in the Medical Officer of Health's report for 1970 of inadequacies in domestic sanitation, although 4004 cesspools or septic tanks still exist in the district.[22]

No information was collected in the household survey on the ownership of household equipment or on the extent to which food was produced or processed by the household. It can safely be assumed, however, that a clear majority of households possess a refrigerator, vacuum cleaner and a washing machine and that the average length of time spent on household chores has been drastically reduced compared to the 1930s. This is a necessary, but not sufficient, condition to produce the employment status pattern shown in Table 4.14. The 124 households where the head of household was not retired produced 223 people in full or part-time work, an average approaching two persons per household. Only 73, or fewer than half the households, included a full-time housewife. It follows that many wives are working either full-time or part-time and that their income is an essential, or at least important, component in the domestic economy.

Table 4.14 Employment Status of all Respondents Household Survey, 1971

Status	Number of people
Working full-time (over 30 hours per week)	176
Working part-time (under 30 hours per week)	47
Seasonal/casual work (under 7 hours per week)	8
Unemployed	2
Retired	35
Full-time housewife	73
Full-time education	90
Under school age	40
No data	9
	480

Source: 1971 Ringmer Survey

Equally, it is clear that compared to earlier periods a greater proportion of the food consumed is purchased, rather than produced or processed in the home. Very few households now keep chickens and even fewer keep a pig. Bread ovens are a rarity and gardens often contain more tricycles and balls of various sizes than vegetables. No respondent in the survey, when asked to estimate the percentage of basic household needs purchased locally, suggested that not all needs were purchased. It is, of course, true that wine-making, vegetable growing and baking flourish (especially as the dates of the British Legion and other produce competitions approach), but almost certainly the proportion of the total food consumed that is home produced has declined enormously. Households now sell more labour to buy more produce, thus contributing to the great trends towards the division of labour and the exchange-based economy.

5 · Social Change in the Village

The analysis of change in the structure and organisation of society, and in the way of life of its members, is clearly a vast field of enquiry. Generalisations concerning change, and subjective comment based largely on personal experience, are commonplace. Well-documented studies of change at the scale of the single settlement, the social microcosm, seem much rarer.[1] The analyses in this chapter, based on data presented in the previous three, will be organised into four sections; changes in the everyday life of individuals and families, in the structure of village society, in the administration of social security and welfare and in the distribution of economic wealth and political power. The chapter, and the first half of the book, will close with a brief review of those findings which seem to have the most significance in giving insight into social change both locally and nationally together with an assessment of the rate at which the various changes are occurring.

CHANGES IN EVERYDAY LIFE

There have been considerable changes in household size as shown in Table 5.1.

In 1871 the most frequently occurring household size was 5, in 1921 it was 3 and in the 1971 survey it was 2. The proportion of households including 6 or more people was 39% in 1871, 16% in 1921 and 6% in 1971. The average size of village households fell from 4·6 to 3·0 over the period.

Table 5.1 Household Size, Ringmer, 1871, 1921, 1971

Number of persons	1871		1921		1971	
	Percentage	Number	Percentage	Number	Percentage	Number
1	5	16	6	20	7	11
2	12	37	21	72	33	49
3	15	44	25	86	21	31
4	14	41	19	67	22	33
5	15	46	13	46	11	16
6	10	30	6	21	4	6
7	11	33	5	16	1	2
8	7	21	2	8	1	2
9	5	14	1	3	—	—
10	3	6	2	8	—	—
11 and over	3	5	—	1	—	—
	100	293	100	348	100	150

Sources: 1871 Census Enumerators' Returns, 1921 Census, 1971 Ringmer Survey

It is difficult to gauge the changes in the availability and use of domestic help. In 1871, 25 of the 293 households had one or more servants living in.[2] The percentage is undoubtedly much lower now, of the order of perhaps 1%, but it seems likely that a rather higher percentage of households employ someone to 'do' for a few hours weekly. In aggregate, it is likely that the number of hours spent on domestic work for others has fallen considerably.

The changes in birth and death rates are shown in Table 5.2. The figures indicate that between the 1870s and the 1930s the village experienced a transition from high to low birth and death rates. Infant mortality rates show a striking change, both at national and at local level (the local rates are consistently better than the national), and some of the implications of this trend will be touched upon later.

Table 5.2 *Crude Birth and Death Rates, Ringmer Area, 1871, 1933, 1970*

	1871–5		1933		1970	
	Local	(national)	Local	(national)	Local	(national)
Crude birth rate (per 1000 pop.)	21·8	(35·5)	12·9	(14·4)	12·4	(16·0)
Crude death rate (per 1000 pop.)	19·2	(22·0)	11·2	(12·3)	14·7	(11·7)
Death rate–under 1 year (per 1000 live births)	44·1	(158·0)	33·1	(64·0)	11·0	(18·0)

Sources: Parish Registers, Annual Reports, Medical Officers of Health, Chailey R.D.C., 1934 and 1971

Marriage patterns also show a consistent change through time, as seen in Tables 5.3 and 5.4. If marriage is taken as one result of social interaction, which seems reasonable, then the tables show a marked decline in the extent to which such interaction was localised, both in terms of the percentage of intra-parochial marriages and in terms of the distance distributions of incoming partners.

The nature of the work undertaken by the head of household is another very relevant consideration in the study of changing life-styles. Table 5.5 sets out comparative data under the present social class allocations used by the Registrar General. To construct this table it was necessary to classify the 1871 and 1926/35 occupations under the present headings. This proved to be rather less difficult than expected, apart from a few unclassifiable cases from 1871 (mole catchers, ostlers, pedlars, whippermen and workhouse keepers are not classified by the Registrar General these days). The change is quite fundamental to an understanding of village life and the lives of individuals. In 1871, 83% of heads of households were manual workers, the vast majority of them in agricultural work. In 1971 the proportion was 34% and the survey of 150 households in the village produced just one head of household classified as an agricultural worker. Manual work, especially agricultural work based on the local area, seems profoundly different in its implications from the clerical work outside the area in which the majority of household heads are now employed. Clearly the physical outputs of the former are greater, but so perhaps

Table 5.3 Percentage of Marriages with both Partners from Ringmer Parish

Period	Total marriages (in parish church)	Percentage in which both partners were from the parish
1857/66	75	58
1926/35	90	46
1961/71	138	25

Source: Ringmer Parish Marriage Register

Table 5.4 Distance Distribution of Incoming Partner to Marriage

Miles	1857/66 %	1926/35 %	1961/71 %
0–10	78	65	55
11–20	8	6	21
21–30	1	2	4
31–40	2	—	—
41–50	8	12	5
Over 50	3	15	15
	100	100	100

Source: *ibid.*

Table 5.5 Percentage Distribution of Ringmer Heads of Households (using Registrar-General's 1971 Social Class Groupings)

Social class	1871	1926/35	1971
I (Professional)	0	0	9
II (Intermediate)	13	16	44
III NM (Skilled non-manual)	2	5	9
III M (Skilled manual)	17	26	18
IV (Semi-skilled manual)	61	40	13
V (Unskilled manual)	5	5	3
Services	—	0	1
Unclassifiable	2	8	3
	100	100	100

Sources: 1871 Census, 1926/35 Ringmer Parish Marriage Register. 1971 Ringmer Survey

are the returns in the form of job satisfaction. This is much too vast a topic to pursue here; it has been discussed by various social theorists dating back to Marx and beyond.[3]

The time available for recreational and leisure pursuits, whether daily, weekly or annually, has enormously expanded. It is not possible to give comprehensive data on the hours worked in various occupations but Table 5.6

Table 5.6 Hours Worked (weekly) and Holidays (annually) of Various Occupations, Ringmer and locality 1860/70s to 1971

Occupation	Hours worked (per week)	Holidays (per year)
1860/70s		
agricultural labourer	c. 100	nil
farmhouse servant	c. 100	nil
police constable	65–70	a few days
vicar	no data	6 weeks
1920/30s		
agricultural labourer (1920s)	50–80	nil
domestic servant	c. 80	no data
carpenter	c. 70	nil
council employee (manual)	60	no data
1971		
5% of all heads of households	<25	generally 2–4 weeks
50% ,, ,, ,,	26–50	
15% ,, ,, ,,	>50	
30% ,, ,, ,,	not applicable	

Sources: 1860/70s – memoirs, etc. 1920/30s – informants. 1971 – Ringmer Survey. (NB. 1971 figures refer to hours away from home; they therefore include travelling time)

contains some fragmentary evidence. Developments in collective bargaining leading to legislation concerning hours of work and holidays have resulted in greatly increased leisure time for virtually everybody.

There have been a number of changes in the way in which this time has been used. A comparison of the relevant sections of Chapters 2–4 shows that the degree to which the recreational life of the village depends upon the initiative of the 'gentry' has declined considerably over time, as has the extent to which participation in the main activities is specific to identifiable social groups. From an analysis of the 1971 survey it is clear that support for the most frequently pursued pastimes is drawn from all parts of the social spectrum, and activities now seem to be rather more age-specific than specific to a particular social group. A second point is that whereas in the 1870s it appears to have been rare for women to be involved in any of the recreational pursuits listed, they now participate fully in most activities including several sports. This stems partly from the fact that several of the most frequent activities involve the family rather than individuals, partly from the greatly reduced incidence of domestic work as a result of smaller families and an increased range of labour-saving appliances in the home, and partly from the general emancipation of women in society.

The standards of comfort experienced in the home, and the adequacy of the physical fabric of houses, have improved enormously over the period. As a result of increasing public control over housing standards, and of rising expectations by residents, central heating has replaced oil stoves and mains electricity, water and drainage have made oil lamps, wells, pumps, buckets and middens mercifully obsolete. Nearly all these changes have been concentrated in the period since the 1930s. The most effective way to appreciate these changes is to acquire a late Victorian house which has been subject to little improvement for the past 30 or 40 years, and to bring it up to modern standards of heating, plumbing and sanitation.[4]

The role of women, both in the household and in village society generally, has evolved quite strikingly. The evidence presented in the previous three chapters can be summarised as follows:

in the late 1860s and 1870s women:

were regarded as a necessary adjunct to the household economy (responsible for the vegetable garden, the pig and the chickens)
had larger families to care for
experienced poor care in confinements and perhaps suffered the frequent devastating grief of losing a child
had little education and virtually no career possibilities
were normally 'in service' until marriage
played no part in politics and little part in recreational activities
seemed more subject to paranoid fears than men

in the 1920s and 1930s women:

still experienced inequality of educational opportunity and a strictly limited career choice
normally worked 'in service' or in a shop until marriage
very rarely worked after marriage (and therefore rarely developed an independent work-based circle of friends)
spent very long periods on domestic chores
participated very little in local political activity

in 1971 women:

have equality of educational opportunity
have a fairly wide range of career possibilities
have increased free time as a result of owning domestic appliances
frequently pursue an independent working life after marriage
participate fully in local social activities and clubs
often participate in local political activities (as local government councillors, etc.)

One hundred years ago, if we may take some of the examples quoted in Chapter 2 as typical, the ordinary village girl could expect to receive perhaps one or two years' education in a Dame School, learning to 'read her book' and to do needlework. She would then go into service, perhaps at age 10 or 11, and work up to 100 hours per week on a variety of heavy manual tasks until she married. She would then have five or six children, several of whom might die in infancy. She would have to combine the housekeeping this entailed with the care of the chickens, the pig and the vegetable garden. She would also be expected to produce a range of basic foods, including bread. If, after all this, she outlived her husband, she would quite likely end up in poor health and in the village workhouse. The contrast between this existence and the life experienced by the average woman in the village today is perhaps one of the most striking conclusions to be drawn from this study.

One final aspect of change concerns the extent to which knowledge of national and world affairs reached the ordinary village resident. In 1870, literacy rates were quite certainly much lower than today; only 40% of 10-year-olds were in full-time education and the total circulation of daily newspapers was about 500,000 copies (see Chapter 1). Few villagers could have afforded to buy a newspaper and there is no record of a reading-room in Ringmer until just after 1900.[5] News would no doubt spread largely by word of mouth and events such as the American Civil War or the Franco-Prussian War can have had little significance compared to such topics as the weather at harvest time or the death of the old vicar in 1863. Even in the 1920s, the village was, by today's standards, isolated from external events. One quotation from Chapter 3 is worth reproducing:

'. . . I don't think we took a daily paper so there was no way of keeping in touch with national events as we do now.'

Several informants stressed the extent to which the wireless broadened people's horizons in the 1930s, thus emphasising, by implication, the degree of isolation previously experienced.

In 1971, of course, we experience what can only be described as 'news bombardment'. Events from the most unlikely corners of the world are reported within hours, discussed on the television by panels of pundits in neatly packaged 40-minute periods enclosed by 'important' music, and then overtaken by news of fresh disasters. 'News', in the daily press, expands by some miraculously Parkinsonian manner until it exactly fills, to the nearest column inch, the space available for its propagation. The significance of an event becomes confused with its newsworthiness.[6] It may be difficult to define the former but it is safe to assume that it is not synonymous with the latter. The implications of the communications revolution for village life cannot be plotted with any precision. But if any valid measurements could be taken of the time spent discussing various issues one would no doubt find that 100 years ago conversation was about local things, people and events actually seen, known or experienced (as the Hardy quotation in the Prologue suggests). Today much of our conversation concerns phenomena known only vicariously through the various distorting filters of the media. This, like so many recent developments, seems to be neither wholly good nor wholly bad, but just inevitable.

CHANGES IN THE STRUCTURE OF THE VILLAGE SOCIETY

Figure 5.1 shows that a number of changes occurred in the age/sex structure of the village. The proportion of residents aged nine and under fell from 30% in 1871 to 15% in 1971; the proportion aged 65 or over rose from 6% to 11%.

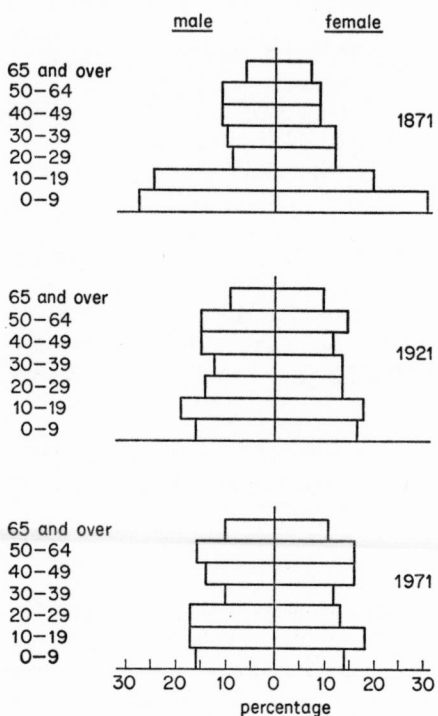

Fig. 5.1 Age/Sex Structure, Ringmer, 1871, 1921, 1971.

Sources: 1871 Census Enumerators' Returns,
1921 Census, 1971 Ringmer Survey.

As might be expected, the median age rose considerably (from 19 to 31). These figures may surprise those who view the present-day village as over-burdened with young families and children. In contrast to the changes in housing standards, nearly all the changes in age/sex structure occurred between 1871 and 1921; the pattern in the latter year is almost identical with that of 1971.

The residential stability of any community, measured in terms of the percentage of its inhabitants locally born, is an important factor which may throw light on a number of other aspects of village life. Table 5.7 gives some comparative information:

Table 5.7 Birthplaces of Ringmer Residents, 1871, 1921, 1971

	Percentage born in Parish	Percentage born elsewhere in Sussex	Percentage born outside Sussex	Total %
1871	53	43	4	100
1921	33	41	26	100
1971	9	no data	no data	—

Source: 1871 and 1921 Censuses, 1971 Ringmer Survey

Unfortunately, data on place of birth are not available for the 1971 sample but the data on previous address given in Chapter 7 show that 65% of the population had moved from elsewhere in Sussex and 29% from outside Sussex. If the process of being born and growing up in a village gives one a particular kind of involvement in it, then the percentage of residents who experience that type of involvement has declined consistently and considerably over time while the influence of values and lifestyles from more distant parts of the British Isles has been increasingly strong.

Changes in the status structure[7] of the village can perhaps best be gauged by a combination of two sources; firstly from inferences that can be drawn from social, economic and political arrangements and events in the village, and secondly, from perceptions of the structure by village residents. In 1871, as shown by the varying recreational patterns, the arrangement and conduct of harvest suppers and 'big house' weddings, the rateable value data, and various other indications, there existed a clearly defined social hierarchy in the village. Evidence was presented of movement up and down through this structure and these examples, in themselves, provide good grounds to suppose that different social levels were perceived to exist. In the 1920s, according to virtually all informants, everybody knew who the 'gentry' were and there was widespread acceptance of different levels in the status structure below this group:

'. . . the differences were much greater then than they are today . . . you were always very particular to be polite to the vicar . . .'

'. . . there was clear class differentiation . . . people accepted the social structure . . .'[8]

In 1971 the perceived situation seems to be fundamentally different. Only 20% of respondents to the survey perceived 'clear signs' of social differentiation in the village, while another 23% saw 'some signs'. The majority of respondents either saw 'no signs' or else did not know, which in the context is arguably a negative response. Of the 43% who did see some signs of differentiation, a sizeable minority based their judgment upon such factors as location in the village or differences in length of residence rather than specifically status criteria. Further analyses showed that it tended to be the higher socio-economic groups, and the age group under 40, who most clearly perceived social status differences. Attitudes towards the 'gentry' show a considerable change, even from the inter-war period. Table 4.8 shows that only 37% of respondents considered them to have any significant degree of importance to village life, 22% accorded them 'minor importance', and 36% considered them to be either irrelevant or non-existent. Even making allowance for the fact that the inter-war sample of informants is small and may be non-representative, there seems to be a considerable change in perception of the status structure generally and in attitudes to the 'gentry' specifically.

The position of the church and the vicar in the status hierarchy seems to have undergone a similar change. There can be little doubt that in mid-Victorian Ringmer the vicar stood near the apex of the social structure. John Constable, vicar till 1863, lived in the largest house in the parish (see Plate 1a) and employed by far the largest domestic staff.[9] His diary shows that he was extremely rich and that he played a pastoral role in both senses of the word; he was active both in the welfare and social support system and he had direct interests in farming. He was also politically significant in view of the importance of the vestry meetings, which had power to levy rates. He participated in the anniversary dinners of the benefit societies and was often present, with his family, at a wide variety of other social events in the village. No doubt there were many occasions when the company had to wait politely upon the vicar's departure before carousing in earnest could begin.

In the 1920s and 30s, as a previous quotation in this chapter has shown, the vicar was still a very significant social figure. At least one vicar in the period gave minor financial handouts to the poor, and the clergy frequently served very actively on local government councils, especially on committees concerned with education, housing and welfare.[10] The recollections of informants concerning the importance of churchgoing seem to conflict, but at least one felt that the church was the cog around which village life revolved, and the comment of another that church attendance was 'voluntary' seems to betray at least the possibility of an alternative attitude; that, socially, it was not.

The present-day role of the vicar and the church is rather different. The survey showed that fewer than a fifth of village households included a regular churchgoer and in exactly one-half of households no member ever went except for weddings, christenings and funerals. Attendance was especially rare among the lower status groups. The present vicar is active and takes his clerical and secular commitments very seriously, but he would probably lay no claims to great political or social significance in the village. Recreational life no longer centres mainly around the church, as it did even in the 1930s, and clerical significance in the social security system is negligible. A recent incumbent did achieve no mean reputation in the appropriate professional circles as a property developer in a nearby village[11] (an honourable successor, in financial *savoir faire*, to John Constable) but was felt by some to be less consistently successful, with his wife, in social relations in the community.

The pattern of recreational pastimes, and the extent to which pastimes are specific to particular groups, is another indicator of the degree of social stratification in a community. As shown earlier in this chapter, in the 1870s recreational activities varied up and down the social scale, whereas today the most frequently carried out activities (visiting a pub, going out in the car, watching or playing sport) do not appear to reflect occupational status differences at all. Similarly, as Chapter 8 will show, the level of membership of the various village clubs and organisations appears not to be significantly biased by occupational status and all socio-economic classes, except Class V, have reasonably high participation levels. It may be true that certain clubs draw their membership from a fairly narrow social base but others, notably the sports clubs and the Dramatic Society, have a very wide cross-section of people in their membership.[12]

CHANGES IN SOCIAL ADMINISTRATION AND WELFARE

Two great changes have occurred in the social security system over the period. The system has been enormously widened to cover a broader spread of need and its administration has been progressively removed from local to external agencies.[13] Care of the poor, the sick, the aged and the very young was largely the province of the poor law system in mid-Victorian Ringmer, and the administration was either at parish level or through unions of three or four parishes. The informal agencies, the benefit societies, private charities and the vicar, were all parochially based. In time of need one was 'on the parish' not 'on the state'. Certain categories of need, for example home nursing, maternity assistance and child care, were simply not recognised, or were met informally by neighbours. The situation between the wars is difficult to characterise. It was, in itself, a period of rapid change which witnessed the near-dismantling of the poor law system, the vast improvement of a number of services, for example child care and the provision of school meals, and the passing of at least 21 Acts relating to unemployment.[14] This was, in effect, one of the main transitional periods between the Victorian social security system and that of today.

The present situation is one which, to all appearances, caters for a very complete range of needs. Unemployment, sickness, disablement, old age and maternity benefits are freely available to those eligible as are family allowances, supplementary benefits and family income supplements. Local authority benefits, for example school uniform allowances, concessionary fares to the elderly, and home-help services are also available. Many of the national and local benefits are on a means tested basis. For this reason, and because of the differences in the level of knowledge about them, differential rates of take-up occur and it is rare for a means tested benefit to reach 50% of those eligible for it.[15] The actual operation of the complete social security system is thus a lot less impressive than its design on paper. Nevertheless, in comparison with the past, it represents a considerable improvement. The administration of the system is, as has been shown, almost entirely external to the parish. Apart from the presumed gains that this brings in efficiency, external administration provides one other fundamental benefit – the applicant for assistance is making use of his legal rights as a citizen of the state. He is not, as he was in the 1870s and to some extent in the 1920s, dependent upon the goodwill of fellow-villagers or of the local squirearchy. Nor does he have to be '. . . of reputed good character for honesty, industry and sobriety . . .' before receiving benefits (as the beneficiaries under the Hays Charity had, and possibly even still have, to be). Socially and politically these seem to be very significant changes indeed.

CHANGES IN THE DISTRIBUTION OF WEALTH AND POWER

For the purposes of this section, 'wealth' is defined to include land, residential and other property, manufacturing or farming capital, and income. These aspects are, of course, closely inter-related since in a predominantly agricultural area the ownership of land, farming capital, and property tend to condition income, at least at the upper end of the scale. In 1867, the 17 farms and holdings of over 50 acres were in the hands of only 11 owners. Three of these owned nearly 40% of the parish. In 1934, of a roughly similar number of farms (as opposed to smallholdings) over half were owned by the Christie family. These amounted to 40–50% of the total land area of the parish. In 1971 five of the farms were still owned by the same family and three by another landowner. The degree to which land, farming capital and productive capacity is concentrated in the hands of a small number of landowners appears to have changed little, if at all, over the 100-year period.

The ownership of residential property, by contrast, has been considerably broadened. In 1867 only 30 of 280 householders were owner-occupiers and in nearly all other cases the occupiers were 'tied cottage' tenants of private landlords. In 1934 there were 105 owner-occupiers in 434 households, and 56 others who were tenants of the local authority. In 1971, 878 of 1263 householders were owner-occupiers and only 152 (or 12%) were tenants of private landlords. Clearly, in the key area of owner-occupation of housing much progress has been made. In fact it is possible to argue that the proportion of owner-occupiers in the village is now too high relative to the national and regional levels; a point to be developed in Chapter 13. Figure 5.2 sets out the residential property ownership distribution for the three dates in question.

The distribution curve of rateable values has also undergone considerable change, as shown in Figure 5.3. Whereas in both 1867 and 1934 the very large majority of properties were concentrated at the lowest levels of the scale, the 1971 distribution approximates to the normal curve with peaks (representing particular homogeneous estate developments) at three points. There is some positive skewing of the curve which reflects the small number of very substantial properties of disproportionately high value that still exist.

Little can be said about the change in the local degree of inequality of incomes over time, since no systematic data for any of the three periods is available. In the 1860s, an agricultural labourer or a farmhouse servant would earn £9–£25 per year. A coachman earned £25, a constable about £60, the schoolmaster (in 1879) £120 and the vicar (prior to 1863) at the very least

£1000–he can hardly have earned less; his meat bill alone was nearly £90 in 1851. While matching data for local workers in these occupations are not available for the present day, we can say, very roughly, that a farm worker

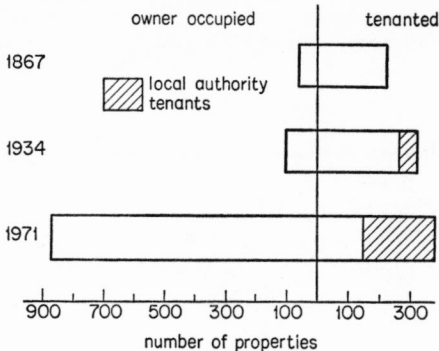

Fig. 5.2 Property Ownership, Ringmer.

earns £1000 or so per year, a driver perhaps £1500, a constable £1800 or so, a schoolmaster, say, £2250 and a vicar a lot less than this. In other words, the factor separating the lowest and the highest is nearer two or three than a

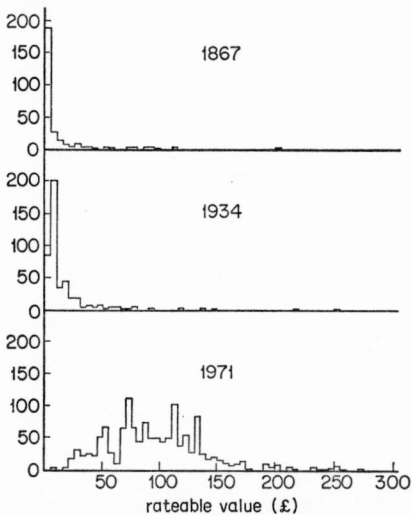

Fig. 5.3 Distribution of Rateable Values,
Ringmer, 1867, 1934, 1971.

hundred or more. In this particular set of occupations, differentials seem to have been considerably reduced. This is obviously a very rough and ready analysis and it appears inconsistent with the more systematic findings of the Department of Employment and Productivity that there has been remarkable stability in the national differential between the top and bottom deciles of the manual income range, at least since the 1890s.[16]

Changes in the distribution of political power over the period are obviously difficult to measure exactly. Nevertheless, certain clear trends are evident. For our present purposes, 'political power' will be defined in terms of the following abilities (all of them vested largely or exclusively in the hands of the local gentry prior to the 1870s):[17]

to vote
to control how others vote
to hold political offices
to command the use of productive capital
to hire and fire labour and set wage levels
to run key social systems (e.g. health and welfare)
to develop land
to influence opinion

Over the period, the right to vote has become virtually universal so that this sort of power is no longer the prerogative of a small élite (see Table 1.7). Similarly, but comparatively recently as certain quotations in Chapter 3 make clear, the power to influence how others vote has largely disappeared. 'Largely', because as people who have canvassed politically in rural areas may know, some fear still exists in the minds of farm labourers in 'tied cottages' that voting socialist may bring some form of retribution from their employer who may, somehow, find out.

The rules concerning eligibility to hold office have been successively liberalised over the period. Before parish councils were introduced in 1894, the vestry meeting was the main formal political body at parish level. Membership was commonly restricted to the small group of property-owners. No manual labourer, craftsman or smallholder would dream of challenging the right of the local squirearchy to man the local administration or to provide the member of parliament. The parish councils from the beginning drew members from a wide range of backgrounds and, partly for this reason, were regarded as an unfortunate intrusion by some members of the gentry.[18] Today, the qualification for office holding in local government generally concerns residence rather than property ownership in the area and candidates come from all sorts of backgrounds. There is, however, a built-in force for reaction in the system in that many county council committee meetings are held during working hours. Manual workers clearly find this less convenient than retired colonels. Candidates at parliamentary elections also now come from a wide range of backgrounds. The constituency of which Ringmer forms a part has, however, been represented by two successive members of the same family with one short break for over 50 years; a charmingly nineteenth-century, not to say feudal, circumstance.

The ownership of 'productive capital', farm land and machinery, appears still to be concentrated in comparatively few hands in this particular parish. Other local examples of persistence in a pattern of concentrated ownership could also be given. But this circumstance no longer carries with it the power to hire and fire labour, at least, not to fire without very good reason, or to set wage levels. These levels, so far as agriculture is concerned, are set nationally and in any case the vast majority of village residents are not employed in either agriculture or any other locally owned enterprise. The growth in trade union power, and the trend towards employment in large national enterprises, whether privately or publicly owned, has virtually removed the power of local landowners to control conditions of employment.

Health and welfare systems, together with services such as roads and power supply, are now run by departments, boards and committees all too aware of their answerability, especially in financial affairs, to the public. Regional Hospital Management Boards, social security offices, transport committees and other respectable and generally incorruptible public bodies have replaced the poor law overseers, the turnpike trusts and the boards of hospital visitors of the mid-Victorian era, many of which were largely made up of local gentry, landowners and clerics. This is not to say that the odd retired colonel or landed farmer does not exert influence out of proportion to his expertise on certain local government committees. By and large, however, because of the complexity of these services, and the economic and technical know-how required to run them effectively, decisions tend to be guided by permanent officials professionally competent to make them. One curious exception to this generalisation seems to be the system of school governors and managers which still exerts influence on decisions that, arguably, should remain within the province of teachers and other professionals in the field.

The development of land, and the use to which it is put, was previously a power that rested quite simply with the landowner. Before this century there was no control over what was built, how it was built or how it was used. This synonymity between ownership and rights to use was successively modified by town and country planning legislation during this century until now any new development, or any alteration to existing buildings, must receive planning approval from the relevant authority. This places a constraint on the use, value and profitability of land, and transfers some development decisions from the private landowner to the publicly answerable planning committee (but see Chapter 13).

The final aspect of 'political power', the ability to influence local opinion, is similarly lost to the local élite. Before the advent of mass circulation newspapers, near 100% literacy rates and the electronic media, opinions on issues of both village and national concern must have been strongly influenced by such leading local figures as the squire, the schoolmaster and the parson, perhaps via his pulpit. The range of information available to most members of the community, and upon which their opinion could be based, was heavily restricted until the mass penetration of radio, newspapers and television during the last 40–50 years (see Tables 1.9 and 1.11). And the range of opinions that could be held, or at least publicly made known, was similarly restricted. It is instructive to recall that a well-known pacifist in the village even in the late 1930s was virtually ostracised and even physically threatened. Pacifism in the face of approaching war would now be a perfectly acceptable view in the total spectrum of views on the subject. If 'public opinion', admittedly a very imprecise concept, is formed on the basis of information one has access to and expressed in inverse proportion to the degree of retribution one fears, then there can be no doubt that the intra-parochial controls on the opinions people hold and express must have dwindled to insignificance.

CONCLUSIONS

It is an almost impossible task to sum up, from the wide variety of phenomena touched upon, the changes that have occurred in this rural settlement over the past 100 years.[19] One way is to reconstruct the circumstances and concerns of a typical village husband and father as he returns home after a day's work.

One can visualise the mid-Victorian agricultural labourer returning at sunset to his four-roomed 'tied' cottage along a muddy, pot-holed lane after a 14-hour day in the fields. He is looking forward to the break in the routine which will occur when they all go to a 'big house' wedding feast two weeks hence. On the other hand he and his wife are desperately worried about their fifth child who, like their second born, looks as if she will not survive more than a few weeks. His widowed mother-in-law, now turned 60, is in the village workhouse because his harassed wife is simply too busy to care for her, his unmarried brother recently joined the army to escape the grind of farm work, and his young sister is in service in Brighton. Last year's harvest was a poor one and wages suffered as a result. He hopes he will be able to continue with his payments to the benefit society because if not, should he be disabled as a friend was recently in an accident with some farm machinery, the family might have to go 'on the parish' and be split up. The vicar referred in church last week to the evils of the war between Prussia and France and he is vaguely aware that there was something about it in the local newspaper but since he reads with great difficulty (he was at the 'national' school for only two years) he does not really know much about it. He does, however, know something about London because last year he went by train from Lewes station as part of a group of agricultural workers taken at the vicar's expense to see an exhibition of new farm machinery at the Crystal Palace. Before that he had never been further afield than Lewes. He hopes the weather, which threatens to spoil this year's harvest too, will improve because if not they will have to endure another hungry winter.

One hundred years later another village resident is driving home from Brighton, where he works as a qualified engineer in a local government department. The news on the car radio contains some items about developments in Vietnam. He is wondering whether to spend the money from the back-dated salary increase he has just received on a deep freeze, or on a holiday at a rather more select resort than the one they visited on the Costa Brava last year. He calculates that on his new salary they might just be able to afford the mortgage on the new four-bedroomed house they have been considering. His elder son is in the top year of the village primary school and may go on to the local comprehensive in Lewes. His daughter is nine, and spends all her time on horses. His younger son is four and will go to school next year. His daughter needed some complicated heart surgery when she was 18 months old but she is now quite recovered. He recalls with dismay that his in-laws, living in comfortable retirement in Bexhill, are visiting them at the weekend. They will have to buy an extra large joint and some more sherry. But then they could use the last three weeks family allowance which they have not yet collected. He hopes the weather, which threatens this weekend's cricket match, will improve because if not he will have to spend all day Saturday on a shopping trip to Brighton with the family.

From the large number of processes underlying these striking changes in village life-styles, three main themes will finally be distinguished; one primarily social and political, one primarily technological, and the third concerned with the rate of change.

1. The Redistribution Downwards of Power, Educational Opportunity and Access to Social Security

The comparative analyses of 'power', of house ownership, of educational opportunity and of health and welfare benefits show clearly that inequalities within the village, in all these respects, have been drastically reduced. Only in relation to land-ownership and the 'tied cottage' system do the last relics of anything approaching feudalism remain. And even in these areas the balancing power exerted by agricultural unions makes the situation less sinister than it might appear. This is not to suggest that there is room for complacency. Glaring inequalities in wealth and incomes still exist and the inequity of 70% of the local population enjoying the security, capital appreciation and tax advantages of home ownership while 30% do not must be continually emphasised.

2. The Transition from 'Closed Cell' to 'Open System'

Developments in technology have profoundly affected life-styles and this is in line with the Marxist position that social organisation reflects the level of productive technology reached. Two specific developments appear to underlie a great deal of the change in the organisation of village society: the internal combustion engine and the electronic media of communication. These two inventions have drastically reduced the 'friction of distance' for the movement of people and goods on the one hand and of information on the other. A thirty minute journey from the village might now mean 20 miles, not two. News from abroad reaches us in fractions of a second, not fractions of a month. The consequence is an enormous enlargement of the distances over which interaction occurs from the village, whether measured in terms of the 'action space' of individuals, or the range from which artifacts and information are imported into, or exported from, the village. This change has been documented in the preceding chapters in terms of marriage patterns, percentages locally born, percentages working and recreating outside the parish, information flows, and in relation to the externalisation of virtually all significant decision-making. It could also be illustrated by an analysis of the area of origin of household artifacts. Few houses would have contained many artifacts from outside the parish in 1871. Now, our houses are full of objects from

Europe, Japan, the United States and everywhere else. In all measurable aspects, the parish is now part of a regional, national or world system of interactions or, to put it another way, the significance of the parish boundary has dwindled almost to nothing.

3. The Rate of Change Appears to Have Accelerated

The midpoints of the three periods analysed were so chosen that the gap between the first and second is 60 years (1871–1931) and between the second and third is 40 years (1931–71). If change in all the phenomena analysed is occurring at a constant rate through time, we should expect to find a 50% greater amount of change in the former interval than in the latter. Of course, relatively few of the changes are susceptible to precise measurement of this kind but in nearly all of them one can discern whether the hypothesis of linear change through time is supported or not. Table 5.9 summarises the findings.

Table 5.9 Rate of Change in Specified Phenomena, 1871–1971

Change in:	60 years 1871 — 1931	40 years 1931 — 1971
demography (vital rates)	←————— apparently linear —————→	
demography (age/sex structure)	←— greater —→	←——— less ———→
population distribution between 'social classes'	←——— less ———→	←——— greater ———→
'firmness' of status structure	←——— less ———→	←——— greater ———→
deference to 'gentry'	←——— less ———→	←——— greater ———→
political power of 'gentry'	←——— less ———→	←——— greater ———→
importance of the church	←——— less ———→	←——— greater ———→
life-style of women	←——— less ———→	←——— greater ———→
hours worked/holidays	←——— less ———→	←——— greater ———→
income differentials	←——— rate difficult to determine ———→	
recreational patterns	←——— less ———→	←——— greater ———→
housing standards	←——— less ———→	←——— greater ———→
home ownership percentage	←——— less ———→	←——— greater ———→
rank/size distribution of rateable values	←——— less ———→	←——— greater ———→
access to social security/education	←————— apparently linear —————→	
knowledge of external affairs	←——— less ———→	←——— greater ———→
land ownership concentration	←————— little change —————→	
control over land use	←————— apparently linear —————→	

Source: previous chapters

'Greater' or 'less' indicate that a larger or a smaller proportion of the total amount of change over 100 years occurred in the interval specified. '*Greater*' indicates that a much larger proportion of total change occurred in the interval specified. 'Apparently linear' indicates that rather greater change occurred in the former (60 years) as opposed to the latter (40 years) interval.

In a few cases it is possible to question this part-quantitative summarisation of mostly qualitative data. But in most cases the analysis is readily substantiated, and the general picture is beyond doubt. The greater proportion of the total amount of change that has occurred has fallen in the second, shorter, time gap. The hypothesis that the rate of social change has accelerated appears to be correct. Extrapolation from this analysis might well be dangerous. Arguably, we have passed through a revolutionary phase of social change in the past 40 years and are now in a phase of comparative stability in the organisation of society. Certainly the village has been subjected to a very large inflow of people during the 1960s, as Part III will show, and this has affected the 1971 situation on some, but by no means all, of the aspects analysed. Alternatively, a repeat study in 1991 might show that the changes in the 20-year period 1971–91 were greater than those of 1931–71. One has a sneaking hope that the latter might be correct since nearly all the changes measured for 1931–71 seem to have been changes for the better. But perhaps those of us who are still here in 1991 will be shaking our heads about all the upstart newcomers, recalling the halcyon days of the 1970s when everybody in the village knew everybody else, and wondering where all this new technology is leading us. *Plus ça change*. . . .

PART THREE

'THERE WAS A FIELD THERE ONCE'

6 · The Planning Context

As was suggested in the Prologue, the physical development of the village and the concomitant social changes are no longer largely a reflection of intra-parochial processes and events. No longer do the changing fortunes of the local farmers and landowners determine whether or not new development will occur; nor do they influence the prosperity and life chances of individual families. The arbiters of these matters are now farther afield and difficult to identify with any precision. What is clear is that the development of the village in the 1960s and 1970s is occurring in the context of a land-use planning system which has evolved gradually since the beginning of the century and which seeks to ensure that development processes are more rational and democratic than those of either the 1870s or the inter-war years.[1] At the time of writing, the main planning decisions are made at county council, or county borough level. These authorities prepare development plans for their areas, zone land for various purposes and exercise development control, in combination with district councils and municipal boroughs to whom some powers are delegated, in approximate accord with these plans.[2]

In the last ten years, this work has tended increasingly to be influenced by the growth of regional planning. From the early 1960s a series of 'plans' was prepared for the various regions of Great Britain[3] although the extent to which these influenced, in detail, what actually occurred is debatable. In relation to the South-East Region, shown in Map 1 on page xiv, the chief concerns have been with the expansion of London and the rapid rate of growth of the region compared to most other regions. Both concerns stem back to the 1930s and beyond (in fact Elizabeth I was worried about the growth of London) and the Barlow Report of 1940[4] and the Abercrombie plans of 1943 and 1944[5] were all serious attempts at a solution. In 1962 a Standing Conference of interested local authority planners was set up. Working partly in parallel with this body, the Ministry of Housing and Local Government produced the South-East Study in 1964.[6] This envisaged an extra $3\frac{1}{2}$ million people in the region by 1981 and proposed to deal with this growth partly by means of a number of 'countermagnets' – large areas of growth situated 70 or more miles from the capital (for example, the Southampton–Portsmouth area).[7] Subsequently, in 1967, the newly set up South-East Economic Planning Council produced a strategy for the south-east which envisaged 'corridors' of growth out along the main transport axes from London. This concept was somewhat in conflict with the earlier proposals of the Standing Conference, which would have tended to concentrate more of the growth closer to London. Finally in 1970 the Strategic Plan for the South-East was produced by a joint team of interested experts.[8] This group, led by Dr. Burns, seems to have combined practical and academic expertise in rather more fruitful proportions than previous groups. Since their plan is the most highly documented and authoritative to have emerged from all the thinking about the region it will be summarised in some detail under the headings of population, employment, social characteristics, housing and growth pattern. The situation in the Lewes–Brighton area will then be examined in relation to these regional projections.

STRATEGIC PLAN FOR THE SOUTH-EAST, 1970

Population Projections

The population of the region is growing only slightly faster, in percentage terms, than that of England and Wales.[9] In 1968 there were an estimated 17,229,600 people in the south-east, just over 35% of the national total.[10] The 'design figures' for population are 18·6 million for 1981, 20·0 million for 1991 and 21·5 million for 2001, an increase of 4¼ million over the present.[11] It is important to realise that this growth will be the result of natural increase and not of immigration into the region. In fact in 1965–6 the region had a net *loss* of 20,000 by migration and this trend seems likely to continue.[12] The high rate of natural increase reflects the population characteristics; there are a high proportion of relatively prosperous people in the younger and middle-age groups.[13] The intra-regional distribution of the expected population growth will be examined subsequently.

Employment

The region has an employment structure that is well suited to above average growth since prosperous manufacturing industries like radio and electronics components, office machinery, photographic products and so on are strongly represented.[14] Similarly the services sector of employment, office and shop activities, are also over-represented. In fact the region has 51% of the total office floor space of England and Wales.[15] Due partly to the age structure, activity rates (the proportion of the total population who work) are high and rising. This means that employment is increasing even faster than population. Despite all this there is evidence that employment growth in the south-east is not as great as one would expect had all the employment groups present grown at their national rate.[16] In other words, certain factors (possibly congestion costs and/or labour shortage) are combining to inhibit what should, on the basis of the industries present, be an even more rapid growth rate.

Agriculture, until quite recently the largest employer of men in the rural areas, now employs fewer than 100,000 farm workers in the entire region.[17] This figure is expected to halve by 1977 and to level off at 20,000–30,000, although this is not to say that agriculture is a declining industry by any criterion other than the size of its labour force.

Social Characteristics

The high incidence of non-manual employment, and of skilled work in the manual sector, means that the region has a disproportionate number of people in the higher socio-economic groups.[18] It also has some problems of social imbalance which have only recently been perceived with any accuracy and which are perhaps as relevant to rural social development as to the more highly publicised and thought about case of Greater London.

As Chapter 3 of the plan points out, we live in an era of rising expectations. More people aspire to home ownership, to a garden, to a decent supply of open space, to car-ownership, to access to recreational facilities, and to a more physically mobile existence than ever before. Each of these trends generates an increased space requirement per head and means that the pressure on land is increasing even faster than is population. In this situation not all will benefit equally. The plan discerns three 'life-styles' for the future although one suspects that, as always in these attempts to distinguish categories, more truth is obscured in the classification process than is revealed.

The 'senior-salariat' (so called in the plan) are more numerous in the region than elsewhere in the country and have the greatest choice over where and how they will live. It is possible that they will opt, in increasing numbers, for rural living, perhaps with a flat in London for the head of household to use during the working week, or for a second or holiday home in the country.[19] There are believed to be 40,000 such homes in the region. This group therefore generate a very large demand for land and housing per person, a situation which the plan appears calmly to accept. The 'middle mass' (the attempt, in this classification scheme, to get away from established terminology is not very convincing) will also aspire to more space such that 'four-bedroomed houses with playrooms may become a minimum requirement'.[20] Since, however, average house prices in the region are about three times the average income of purchasers[21] (and are rising at the time of writing at the rate of 2% or 3% *per month*) this aspiration leads to an abnormally large proportion of income being spent on mortgage repayments.[22] This in turn, has repercussions on social life and the pattern of leisure activities. The 'less privileged', by and large, do not own their own houses, suffer the greatest privations from the way in which the housing market works as will be seen later, and also suffer disproportionately from the decline in public transport services.

This crude three-fold division does at least illuminate one important point. The difference in prosperity between the best-off and worst-off is greater in the south-east than any other region.[23] Not only that, but a vicious circle of causation encourages these differences to be perpetuated from generation to generation.[24] This, of course, is not an original piece of detection. Most of our institutions, especially those concerned with education, seem to be contrived to perpetuate this circle. What is remarkable is that, for the first time in an official planning document, the circle of deprivation is seen to have a *spatial* component:

'. . . planning affects the distribution of resources in a particular spatial context and thus affects the access of people at different locations to these resources . . .'[25]

This is a point which geographers have been trying to make to economists for years and it is a view that car-less old ladies living in now bus-less villages will echo, as will harassed mothers on shop-less council estates. The most crucial aspect of all planning procedures is also, perhaps unexpectedly, made explicit:

> 'planning in the south-east cannot benefit everyone equally, therefore whom should land-use planning benefit most?'[26]

This question, and the related one of the type of positive discrimination in favour of lower income groups that might be possible and appropriate, must now be exercising all those interested in the social development of the region and of society generally. The view that land-use planning is largely a technical matter to be managed by surveyors and engineers in an atmosphere largely devoid of social values and political judgments is at last 'officially' exposed for what it is – a naïve and damaging myth.

Housing

The plan calculates that there were potentially 164,000 more private households than dwellings in 1966.[27] Taking into account the present number of dwellings technically unfit for use, the shortfall for the region was over 700,000 dwellings compared to the total stock of about 5·5 million dwellings. About 70% of the shortfall was in London but housing shortage is a characteristic of the entire region. In the last 30 years there has been comparatively little building for private renting (apart from luxury flats which are no doubt lucrative to develop but which supply a low priority need). Consequently those who cannot afford to buy, and at present house purchase for those without capital requires an income well above the regional average, and who are not eligible for local authority housing, find that they are competing in the privately rented sector; a very obvious sellers' market. One consequence of this is that the lower paid in the region are finding it necessary to spend an ever-increasing proportion of their income on housing. In 1967, for example, households with an income of less than £10 per week had to spend nearly a quarter of it on housing and for those in the privately rented sector the proportion was nearly one-third.[28] It is expected that by 1981 the total demand for dwellings will total 6,238,000, an increase of 625,000 on the present figure.[29] The plan predicts, however, that: '. . . there could well be an end to the housing shortage outside London well before 1981 . . .'[30] and that, as the region moves to a housing surplus: '. . . developers will find their customers more discriminating both as to quality and size of the house and as to the quality of the environment . . .'[31] which the cynic may possibly regard as an over-sanguine view.

Growth Pattern

Given that a large increase in population and economic activity is expected in a region which many people feel is overcrowded already, it is clearly necessary to give very careful thought to the way in which the growth is accommodated. The 1964 South-East Study envisaged a set of 'countermagnets' arranged at more than twice the distance from London of the original ring of post-war new towns. One aim of this idea was to produce large 'free-standing' centres of population that would not act largely as dormitories for London (which some of the original new towns are tending to do). The regional Economic Planning Council document of 1967 envisaged corridors of growth radiating out from London. This idea carries with it the obvious dangers of encroachment on the green belt and of adding to London's growth problems.

The 1970 plan takes as its starting point the trends already powerfully present in the region. The region is divided into three main zones; Greater London, the Outer Metropolitan Area (OMA) and the Outer South-East (OSE). Map 1 on page xiv maps these zones. It will be noted that Ringmer falls in the OSE. Over the period 1961–8 there was an average net *outflow* from Greater London of approximately 82,000 people per year,[32] whereas from 1951 to 1968 the OSE gained 785,100 in population.[33] During the last three years of this period the OSE was gaining population at a rate of nearly 63,000 per year. The proportions of the regional population to live in Greater London and the OSE were as follows:[34]

	1951	1969
Greater London	54·0%	44·5%
OSE	23·0%	25·1%

Over the period 1961–6 the number of jobs in Greater London increased by 1·53%, while the corresponding figures for the OMA and the OSE were 18·39% and 13·03% respectively. The implications of these figures are clear. The rest of the region has grown, and will continue to grow, much faster than London. In fact, in terms of population, London is in decline and Good Queen Bess can sleep a little more easily. The 1981 distribution of population, based upon existing development plans is expected to be as follows:[35]

	1966	1981
Greater London	7,825,000	7,336,000
OMA	5,004,000	6,190,000
OSE	4,160,000	5,161,000
	16,989,000	18,687,000

Further analyses devoted to a comparison of the rate of growth of the OMA and the OSE show that the latter has recently begun to gain population at a greater rate than the former.[36] In other words, more of the growth is tending to occur towards the periphery of the region. This trend can be partly explained by specific growth centres in the OSE (such as South Hampshire and Milton Keynes).[37] But there is, in any case, a spontaneous 'ripple' migration movement by which the OMA is a net gainer by migration from London but has a net loss to the OSE.

To put the entire problem dramatically, the accommodation of an extra five million people outside London (regional growth plus London's outflow) by the end of the century involves the urban development of another 600–700 square miles.[38] This assumes a density of roughly 12 people per acre, which many would regard as the upper limit that is socially acceptable. The present area of Greater London is 620 square miles. In other words, another Greater

London has to be fitted in to a region which has a total area of only 10,500 square miles. The manner in which this growth is arranged is crucially important for the preservation of a decent social and physical environment. The 1970 strategy, after exhaustive analyses, argues that: '. . . there are a number of advantages in concentrating rather than dispersing urban growth . . .' [39] that is to say, of encouraging the larger urban centres to grow faster than the smaller, always omitting London which everybody expects to decline further. The argument is based on grounds of economic efficiency since large towns have a good supply of labour for industry and can supply essential social services more economically. The concentration of people and jobs in limited areas also tends to reduce the aggregate amount of commuting required and makes it more possible to arrange mass transit systems which are, beyond all doubt, more effective ways of transporting people than the private car. They are, moreover, less damaging environmentally per passenger/mile of movement achieved. Since the number of cars in the region by 1981 is expected to be more than double that of 1966 (7·1 million as opposed to 3·1 million), [40] it is clearly extremely important to try to reduce the extent to which car journeys are necessary to reach work.

The effect of this general strategy on smaller centres and villages would be to ease the existing growth pressures. The plan devotes very little space to questions of village planning specifically. It does allow that 'visual factors' may constrain the rate of growth in some small settlements [41] but does not examine the effect that the scale of growth may have on the social organisation of villages. It finally concedes that the countryside is: '. . . an essential element in the structure of the region, separating and giving a distinctive setting to urban settlements.' The country lover and the farmer may feel that some urban backgrounds and value systems are apparent in this assessment of the main uses of rural areas. [42] Within the general strategy of concentrating growth in the larger centres, the plan suggests two alternative formats for 1991. The first, based on the 1967 strategy of the Economic Planning Council, suggests equal growth in the period 1981–91 for the OMA and the OSE with an emphasis on the radial routes from London and especially rapid growth in the South Hampshire, Milton Keynes and Crawley–Horsham areas. The second format suggests a heavier concentration of growth nearer London, specifically in south Essex, north Kent and the area around Reading and Aldershot. This would mean much more rapid growth in the OMA than the OSE and, partly for this reason, attracts the support of rural preservationists.

IMPLICATIONS FOR THE LEWES/BRIGHTON AREA

Both Lewes and Brighton suffer from a shortage of land for development. Much of the surroundings of both towns consist of chalk downlands, large areas of which are barred from development as Areas of Outstanding Natural Beauty. The sea, in the case of Brighton, and the Ouse floodplain at Lewes further constrain expansion. The axis northward from Brighton is, however, a zone designated for growth. By contrast with Brighton, which grew very slowly in employment in 1961–6, [43] Haywards Heath and the Burgess Hill-

Hassocks area have been experiencing rapid growth. In particular, much office employment has moved from London to Haywards Heath.[44] Apart from this employment growth centre, Crawley and Lewes have both been experiencing a marked labour shortage, the latter in particular has been designated an 'employment pressure area' and its acute shortage of housing was especially noted.[45] Since, in 1966, both Lewes and Brighton had more than 70% of their labour force in service industries one can expect continuing labour shortage in these towns.[46] It is significant to note, in view of the rather imprecise use of the term 'commuter village', that in the Ringmer area fewer than 5% of the workforce commute to London[47] and that in most towns in the locality 65% or more of the residents work in the town in which they live (for example the figures for Lewes and Brighton are 69·5% and 74% respectively). This area should not, therefore, be regarded as part of London's commuting belt.

The growth outlook, as seen by the strategy, for the local area is best shown in the following table which makes use of the planning areas adopted by the plan. The four zones together constitute what might reasonably be considered as the Ringmer commuting belt, that is, the area within which most village residents will work. Conversely, employment growth anywhere in this zone might well have a direct impact on demand for housing in the village.

Table 6.1 Scale of Growth for Ringmer Commuting Area

Planning area	Population (000s)			
	1966	1981	1991	2001
4 Uckfield	48	60	70	70
6 Crawley–Burgess Hill	227	280	400	470
21 Eastbourne–Hastings	256	330	380	420
22 Sussex coast (Bognor–Brighton)	526	590	600	610
	1,057	1,260	1,450	1,570
S.E. Region total	16,989	18,686	20,086	21,586

Source: Burns Plan, Appendix D, Table 1

These figures are described as neither projections nor targets but rather as 'indicative of the scale of growth'. The commentary that accompanies them (in Appendix E of the plan) suggests that rapid employment growth is unlikely in Uckfield but that that area, like the Burgess Hill area, will come under heavy pressure from the Crawley–Gatwick growth. It points out also that Brighton is hemmed in by the sea and downs, and will reinforce the pressure in the area to the north of the downs. Eastbourne–Hastings has a somewhat different problem. Here the need is to increase employment and, if possible, to adjust the rather top-heavy age distribution. Any great increase in employment in Eastbourne (less than 30 minutes from Ringmer by car) would introduce a new pressure on housing in the village.

In summary, the area within an approximate 25-mile radius of Ringmer is likely to increase in population from 1·0 million to 1·5 million by the end of the century. This 50% increase is likely to be much greater than the growth in the region as a whole. Lewes and Brighton are virtually powerless to cope with an increase of this magnitude. The Crawley–Gatwick–Burgess Hill area may well double in population size and the percentage growth rate in East-bourne–Hastings may be of a similar order. In this climate of expectation there seems little prospect of any reduction of pressure for housing in the village and little chance of the growth curve levelling off unless development control policies induce it to. It seems much more likely that the dramatic growth pressures in the immediate area of the past decade will continue, with little modification, well into the future.

For the village this is a matter of the greatest significance. Strategies are currently being worked out in the county planning office which will determine whether the village is allowed to expand beyond the estimated 4400 by the mid-1970s (see Chapter 13). In the absence of the development control machinery there can be no doubt that natural pressures would lead to a much higher population figure. But it seems, both intuitively and from various findings in the following chapters, that beyond a figure of 4000–5000 the concept of 'village' begins to evaporate and the concept of 'small town' begins to emerge. Many people hope, on a variety of grounds, that this irrevocable transition will not occur and that the growth strategy will seek to accommodate the development in a range of other villages.

Unfortunately it seems probable that, as often happens, technical, accessi-bility and landownership considerations will weigh more heavily in the choice of villages for growth, and the rate at which they are expanded, than will any scientific evaluation of the rate at which any given village is likely to be able to assimilate newcomers without feeling undesirable social effects. There are a number of reasons for this. One of them is that the sort of evidence that would be required to make well-informed decisions on these complex social issues, evidence such as is presented in the next four chapters, is simply not available for any other village in the county. And until more money is spent on ob-taining it decisions on village expansion will continue to be made on the basis of inadequate information and insufficiently detailed social analysis.

7 · The Newcomers

The recent growth curve of the village is shown in Figure P.1. From this one would expect the 150 sample households surveyed to show a high proportion of recent arrivals and this expectation is borne out. Households have been regarded as 'newcomers' where the head of household arrived in the village in 1963 or later, that is, in the nine years previous to the survey date. This is clearly an arbitrary threshold but it does mark a quickening in the growth rate of the village and the first of the new private developments, which are now characteristic, occurred about this time. The division of the sample between those who arrived before, and after, the threshold date is as follows:

	Arrived before 1963	Arrived 1963 and after	Total
Heads of household	67	83	150
Total sample population	200	280	480
Average size of household	2·99	3·37	3·20

The general socio-economic characteristics of newcomers to villages of this sort, located near large employment centres in regions subject to growth pressures, are by now quite well known. Numerous studies have documented the differences between the incoming group and the 'indigenous' population. These studies include a variety by Pahl,[1] several by county planning authorities (including Hampshire,[2] Kent[3] and Cambridgeshire[4]) at least one by a Rural Community Council (Suffolk)[5] and others by individuals and research groups (for example, Crichton[6] and Radford).[7] The field has been usefully summarised recently by Connell[8] and the concept of a 'discontinuous suburb', a form of settlement with certain 'suburban' characteristics but which is not contiguous to a town, has been established and discussed. It would be wearisome and unnecessary to document, for every point of comparison, the similarities between the Ringmer findings and those of the previous studies. Many of the points have been substantiated elsewhere although of course the form and content of the questions put to the respondents varies considerably in each of the studies. Ringmer is rather larger than most of the expanding rural settlements previously examined and with a population of over 3700, it is one of the largest villages in the county. Similarly, its rate of expansion is rather greater than the villages examined in, for example, Hampshire, Suffolk and by Radford in Worcestershire.

The following sixteen brief sections review the respects in which the incoming group differs from, or is similar to, the pre-1963 residents. Clearly one set of pre-1963 residents have not been interviewed; those who have left the village (or died) between 1963 and 1971. Their reasons for leaving, if not for dying, may well be very significant to the work. In fact it could be argued that the pre-1963 residents still remaining are self-selected by an important characteristic—that of acquiescence in the situation—and that the survey thus gives only a partial view. However, since the mechanics involved in interviewing a representative sample of those who have left seemed fearsome, and since all social scientists live in a world of partial views anyway, the decision to omit an analysis of this group was fairly easily taken.

COMPARATIVE ANALYSES OF HOUSEHOLDS ARRIVING BEFORE AND AFTER THE BEGINNING OF 1963

The differences between the 'newcomers' and the longstanding residents are shown by means of bar-graphs. The original tabulations upon which these bar-graphs are based had five possible categories of arrival time. These were reduced to two categories for the purpose of graphing the data. A statistical test (chi-square) was carried out on the original tables and in nearly every case the differences between the households in the various arrival time categories were found to be significant at the 1% level, that is to say there was only one chance in a hundred that the differences observed would have been due to chance. Where the statistical significance of the result falls below this figure a note to this effect has been included after the section title.

Age/Sex Structures

As Figure 7.1 shows, the age/sex structure of the two groups varies fundamentally. Nearly half the members of pre-1963 households are aged over 50 and there is a striking lack of children under 10 (only eight in all). Taken in isolation, and disregarding the age/sex structure of more recent arrivals, it appears that the pre-1963 demographic structure would lead to a fall in the population level by natural decrease resulting from an ageing population. This hardly seems to be a phenomenon normally associated with a settlement in the south-east region, with its chronic growth pressures. Yet as Jay et al. have pointed out,[9] 57 of the 127 rural parishes in East Sussex remained static in population or declined between 1951 and 1961. Hard-line preservationists, and others concerned to prevent any migration into small settlements, may well ponder the implications of these figures. The mid- and late-Victorian demographic structure of the village (see Chapter 2) which was vastly more 'bottom-heavy' than Figure 7.1(A)., was even so just sufficient to lead to a slow growth. It would have been very interesting to see the 1971 and 1981 demographic pyramid for Ringmer had no immigration occurred after 1963.

Figure 7.1(B) presents the complementary component of the population which, in combination with (A) produces a reasonably balanced structure (C). The newcomers' structure shows a high proportion of people, evenly balanced by sex, in the child-rearing age groups, a predictably large number of young children and relatively few people over 50.

Behind the basic population data, several possible conflicts of interest may be guessed at. Clearly, long-established village residents will be much concerned with issues and facilities concerning the old (for example, special housing provision and home-help) whereas more recently arrived families are likely to be concerned with issues like education, playgroups and children's recreational facilities. It is instructive that the Parish Council (predominantly longer-established residents) are distinctly unenthusiastic about spending more money on more play facilities for children, since they appear to feel that

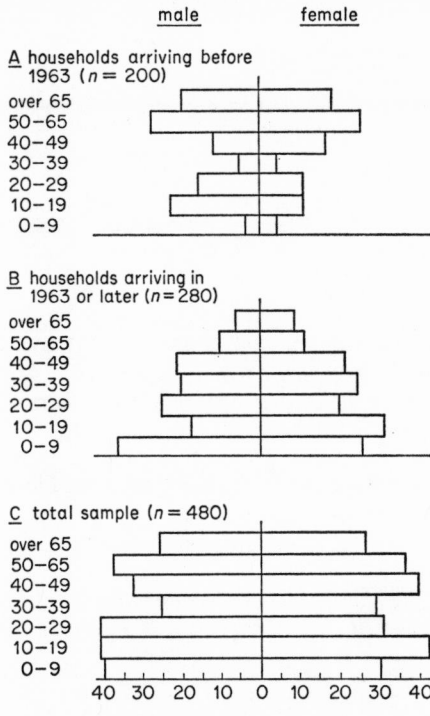

Fig. 7.1 Age/Sex Pyramids in Relation to
Arrival Time.

enough has been spent on the young already. Other village issues, for example traffic on the main road and refuse collection, may concern both groups equally. But generally where a conflict does arise about some matter of policy, reference to the widely differing age/sex structures shown in (A) and (B) may give some insight into the situation.

Life-Cycle Stage

Figure 7.2 shows a situation which could have been predicted from the age/sex structures. Over 60% of recently arrived households have at least one dependent child still at home. Another 11% are currently childless but probably most of them will soon have children. Thus nearly three-quarters of the group can be said to be directly or potentially interested in the provision of educational, welfare and recreational facilities for the young. The older-established households are almost equally divided between those who still have children at home and those whose children have left home, or who have suffered the loss of a spouse. Only a small proportion of households consist of a person who has never been married. This reflects a distinct lack of flats

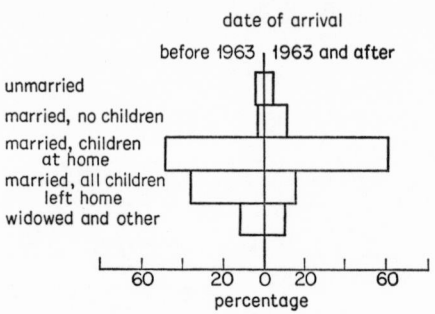

Fig. 7.2 Stages in Life Cycle.

and apartments in the village, and it means that a large and distinctive element to be found in any large town, single office workers, students and nurses, etc., living alone, is almost entirely absent from the village.

Size of Household

Figure 7.3 shows some points of social significance. The small proportion of single-person households is again evident, and the vast majority of households, regardless of arrival date, fall into the two-, three- or four-person

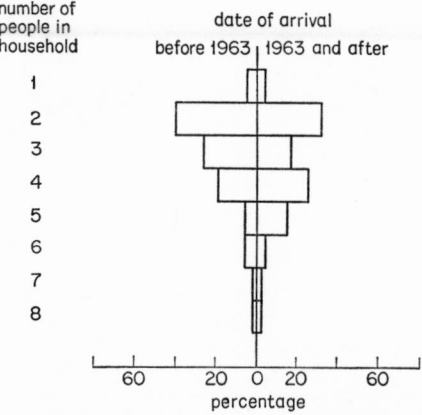

Fig. 7.3 Household Size Distribution.

categories. The older-established group have a greater proportion of two-person households, which is consistent with the life-cycle stage data, while the newcomers have a larger representation of four- and five-person households. This is, to some extent, a reversal of the traditional picture of rural families tending to be larger than urban (most of the newcomers are ex-urban as will be seen later). But, as will become clear from several subsequent analyses, the 'urban–rural continuum'[10] is a rather imprecise and over-simplified dimension for differentiation and the slightly different pattern of family size evident from the sample is much more likely to reflect the age or social status of the households concerned than anything so hazy as 'urbanity' or 'rurality'.[11]

Previous Place of Residence

The data shown in Figure 7.4 on place of residence immediately prior to coming to the village substantiate the general conclusion of various other surveys (for example, the Suffolk[12] and Hampshire[13] studies) that migration

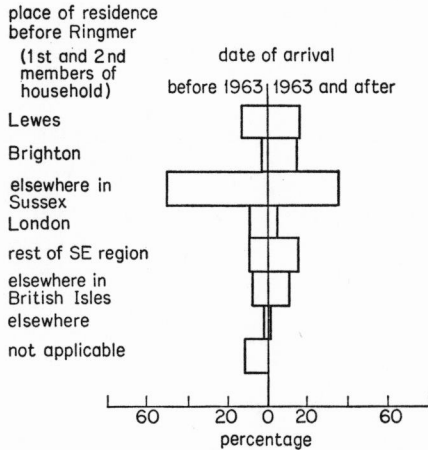

Fig. 7.4 Previous Place of Residence.

into growth villages of this kind is a fairly short-distance phenomenon. Of the sample of 277 (information was collected from both first and second members of each household), 65% had previously lived in Sussex, 6% in London, 11% elsewhere in the south-east region, only 12% had come from further afield and the rest were lifelong residents. Clearly such highly pub-licised trends as overspill from London and 'the drift to the south-east' are very minor factors in the growth. The 'drift' is, of course, a myth rather than a trend since various regional studies have shown recently that the south-east region actually experiences net out-migration in some years.[14] Arrivals from Lewes and Brighton are much more numerous since 1963 (51) than previous to that date (18) as are arrivals from outside the region (23 as against 8). The former trend may be an indirect reflection of the mounting shortage of land for urban development in the towns concerned.

Previous Mode of Life

Figure 7.5 shows two clear points. The first is that the vast majority of village residents have previously experienced an urban life-style. In fact only 17% of the total sample of first and second members of households had never lived in a town. Thus most adults in the sample were well placed to compare the relative merits of town and country life (see Chapter 9). The second point is that there are marked differences between the earlier and recent arrivals. Of the recent arrivals, about two-thirds had lived as a family unit in a town before

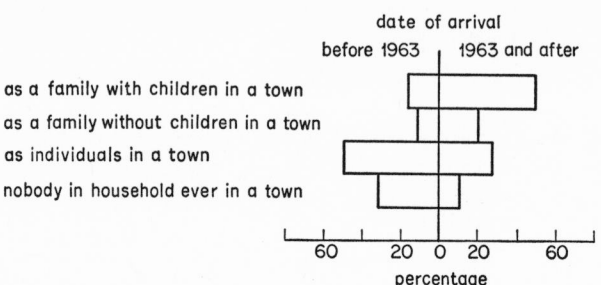

Fig. 7.5 Previous Mode of Life.

coming to the village. In relatively few cases had the first two household members lived as individuals in a town and even fewer had a purely rural background. The earlier arrivals show a different pattern in that a smaller proportion of them had any urban experience and, of those that had, it tended to be as individuals rather than as a family unit. The implications of these results may become clearer if they are considered in conjunction with the reasons given for moving to the village.

Reasons for Coming to the Village

Any attempt to sort out why people make a migratory movement, or indeed why they do anything else, is fraught with difficulties. In this study the usual range of pre-coded answers was available on the interview schedule and the respondents' reasons were recorded either as 'strongly stated' or 'weakly stated'. The intention was to try and distinguish between major and subsidiary reasons. The coded reasons were hopefully a little more specific and precise than those of a previous survey where the pre-defined reason 'convenient home' attracted a predictably large measure of support.

Figure 7.6 shows the distribution of reasons given and indicates the extent to which each was strongly stated. As is usual in these cases, employment was the most frequently cited reason for the move by both groups (although, from the wording of the reason, this did not necessitate that the job was actually in the village). Following this, however, the relative importance of other reasons varies greatly with arrival time. For the pre-1963 arrivals, movements on marriage, being born in the village and movements to be near relatives were next most frequently mentioned. This set of reasons might reasonably be termed 'familial'. Few people mentioned reasons such as the desire for rural amenities and community spirit or the liking for a particular house, while the comparative cost advantage of property was hardly given as a reason at all. Subsequent arrivals quoted these three latter reasons almost as frequently as they quoted employment. Movements to relatives or a spouse on marriage were much less significant. There thus seems to be a shift over time from reasons connected with the family and extended kinship networks towards reasons based on more material considerations and upon choices (for example, concerning house type and rural amenities) unconstrained by factors outside the nuclear family.[15]

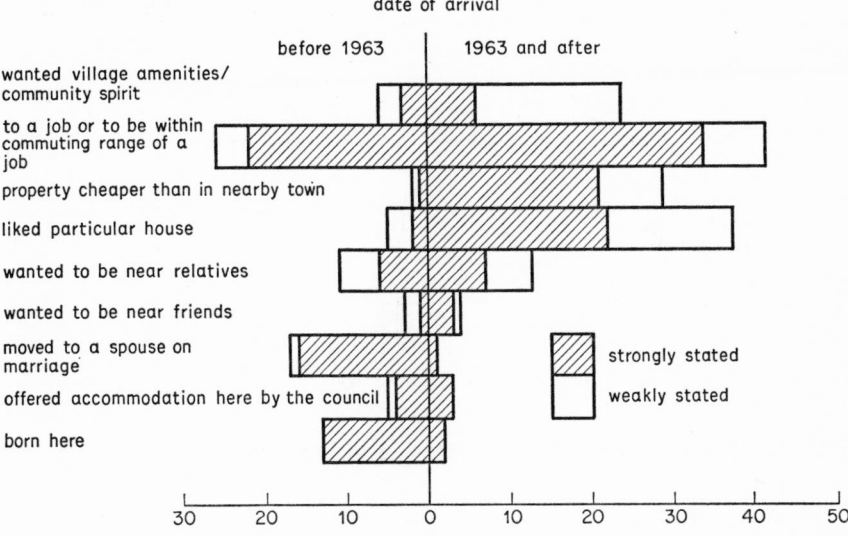

Fig. 7.6 Reasons for Coming to the Village.

Another insight into the situation can be gained by considering the ratio between the number of times each reason was 'strongly' and 'weakly' stated, although obviously interviewer interpretation provides an unknown bias here. 'Born here' was quite understandably given as a strong reason whenever it was quoted. It thus had a 'strong to weak ratio' of 100%.[16] The employment reason had a ratio of 72% and the 'cheaper property' reason one of 71%. By contrast the 'village amenities' reason was strongly stated on only 30% of the occasions on which it was mentioned. It thus seems to be a consideration frequently in the minds of recent arrivals, but mostly in a subsidiary capacity. The liking for a particular house (56%) stands intermediate between the two extremes. 'Movement to a spouse on marriage' provides a moment of diverting relief. For 17 spouses this was accorded its expected strong significance. For one less enthusiastic respondent it constituted only a weak reason for the move. Since he or she has been here for a long time one can only surmise that the move was perhaps important at the time but that retrospection has lent disenchantment to the view.

Number of Close Relatives in the Village

'Close' in this context was defined to mean parents, grandparents, siblings, children, grandchildren, uncles and aunts, nieces and nephews and first cousins of any household member. Relationships within the household were, of course, not counted. As would be expected, there is a clear difference in the strength of local kinship networks between the two groups. The clear majority of pre-1963 households had at least one close relative in the village and 17% had five or more. By contrast, over 80% of more recent arrivals had none. The importance of kin-based social networks and family feuds as cementing factors in more 'traditional' small rural, and some urban, communities is well established.[17] It is evident, in the virtual absence of these factors, that social

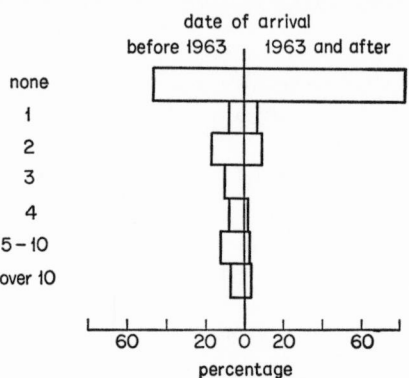

Fig. 7.7 Number of Close Relatives
in the Village.

relationships and styles of interaction are tending to be grounded on more ephemeral bases than blood relationships. This may produce subtle changes in the expectations people have in their social relationships (one probably makes different assumptions about the readiness of a near neighbour to help out in some emergency depending on whether she is a cousin or not). The new situation also seems to include an inherently wider range of choice concerning which relationships can be made and developed. Against this must be set the reduced degree to which individuals can rely upon kin-based support in time of need.

There is some fragmentary evidence that the proportion of recent arrivals with close relatives in the village may be increasing. The invaluable efforts of one of the research assistants on this study were partly interrupted while she helped various sets of relatives, including her parents, to move into the village. Various other examples are known where parents of near retirement age have settled near their married children in the village. The new pattern seems to be neither patrilocal or matrilocal but 'puerlocal' (for those parents fortunate enough to be able to cope with spiralling local house prices).

Educational Level

The differences shown by Figure 7.8 between the two groups are quite fundamental and may be closely related to differences in the social structure. Two thirds of the pre-1963 residents left school at 15 or younger and presumably experienced their schooling before the 1944 Education Act. Apart from the generally lower standards of the time, this was an era in which secondary education opportunities were better for boys than for girls[18] (a situation the Act sought to redress) and one which thus still maintained some Victorian assumptions about conjugal roles. Many of the beliefs and opinions of older residents, concerning for example power structures and what can be done to change them, must surely be coloured by an educational experience which was more formal and disciplined, less varied and imaginative and, in terms of years, briefer than that experienced today.

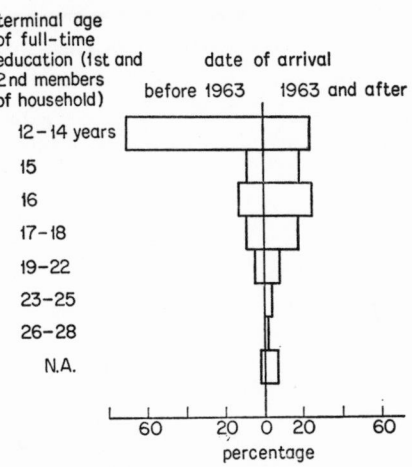

Fig. 7.8 Educational Levels.

The newcomers show a completely different educational profile. Only 22% left school at 14 or younger and the clear majority (59%) were in full-time education until the age of 16 or more. In terms of higher education similar differences are apparent. The proportion of newcomers with a degree or other professional qualification is 25% against the corresponding proportion of 7% for pre-1963 arrivals.[19] It is not known whether these great differences in educational level between the two groups is reflected in different educational aspirations for their children.[20]

In any situation of actual or potential conflict of interests, and the rapid expansion of a rural community is such a situation, marked educational differences do not help. It is all too easy for the incoming family, highly educated and with consequent high income and social skills, to make incorrect assumptions about older-established families and to approach them as if they had enjoyed similar educational opportunities, which is likely to be simply incorrect, or as if they were totally without education, which is both incorrect and insulting. Similarly, older residents may be, quite wrongly, overawed by the easy articulation of newcomers on club committees and may opt out with a feeling of resentment at the newcomers' 'takeover'.[21] Both attitudes would be modified if it were more generally accepted that an individual's education is a lifelong process based partly on formal and partly on informal learning and that the number of years spent in formal education cannot be relied upon to give an accurate indication of one's ability to synthesise, and profit by, experience.

Social Status

For the purpose of this comparison the 'social classes' recognised by the Registrar-General have been used. The most striking characteristic of the village as a whole is the preponderance (53%) of the total population who fall into social classes I and II. The comparison with national data is given in Table 7.1.

Table 7.1 Distribution of Population Between the
Registrar-General's Social Classes

Social class	Ringmer	Great Britain
	%	%
I	9	3
II	44	15
III NM	9	} 49
III M	18	
IV	13	22
V	3	8
Unclassified, etc.	4	3
	100	100

Sources: 1971 Ringmer Survey. Social Trends, No. 3, 1972, H.M.S.O. Table 16

Within the village, the status structures of the older and more recent arrivals are quite distinct. Figure 7.9 shows that, of older residents, 51% of heads of

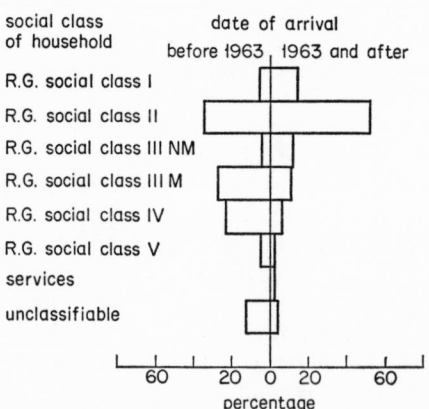

Fig. 7.9 Occupational Status.

households are engaged in manual work as compared to only 18% of more recently arrived heads of household. The complementary proportions engaged in non-manual work were 37% for pre-1963 arrivals as against 77% for the newcomers, 64% of whom were in social classes I and II. The 'top-heaviness' of the village status profile is thus clearly a result of the recent influx. This is part of a significant socio-spatial trend which, from the present pattern of house building, is likely to continue and accelerate. Its broader implications will be discussed in Chapters 13 and 14.

Distance of Households from the Village Centre
(differences significant at the 5% level)

For the purpose of this analysis, the centre of the village was taken to be the new shopping centre which lies almost adjacent to the village green and the distance of each sample household was measured from this point by straight-line distance. Nearly 60% of the newcomer households were found in the most central zone (within 500 yards of the centre) as opposed to only 40% of the older households.[22] The inevitable consequence is that more of the pre-1963 residents are distributed peripherally in the village. This finding is surprising, since one normally expects more recently added development to be more peripheral, and it stems from the rather linear and loose-knit pattern of the pre-1963 village which had large open gaps suitable for infilling. No great social significance can be ascribed to the result at this stage (later analyses in Chapter 8 will compare the degree of integration into village life with distance from centre). It may well be, however, that these locational factors are significant and that the capacity of a village to absorb new growth in a social sense is in some way related to the location of the new population in a physical sense. If so, the Ringmer situation seems preferable to a situation like that researched by Pahl in 'Dormersdell'.[23] The possible planning implications of these questions of village design will also be discussed in Chapter 12.

Property Tenure

Figure 7.10 shows that the vast majority (85%) of post-1963 arrivals live in owner-occupied property and only 8% live in local authority housing. This

date of arrival

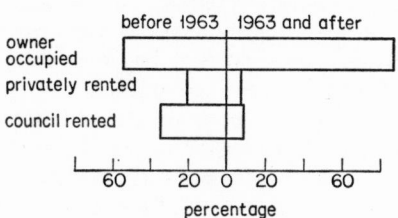

Fig. 7.10 Tenure Type.

has had the effect of distorting the pre-1963 pattern, which was not far from the national average, to a pattern where 70% of households are owner-occupied. This is considerably different from the national average (52%).[24] Simultaneously, the importance of privately rented accommodation, which was the norm up to 50 years ago (see Chapter 3), is declining and only 7% of new arrivals fall into this category.

Household Mobility

Newcomer households tend to be more mobile than others. Only 10% of them are without any form of private transport whereas the corresponding proportion for pre-1963 households is 24%.[25] Given the increasing tendency of various facilities to be centralised into large settlements, and the steady decline in the provision of rural public transport, those without cars are placed at a considerable disadvantage. This disadvantage is much more widely felt among long-standing residents than among newcomers. Various authors, including Pahl, have recently begun to question the partly subconscious assumptions about car-ownership rates made by planning authorities and others.[26] Clearly, any policy assumptions that private transport is ubiquitously available to rural residents are less accurate for older than for more recently arrived residents.

Location of Work
(differences significant at the 5% level)

Older residents are much more locally oriented in their place of work. About three-quarters of pre-1963 heads of household work in either Ringmer or Lewes compared to fewer than half of the post-1963 arrivals. Employment in London and, surprisingly, Brighton is virtually confined to newcomer heads of household. As noted in Chapter 4, the largest single-work location is the village itself, which employs nearly one-third of heads of household.

Shopping Activity
(differences not significant)

The household survey showed that the pattern of shopping activity, as measured by the proportion of basic household needs (food, cleaning materials, chemist goods, etc.) purchased within the village is virtually unbiased by arrival time and the differences between the two groups are nowhere near significant. The fourteen-shop parade built in the village in 1968–9 (see Plate 5a) appears to be operating quite successfully since nearly half of both groups of households estimate that they buy over 80% of their basic needs there. One curious feature is that the intermediate percentage categories attracted only a small proportion of respondents. It seems that people either do virtually all their frequent shopping in the village or else virtually none. The latter tendency is stronger in recent arrivals than in others, which might have been expected from the findings on, for example, car-ownership rates.

Recreational Activity
(differences not significant)

Evidence was presented in Chapter 5 indicating that car outings of one sort or another are the most frequent of recreational activities, followed by watching or playing sport, and by visits to the pub or licensed club (in the case of Ringmer the club would most likely be the football club). The more 'formal' activities such as visits to a restaurant, theatre, dance or cinema occur much less frequently. Comparison between the two groups shows that they each have a remarkably similar pattern. The average number of recreational activities per household was almost identical (3·0 in the previous month for pre-1963 households and nearly 3·1 for the others) and the distribution between categories showed very little difference. The newcomers had a slightly greater propensity to participate in sport and to go to the cinema, theatre or a dance but the differences are marginal and have no statistical significance.

Length of Stay Expected in the Village

The most surprising feature of this analysis, in view of the literature on the upwardly mobile, transient families which villages like Ringmer are supposed to attract, was the overwhelming frequency with which the question 'Can you say how long the household expects to be in the village?' was met with the response 'We do not expect to move out.' This was given, as might be expected, by a large majority (86%) of pre-1963 households. It was also given by very nearly half (46%) of the newcomers. In all, 95 of the 150 households (over 63%) did not expect to leave the village. Of the newcomers, a further 21% expected to be in the village for 5–10 years and only 16% expected to leave in four years or fewer.

Precise comparison of these data with national rates of residential mobility is difficult. The survey question concerned future intentions in what might have appeared to the respondents as an ill-defined and hypothetical situation. Nevertheless, only nine of the 150 households (or 6%) expected to leave the village within the next two years, which would imply a population turnover rate, given no new growth, of about 3% per year. This compares with a rate of 5·7% for Rural Districts in England and Wales for 1960–1.[27] No firm conclusions can be drawn from this comparison. A more thoroughgoing analysis of changes in the Electoral Roll from year to year would be required for any valid comparisons to be made. But it does appear that, in intention at least, the residential mobility rate of the newcomer households in the village is lower rather than higher than the national rate for rural areas. There is fragmentary evidence to support this idea from the Worcestershire study. Radford found that, in her two villages, 37% and 16% respectively of newcomer households had lived in their previous houses for more than 10 years.[28] In addition, the village studies in both Hampshire and Suffolk found very low expectations of moving out (two-thirds and 71% of the population respectively had never considered moving).[29] The emerging picture of the behaviour of newcomers to growing villages hardly accords with the idea that most of them are 'spiralists' moving around the country as they move up through the promotion structure of some large organisation.[30]

SUMMARY

From the various analyses carried out, it is possible to arrive at a summary of the ways in which the newer households in Ringmer differ from the old. The findings fall into six main areas:

(i) *Demographic*–new households tend to be younger, more of them are in the 'married, children at home' stage of the life-cycle, and the average household size is larger.

(ii) *Previous Life-style Experience*–a larger proportion of the new households have lived in towns and especially as family units in towns.

(iii) *Reasons for Coming and Future Migration Intentions*–disregarding the employment reason, which was very important for both groups, the newcomer households tended to come to the village for considerations based on the needs of the nuclear family unit as opposed to considerations based on extended family networks or marriage; very few of either group envisaged leaving the village in the near future.

(iv) *Education, Employment, Status etc.*–the newcomer households have much more formal education, more professional qualifications and household heads are employed in jobs which place them much higher, on average, in the occupational status structure; they are almost entirely involved in non-manual work as opposed to the almost equal manual/non-manual distribution of the older residents; they are, in addition, more likely to work further afield than the village.

(v) *House tenure, Location and Household Mobility*–newcomer households are almost entirely owner-occupied as opposed to only half of older households, they tend to be located more centrally in the village and they command greater access to private transport.

(vi) *Shopping and Recreational Activities*–there is very little difference in the pattern of shopping or recreation between the two groups; this finding, while negative, was interesting and unexpected in view of the clear distinctions between the groups in more structural terms; it appears that wide socio-economic differences do not translate themselves into differences (as observed in this study) in two important aspects of behaviour; as Chapter 2 has clearly shown, the situation 100 years ago was very different.

Attempts have been made in the preceding sections to point out some of the implications of the differences between the two groups. Date of arrival will be used with other presumed explanatory variables in several of the following chapters and other aspects of the 'grafting on' of a new population, with very different characteristics from those of older residents, will be examined in Part IV.

8 · The Process of Integration

This chapter seeks to measure the degree to which the various households in the sample survey are integrated into the life of the village, to seek relationships between the development of integration and certain other socioeconomic attributes of the households concerned, and to examine some aspects of the process of integration. 'Integration' into a community is clearly an imprecise and many-faceted idea. Nevertheless, any attempt to relate the degree of involvement to other, possibly explanatory, variables must depend upon some quantitative evaluation of it. Various previous attempts have been made to quantify integration.[1] At least one of these has combined both 'objective' variables (such as whether or not the respondent knows the Chairman of the Parish Council) with less tangible 'subjective' assessments ('do you feel you belong here?').[2]

AN INTEGRATION INDEX

Construction of the Index

The present study uses an index of integration which combines a limited number of quantifiable objective variables as follows:

(a) For every 10 people known in the village to a defined level ('well enough to call on or stop and talk to')   1 point

(b) For every 10% of the respondent's total set of friends who live in the village rather than elsewhere   1 point

(c) For every 'key resident' known by name (from a list of eleven)   1 point

(d) For every club/society membership (all household members aggregated)   2 points

(e) For every club/society committee membership (all household members aggregated)   2 points
(in addition)

For all households (a), (b) and (c) were summed for each of the first two members. These additions were then summed and (d) and (e) were added to produce the 'integration score' (I.S.) for the household. In households headed by a married couple, the sum of the first three elements was calculated separately for husband and wife and these indices were termed the 'husband integration score' (H.I.S.) and the 'wife integration score' (W.I.S.) respectively. This was done since it was believed that in a village like Ringmer, where many of the husbands work elsewhere, conjugal differences in the level of integration might exist. The I.S. for the household has obvious defects (for example, the possibly large number of local friends acquired by a gregarious teenage son or daughter does not count). But the practical difficulties in constructing a more complex index were considerable. The way in which the various aspects of integration are weighted is arbitrary but it could hardly be otherwise since no clear empirical basis for weighting is available. Research evaluating the precise social significance of, for example, knowing ten other people to a defined level as opposed to belonging to a horticultural society, appears not to have been done, although it conceivably could be done.

The Distribution of Scores

The distribution of household scores was as follows:

I.S.	Number of households
0–9	35
10–19	22
20–29	31
30–39	20
40–49	26
50–59	8
60–69	4
70–79	2
80–89	1
90–99	1
	150

The average of these scores is approximately 28. The integration scores for husbands and wives were distributed as follows:

H.I.S./W.I.S.	Husbands	Wives
0–4	29	29
5–9	25	19
10–14	27	28
15–19	23	31
20–24	21	21
25–29	11	15
Not applicable	14	7
	150	150

N.B. 'Not applicable' indicates the number of households without a husband or a wife (e.g. households headed by widows or widowers).

The W.I.S. mean (13·4) is marginally higher than the H.I.S. mean (12·6) which indicates a slightly higher degree of involvement, a result at variance with a finding of the Community Attitudes Survey carried out by the 1969 Royal Commission on Local Government in England.[3] It seems likely that the difference in the degree of conjugal involvement might well be understated by these scores because membership of clubs and societies, in which women appear to be marginally more participatory than men, is not included.

Relationship to Other Variables

It was thought that the level of integration might be influenced by certain other variables, such as length of residence. To test this idea, the household scores were cross-tabulated with scores on each of these variables. The results in relation to those variables which a chi-square test showed to have a statistically significant biasing effect are as follows:

(i) *Length of Residence.* As expected, a biasing effect is evident but it is by no means simple. Households of fewer than two years' standing tend to have low scores and those of twenty-five years or more to have high scores. Between these extremes, however, the relationship is irregular, households of three to six years' standing tending to have higher scores than those of seven to ten years. It was believed that it might be the wives in recently arrived families, rather than the husbands, who acted as a 'spearhead' of social involvement in the village. Husbands work elsewhere in the vast majority of these households while, in most cases, the wives are at home with the children and might well be more dependent on the village for their social life. This general expectation was borne out. Figure 8.1 shows

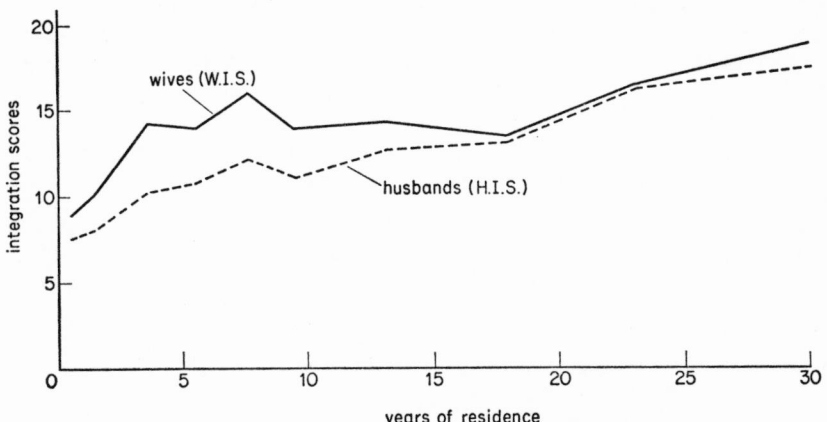

Fig. 8.1 Integration Scores for Husbands (H.I.S.) and Wives (W.I.S.) in Relation to Length of Residence (3-year moving averages).

that in recently arrived households there is a considerable discrepancy between the mean H.I.S. and W.I.S. scores. This discrepancy slowly decreases with length of residence as the H.I.S. scores make up the leeway.

(ii) *Social Class.* The effect here is also irregular. Class I and Class III Manual households had high average scores (36 and 39 respectively). Classes II and III Non-manual rather lower (both 24) and Class V lowest of all (20).

(iii) *Education.* Terminal age of education and degree of integration appear to be negatively related. In fact in no case in a sample of nearly 300 (the first two people in every household) did a person with a terminal age of education of 19 or more have an above average integration score. This result is corroborated by the indication (not statistically significant) that whereas only 18% of households including someone with a degree or professional qualification had a score of over 40, the corresponding percentage for the rest of the sample was 31%.

(iv) *Life-cycle Stage*. The eleven households consisting of unmarried or widowed people living alone all had scores of 9 or fewer while the scores of the 83 households with children living at home averaged 32. Married couples with no children averaged 20 and couples whose children had left home averaged 31.

(v) *Household Size*. There was a generally positive relationship between household size and the integration score although this relationship was less strong towards the top end of the size scale since households with five or more members tended to have average rather than high scores.

(vi) *Household Mobility*. Households without cars averaged a score of only 21, while two car households averaged 31.

(vii) *Church Attendance*. Households including a regular church attender averaged 38 (the highest average for any subset tested), those with an infrequent attender 29, and those including no churchgoer averaged 24. There is thus a clear relationship between church attendance and integration into village life. From later analyses in this chapter, however, it would seem wiser to conclude that the two tendencies are concomitant rather than that a high degree of integration *results* from church attendance.

Certain other variables which it was thought might have had a bearing on integration scores appeared to have very little, or no, biasing effect. These included the following:

location of work
number of hours the head of household is away at work each day
reasons for coming to the village
length of stay expected in the village
distance from village centre.

There are reasonable arguments why each of these variables might have had some bearing on people's desire, ability, or both to become involved in village life. Their lack of systematic effect on the pattern of results is probably as socially revealing as some of the positive results. For example, households where the husband spends many hours commuting, or who had no particular preference for Ringmer as a place to live, or who expect to leave in the near future appear to suffer no adverse effects so far as their level of involvement in the village is concerned.

One problem in analysing any social process as complex as integration into a village concerns the interdependence between the various 'explanatory' variables. There appeared to be a number of cases where the effect of two variables tended to cancel out. For example, holding all other factors constant it seemed plausible that both social status and length of residence would be positively related to the integration score. But, by and large, recent arrivals are of higher status than old-established villagers so the effects tend to be self-cancelling. Similarly, the effect of increasing distance from the centre may be masked by the fact that, paradoxically, the new estates tend to be located at a lower mean distance from the centre than the earlier pattern of settlement (as shown in Chapter 7). Attempts to disentangle the effects of the various factors by means of multiple regression analysis were unsuccessful, largely because the sample of households was too small. Further research is required on this complex issue.

Husband/Wife Variation in Integration Scores

There is an extensive literature on the degree to which the social roles played by the husband and wife may differ from each other according to the circumstances of the household.[4] By calculating the integration scores of husband and wife separately in this study it was possible to carry out some analyses to extend this literature. As noted earlier in this chapter, the two indices (H.I.S. and W.I.S.) are composites which incorporate the number of 'key residents' named, the number of people in the village known to a defined level, and the percentage of one's total set of friends who live in the village rather than elsewhere.

When H.I.S. and W.I.S. values were graphed, with the former along the y (vertical) axis and the latter along the x (horizontal) axis, the expected positive relationship emerged. There was, however, a tendency for the points to scatter on the x side of the diagonal. These are households where the wife scores much higher than the husband in terms of local involvement. The statistics of the distribution are as follows:

Correlation coefficient (r)	Regression coefficient (slope)	Mean	Standard deviation
0·75	0·69	13·1	7·8

The regression coefficient measures the degree of association between the scores in the sample households. A value of 1·0 (a 45° slope) would indicate that the two sets of integration scores are identical to each other while much steeper or shallower slopes indicate the reverse. Arguably, the first situation reflects similarity between husbands and wives in social activity while the second reflects wide differences in the degree to which the social lives of husbands and wives are locally based. The correlation coefficient indicates the reliability of the relationship, values approaching 1·0 indicating consistency in the conjugal association of scores and lower values indicating the reverse.

A similar analysis carried out on various subsets of the sample population revealed considerable differences in these general relationships. The complete set of results is given in Table 8.1.

Table 8.1 Analysis of H.I.S. and W.I.S. Scores by Various Population Subsets

Grouping criterion and group	Correlation coefficient (r)	Regression coefficient (slope)	Mean	Standard deviation
Mobility				
no cars	0·73	0·73	12·8	8·8
1 car +	0·73	0·66	13·3	7·6
2 cars+	0·69	0·59	14·0	9·4
Social Status				
R.G. Class I and II	0·72	0·68	11·2	7·0
R.G. Class III	0·82	0·71	14·4	8·6
R.G. Class IV and V	0·56	0·75	18·0	6·2
Educational Level				
Aggregate T.A.E. <30	0·79	0·74	15·6	7·8
Aggregate T.A.E. 30–34	0·71	0·66	12·1	7·8
Aggregate T.A.E. >34	0·68	0·87	8·7	5·0
Life Cycle Stage				
No children	0·92	0·95	10·6	7·7
Children at home	0·66	0·60	13·0	7·6
Children left home	0·85	0·96	14·6	8·3
Total Sample	0·75	0·69	13·1	7·8

Source: 1971 Ringmer Survey and Analyses

The results of each grouping operation will be considered in turn.

(i) Mobility

The main systematic effect here was the reduction in slope angle with increasing mobility. For example, in two-car households wives' scores tended to be very high in relation to husbands. One inference that might be drawn is that highly mobile wives tend still to develop a village-oriented social life, even though they presumably have the means, during the day, to engage in social activities further afield.

(ii) Social status

Class IV and V households appear to be much less consistent in the degree of conjugal association, and this particular distribution was also unusual in that the H.I.S. mean was marginally higher than the W.I.S. mean showing, overall, a greater local involvement by husbands than wives. The three group mean values are widely and systematically differentiated, high social status being associated with low local involvement and vice versa (perhaps it should be repeated that these scores do not include participation in clubs and societies).

(iii) Educational Level

A higher educational level appears to be associated with rather less consistency to the subset slope. A rather more startling result is that the mean score of highly educated households is little more than half that of the mean of the less well educated. This is consistent with the pattern of mean scores in the social status groupings. This implies that highly educated/high status families have less local knowledge and fewer local friends than others. One possible explanation is that their social activity is territorially more broadly based.

(iv) Life-cycle stage

The three stages exhibit clearly differentiated patterns as shown in Figure 8.2. The scores of married couples without children are very closely and consistently related and their mean value is below average. Households with

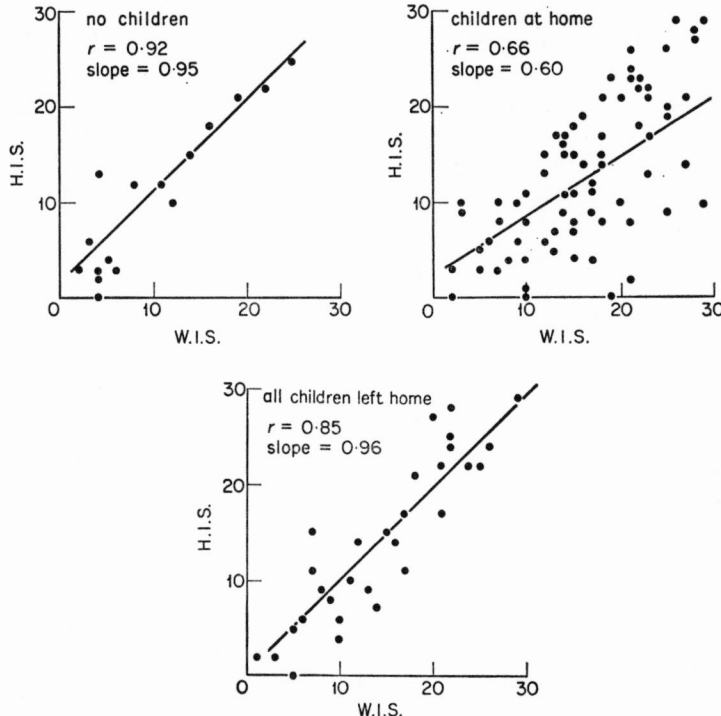

Fig. 8.2 Husband Integration Scores (H.I.S.) and Wife Integration Scores (W.I.S.) by Life Cycle subsets.

young children have a higher mean score, there is a sharp movement towards the primacy of wives' scores over those of husbands but there is also a reduction in the consistency of the conjugal score comparisons. Households where the children have left revert nearly to a pre-children level of slope and the mean value of the score increases a little. All these statistical findings show a comforting relationship with expectations based upon general observation.

These results stem from research which is exploratory. Many questions remain to be answered. For example, do nearly identical conjugal scores imply that there is a strong overlap in the actual people comprising the husband's and the wife's set of friends? Would other factors apart from the four analysed reveal significant differences in the pattern of scores? And why is it that better educated couples have a fairly upright slope, showing relatively high male scores compared to female, while the slopes in the social status subsets would lead one to a different conclusion (the slopes get steeper as one goes 'down' the scale)? More research is required to illuminate these questions and a number of others.

ASPECTS OF INTEGRATION

Meeting Friends

Respondents in the survey were asked to identify, in their minds, their three closest friends in the village (counting a household unit as one 'friend'), and to recall the manner in which each friend was first met. Clearly the manner of meeting does not tell us much about the context in which the friendship developed, but it does at least tell us something. Separate responses were recorded from husbands and wives, or from the two most senior adults in households not headed by a married pair. A range of possible modes of meeting was available on the interview schedule, together with an 'other' category. A perusal of the responses in this category reinforces one's faith in the infinite variety of man's social behaviour (and calls into question the whole issue of a 'scientific' approach to it). A former police dog-handler made friends via his dog, someone else originated a close friendship when learning to drive, which seems inherently unlikely, while other friendships began on the bowling green, through people simply introducing themselves, or by way of a wife's milk round. Apart from these methods, and the pre-coded categories, the most frequent ways of bumping into people were either in the pub or through the activities of one's children.

The distribution of first contacts between the pre-coded categories was as shown in Table 8.2. Physical contiguity ('very near neighbour' was defined as next door, next door but one, or immediately opposite) is clearly the most important factor in conditioning the pattern of friendship in the village. This finding confirms many previous results.[5] Associations made through work are the next most frequent, followed by those made in clubs and societies. The relative unimportance of casual meetings outside the school, at the shops, doctor's surgery, playgroup or clinic was rather unexpected; these contributed a total of only 39 first contacts in a total of 808. The church provided fewer first contacts than expected; rather a change from former times when one's first social contact in a village might be a call from the vicar, or alternatively a bunch of clerical carrots left on one's doorstep.

In those households headed by a married couple, the pattern of responses was noted separately for husband and wife. As expected, considerable differences exist. For husbands, work and territorial proximity were almost equal as the two strongest modes of contact; whereas for wives, proximity was far and away the strongest, more than twice as important as any other means.

Contact via a mutual friend was much more important for wives than for husbands, which tends to confirm the importance intuitively ascribed to such informal events as coffee mornings, while husbands seem to have retained more of the friends they made at school.

Table 8.2 Modes of Initial Contact with Close Friends

| | Total of all respondents | Husband/Wife Households | | |
		Husband	Wife	Total
Very near neighbour	185	69	103	172
At work	125	72	50	122
At specified club/society	97	47	40	87
Introduced by mutual friend	61	19	37	56
At church/church function	45	19	25	44
When at school	44	23	9	32
Outside school/school function	20	8	12	20
At shops	10	4	6	10
Other	107	46	55	101
Not applicable/unable to remember	114	47	36	83
	808	354	373	727

Source: 1971 Ringmer Survey

Cross tabulation between mode of contact and a range of possible explanatory variables was also carried out to see whether such factors as educational level, location in the village and so on had any significant effect on the pattern. These cross tabulations were prepared separately for husbands and wives (in households headed by a married pair) to see if any significant conjugal differences could be detected in the effect of the chosen variables. The results are summarised briefly below and are discussed more generally later in the chapter.

(i) Educational Level

(a) *Husbands*–All the 23 friendships first made when at school occurred among those who left school at 15 or younger. The 'old school tie' syndrome, normally associated with later leaving ages, appears not to exist.

(b) *Wives*–There was a strong inverse relationship between the level of formal education attained and the propensity to make friends via work. Conversely, there was a direct relationship between education and making friends via church activities.

(ii) Social Status

(a) *Husbands*–Only 6 of the 39 first contacts of Social Class I respondents were by neighbours or at work. Contact via the church, formal organisations or mutual friends were much more frequent.

(b) *Wives*–The same trends were evident; very few Class I women made contacts at work.

Overall, it was evident that territorial propinquity is much more significant socially for Classes II and III (non-manual) than for the others. Possibly most Class I families live at a density which makes a chat over the garden fence impracticable unless one has a megaphone.

(iii) Age

(a) *Husbands*–For the under-40s, neighbour contact is much the most significant whereas for the over-40s, work contacts were more frequent bases for friendship.

(b) *Wives*–Neighbour contact was again highly important for the under-40s and also for the over-65s but less insignificant for the ages between. For the latter group, clubs and societies and work contacts were the more important.

The significance of church activities as a means of first contact was not particularly affected by age, either for husbands or wives.

(iv) Life-cycle Stage

(a) *Husbands*–Neighbour contact was most significant for families with children at home whereas work contacts were more important in later stages of the life-cycle.

(b) *Wives*–As expected, neighbour contact was even more significant for wives with children at home. Work contacts were more important for those without children while clubs and societies provided more contacts for those whose children had left home.

(v) Length of Residence in Village

(a) *Husbands*–Contact via neighbours was most significant for arrivals in the last six years whereas for residents of longer standing, clubs and societies had been the most frequent means of making friends. The significance of school contacts is directly related to length of residence.

(b) *Wives*–Neighbour contact was again of most importance for recent arrivals; clubs, societies and mutual friends provided very few contacts. For longer-term residents the pattern changes and the latter means assume greater importance.

(vi) Size of Household

(a) *Husbands*–This variable appeared to have no systematic effect.

(b) *Wives*–Increasing family size leads to an increase in the significance of neighbour contacts and (predictably) of contacts made at school functions. Work, and clubs and societies, become less important with increasing size. In fact wives in families of six or more did not mention clubs and societies at all–which may occasion no surprise to wives in families of six or more.

(vii) Location of Work

It was believed that there would be an inverse relationship between distance to workplace and the significance of work as a means of meeting friends who subsequently became close ones. This relationship was found to be marked, both for husbands and wives.

(viii) Household Mobility

(a) *Husbands*–The only clearly marked result was the unexpected one that husbands without private transport made virtually no close friends via contact with neighbours but relied much more on other means, notably work contacts.

(b) *Wives*–The pattern here was quite different in that increasing household mobility, and especially the possession of two cars, led to a much reduced degree of dependence on propinquity as a basis for friendship. Highly mobile wives also made more contacts by means of work and mutual friends.

(ix) Residential Layout

Four possible categories of layout were identified for the position of the house; on a through road carrying traffic, on a cul-de-sac road, arranged around a communal green space designed for social use and, finally, 'other'. It was expected that layout design might have some significant effect on the pattern of first contacts, particularly for wives. This expectation was partially borne out. First contacts via near neighbours for wives living in cul-de-sac locations were significantly more frequent than for those in 'through traffic' situations. So were contacts by means of mutual friends. It might be inferred that the risk from traffic on through roads (see Plate 5b) is having some effect on the development of social contacts with near neighbours (which include those immediately opposite). For those on through roads, more friendships were based on contact made via clubs and societies and at work. This evidence supports comments made in Chapter 13 concerning residential layout. The effect of this variable on the pattern of contacts made by husbands was indeterminate.

(x) Distance of the Household from Village Centre

This variable was the only one of the ten used in the cross-tabulations which produced no statistically significant biasing of the pattern of first contacts, either for husbands or wives.

Joining Clubs and Societies

As is characteristic of villages, Ringmer has a wide variety of clubs and societies which together form an important means by which newcomers integrate into village life. As always, definitional problems arise. For example, bell-ringing and Sunday School have been counted as a club/society whereas, strictly speaking, neither is either. The various churches have not been included, neither have evening classes or WEA classes (although one respondent reckoned that, socially, her cookery class was 'as good as any club'). The 150 households produced a total of 245 memberships in these various organisations, an average of over 1·6 memberships per household. These memberships were distributed as shown in Table 4.11. From that table it can be seen that 88 of the households (or nearly 60%) had at least one member participating in one of the village clubs or societies. Committee membership is naturally less frequent, being confined to 22% of the households. Their distribution, incidentally, undermines the notion that village organisational life is run by a small group of people who sit on all the committees. The majority of households containing committee members in the sample (21 of the 33) are connected with only one organisation while only two households were involved in the executive of more than four. Overall, there appears to be a healthy and widespread degree of participation in formal social organisations, arguably (although no research on this point appears to have been done) a much greater degree than would be found in an urban suburb or 'neighbourhood' of similar size.

Various cross-tabulations were carried out to analyse the effect of certain variables on the level of involvement in village organisations. Length of residence had some biasing effect but the expected direct relationship between length of residence and involvement had certain aberrant features. For example, the two most deeply involved households (nine or more memberships) both arrived between five and ten years previously in the first phases of village expansion. And the thirteen households whose head had lived in Ringmer since birth tended to be no more involved than the almost equal number who had arrived from one to two years previously. Clearly, however, these two subsets of the sample population have very different social characteristics (see Chapter 7). As was pointed out in Chapter 4, occupational status has only a weak biasing effect on involvement in village clubs and societies except that Class I households have a disproportionately high rate of participation. Committee memberships are, however, strongly biased by social status. Of the total of 65, 24 occur in the Class I households and 19 in the Class II, leaving just 22 for the other four classes. Clearly there might be some support here for the notion (sometimes somewhat loosely referred to as a 'middle-class takeover')[6] that incoming families of high social status play a disproportionately large part in running village organisational life. This, like most statements about the 'middle class', would be insufficiently precise. No firm statements can be made about the relationship between length of residence and committee membership because of the limited size of the sample. Nevertheless, it appears that it is rare for newcomers to play an executive role in clubs and societies (only seven of the 65 committee memberships occurred in households of fewer than five years' residence). The Class I dominance of committees stems primarily from old-established farming and professional families in the village, not from high-status newcomers.

Life-cycle stage was also cross-tabulated with the distribution of memberships. The average number of memberships occurring in households of various stages in the life-cycle is shown on the opposite page. It is evident that two-generation households are significantly more active in village organisational life than others. This is partly a reflection of the greater size of households with children, and therefore the greater likelihood that some member of the household will join a club or society. It is also a reflection of the link between the whole process of bearing and raising children and of integration into village life. Households with children are, for that reason, more likely to be involved in such organisations as the Cubs, Brownies, Guides, Scouts,

Playgroup, Road Safety Committee, Youth Club, Mothers' Union and Sunday School while their propensity to join more adult-oriented clubs remains undiminished. The importance of children as means of integration into the formal social life of the village is matched by their social significance in less formal ways, as will be discussed later.

Stage in life-cycle	Average of memberships per household (number of households in brackets)	
Unmarried	0·6	(5)
Married, no children	1·4	(11)
Married, children at home	2·1	(83)
Married, all children left home	1·1	(34)
Widowed	1·0	(6)
Other	0·7	(11)

Source: 1971 Ringmer Survey

This argument concerning the social significance of children is substantiated by an analysis of the distribution of membership between the various members of the survey households. Of the total of 245 memberships, 237 occurred in households headed by a married couple. In these households memberships were distributed as follows:

Husbands	74 memberships
Wives	80
Children	83
	237

Since only 83 of these households included children (see above), it follows that the younger generation in two-generation households are producing a collective average of one membership per household. Since, presumably, parents take at least some interest in the clubs and societies their children have joined, this degree of participation by children appears to be an important integrative force. In fact in nearly 16% of the households with children (13 out of 83), the children provided the *only* membership occurring in the household.

For the purposes of this chapter, the most crucial aspect of village organisational life is the means by which newcomers are drawn into the various clubs and societies. In Table 8.3 overleaf, eight different ways of becoming involved are distinguished and the manner in which each of the organisations acquired members from the sample households is set out. The total (210) is less than the total of memberships (245) because in some cases the respondent could not recall how his or her membership began. Taking membership origins collectively, the most frequent means of introduction to a club or society is by way of a friend or neighbour who is already a member. Joining on one's own

Table 8.3 Mode of Introduction to Clubs and Societies

	Founder Member	Introduced by friend or neighbour	Introduced by relative	Own initiative	Club/Society's initiative	Previously a member elsewhere	Via church or vicar	Via another club or society	TOTAL
Bell-ringing				2			2	2	6
Bowls Club		2							2
British Legion		3	1		4				8
Brownies		1	2			1			4
Choir		1		1			4		6
Conservative Association		4	3		1			1	9
Cricket Club		3	4	2	2				11
Cubs			4	1					5
Darts Club		1	2	1					4
Dramatic Society	1	2	1						4
Evergreen Club	1	2		1				1	5
Football Club	2	13	7	10	3			3	38
Guides		1	2	1		3			7
Horticultural Society	1	3		2	3				9
Men's Club	1	1		1			2		5
Mothers' Union		1					1		2
Playgroup Committee	1			1					2
Red Cross	1	2		3	1		1		8
Rifle Club		2	1	2					5
Road Safety Committee		1						1	2
School Band		3		1					4
Scouts		4	1	1	1				7
Sisterhood		2		1					3
Southdown Hunt				1					1
Stoolball Club		2		4					6
Sunday School			1				1		2
W.I.	1	11		4		2	1		19
Young Wives		4	1	1	1		2		9
Youth Club		13	2	1			1		17
TOTAL	9	82	31	43	16	6	15	8	210

Source: 1971 Ringmer Survey

initiative ('I just went along') was the next most common means. The South-down Hunt membership ('They were hunting across my land, so I joined') is presumably a case of 'if you can't beat 'em, join 'em'. Introduction by means of a relative, including parents, was also quite significant. A club by club analysis reveals that patterns of first contact vary. Some clubs, for example the British Legion, appear to have greater missionary zeal than others, for example the Football Club, as measured by the proportion of membership resulting from an approach by the club. The Youth Club is heavily dependent upon introductions by existing members, while other organisations, such as the Guides, acquire members who have already joined the organisation elsewhere. The vicar is a significant agent in recruiting members to the church choir, bell-ringing, the Men's Club and the Young Wives. Finally, the extent to which clubs acquire members on the initiative of the individual varies from the sports clubs, where it is relatively common, to the Conservative Association where no membership in the sample arose in this way.

The relative unimportance of the church and/or the vicar as agents of social integration is worth further consideration. In Table 8.2 it was shown that only 45 of 808 first meetings with friends occurred in this way while Table 8.3 shows that few memberships of clubs and societies originate via the church. This situation is certainly different from the (no doubt selective) recollections of the inter-war period and is probably at variance with the presumed desire of the various churches to be helpful social agents in the process of assimilating large numbers of newcomers to the village. However, as was established in Chapter 4, contact with the churches is more frequent towards the upper end of the social scale and relatively few households in the lower occupational groups contain a regular churchgoer. This corroborates the finding earlier in this chapter that friendships based on meetings via the church were significantly more important for Class I than for any other class.

Regular church attendance is by no means confined to old-established residents, in fact attendance is not significantly biased by length of residence at all. Neither is it particularly biased by life-cycle stage or distance of the household from the church (although the very peripheral households are poor attenders). If the aim of the church is to make a universal appeal it appears that its partial failure at present in the village relates to the relative narrowness of the social base from which it draws its regular attenders rather than from any lack of success with incoming families.

Knowing Who's Who

One element in the composite integration index was knowledge of various 'key residents' in the village. Respondents in the survey were asked which of eleven such individuals they could name. The results are shown in Table 8.4 overleaf. The best-known individual was the owner of Glyndebourne. Apart from being the largest house in the vicinity, Glyndebourne is also the home of the famous annual opera festival. The owner is probably the nearest approach to a 'squire' the village has but it was unfortunately not possible to ascertain whether he was known primarily in that capacity or in connection with the opera. The two headmasters and the vicar were the next best known, well ahead of the local government representatives and the police constable (strictly speaking, 'village bobbies' do not exist under present organisational arrangements). The patterns of response from husbands and wives, in households headed by a married couple, were significantly different. More husbands could name the political figures and the officers of sports clubs whereas the vicar, the headmasters and, predictably, the W.I. President were much better known among the wives.

Table 8.4 Knowledge of 'Key Residents' in the Village

'Key Resident'	Percentage of respondents able to name		
	Husbands	Wives	Total
Owner of Glyndebourne	82	88	85
Head of the Secondary School	57	72	64
Vicar	47	68	57
Head of the Primary School	45	60	53
Chairman of the Football Club	47	34	40
Village resident on Chailey R.D.C.	38	29	34
Village Police Constable	31	34	33
Chairman of Parish Council	34	23	29
Secretary of the Cricket Club	31	20	25
President of the W.I.	8	27	17
Leader of the Youth Club	1	2	2

Source: 1971 Ringmer Survey

Notes: There were two village residents on the R.D.C. Either was accepted.

The officer chosen for the sports clubs was the one thought to be the best known in each case.

Either the afternoon or the evening W.I. President was accepted.

SUMMARY

From the wealth of rather complex material presented in this chapter certain broad themes emerge. Some of them will be taken up again in Part IV but for convenience they are briefly summarised now. Residential propinquity and work contact appear much more important than the formal social organisations in conditioning the pattern of close friendship in the village. This is true despite the very widespread involvement in village clubs and societies. Certain structural variables, and especially social status, life-cycle stage and length of residence, were effective in biasing the degree of social integration, especially in organisations such as the church. The evidence, however, did not support the notion of a 'newcomer middle-class takeover' of organisational life. The pattern of involvement of the Class I households seemed more distinctive than that of others. They were disproportionately represented on committees yet the mean of the H.I.S. and W.I.S. scores was very low, showing a low average participation in the less formal aspects of village social life.

The analyses of conjugal differences reached certain broad conclusions. Wives build up an involvement in social life more quickly than husbands and they appear to be slightly more participatory overall, both in clubs and societies and informally. The degree of disparity between the strength of husbands' and wives' involvement is related to various factors but notably to life-cycle stage and household mobility. The means of originating close friendship also shows a marked conjugal variation.

Some insights were gained from the finding that the reason for coming to the village, and the length of stay expected, had no biasing effect on integration nor did the distance a husband had to travel to work. This undermines the commonly held view that growing villages are full of 'spiralists' who contribute nothing to village life because they view it only as a convenient 'bus stop in the country'[7] for a few years and do not bother to get involved. There is no evidence at all to support this view. Children were found to be very important in affecting the degree and type of involvement. Apart from their own membership of youth-oriented organisations, which increased integration scores, they tended to affect other aspects of integration, notably the pattern of means by which their parents met close friends and the degree of disparity between the integration scores of husbands and wives (which was higher for families with children at home).

Despite all these results, and others not summarised, one is left with an uncomfortable feeling that the whole area of enquiry is much more complicated and subtle than the research methods with which it has been approached. It seems that certain personality attributes, untouched in this research, might have greater explanatory power and that the well-known distinction 'joiners' and 'non-joiners' incorporates aspects which have not here been identified. Intercorrelation between the so-called 'explanatory variables' has also posed severe problems. Probably, in all, more questions have been raised than have been answered. The consolation, given the existing growth situation in the area, is that they are at least interesting and relevant questions.

9 · Perspectives on Village Growth

This chapter is concerned with the pattern of responses in three general areas of enquiry; how do the sample households, and various subsets of them, feel about the rate at which the village has expanded; how friendly and pleasant a place do they find it; and how strongly do they perceive social divisions and tensions within it. Each of these three general areas consists of several rather more specific questions. The chapter ends with a selection of verbatim comments made on these issues.

ATTITUDES TO THE RATE OF GROWTH

General Opinions on Growth

The first two members of every household (provided they had lived in the village for two years or more) were asked:

> 'The recent rapid growth has changed the village in many ways; on the whole, how do you feel about these changes?'

The responses were as follows:

Generally approve	116 (51%)
Mixed feelings; didn't really mind	78 (30%)
Generally disapprove	37 (15%)
Don't know.	10 (4%)

This indicates a perhaps surprisingly high degree of approval, certainly a somewhat more favourable response than that obtained in the Suffolk villages survey (where 30% were generally unfavourable to the changes taking place).[1]

Various cross-tabulations were carried out to see whether the pattern of responses varied in different population subsets. Length of residence was not significantly related so it would be incorrect to suppose that opinion is divided along 'newcomers' versus 'established' lines; a result which undermines some widely held views. There was a roughly positive relationship between the integration score and the degree of approval and it appears that the more a household is involved in village affairs the more tolerant of growth it will be. This applied both to husbands and to wives. There was no significant biasing effect, either for husbands or wives, arising from the respondent's perception of social tensions and divisions in the village, from the degree to which social life was locally based, or from the level of involvement in clubs and societies specifically. Finally, the distribution of opinion was about identical for husbands and wives. The cross-tabulation of responses for husbands and wives is shown in Table 9.1. Incidentally, in this table 78 of the 109 responses fall along the diagonal indicating agreement between husband and wife, a 'unanimity rate' of about 72%. This rate will be calculated for various subsequent conjugal cross-tabulations of opinion.

Table 9.1 Husbands' and Wives' Opinions on Village Growth

Husbands' Opinions

		Generally approve	Mixed feelings	Generally disapprove	Don't know	Total
Wives'	Generally approve	44	7	1	—	52
Opinions	Mixed feelings	8	22	5	1	36
	Generally disapprove	3	2	10	3	18
	Don't know	—	1	—	2	3
	Total	55	32	16	6	109

Source: 1971 Ringmer Survey

Respondents were also asked *why* they approved or otherwise of the growth. Table 9.2 shows the results. Clearly the improvements in shops, services and

Table 9.2 Reasons Given for Opinion on Growth Rate

	Percentage of sample mentioning this reason
Approving comments	
More shops and services	36
Improvement in school facilities	12
Clubs and societies have benefited	12
More young people around	6
Disapproving comments	
Village atmosphere changed	23
Village becoming suburb of Lewes	6
Village socially divided	3

Source: 1971 Ringmer Survey

schools are much appreciated while regret was expressed for the change in village 'atmosphere'. Only a tiny proportion, however, saw this change as an increase in the degree to which social divisions exist in the village.

Opinions on the Rate of Growth

Respondents were asked:

'The village has grown from about 2000 in 1961 to well over 3000 now. Do you think it is growing too fast?'

The replies were:

Yes	102 (37%)
No	145 (52%)
No opinion	30 (11%)

It was noteworthy that this pattern of response was not significantly biased by length of residence, occupational status, age, previous residential background, educational level, location in the village or by the integration score. Marginally more wives than husbands were concerned at the growth rate but the degree of conjugal agreement was very high at 78%. There seems to be no evidence in these figures for the idea that rapid growth has suited some groups in the village more than others or of conflict between newcomers and established residents concerning the rate of expansion. Overall, the level of concern expressed when opinion has to be fitted into a simple 'yes/no' scheme is perhaps surprisingly low in view of the frequency with which more open-ended questions were met with comments which reflected disquiet.

Those who considered that the rate of growth had been too fast were asked the subsidiary question:

'Why does this rate of growth matter?'

Replies were unprompted and the interviewers recorded as many reasons as the respondent gave. Table 9.3 shows the percentage mentioning each of the

Table 9.3 Reasons for Opinion that the Village was Growing too Fast

Reason	Percentage mentioning
Loss of 'village character' visually	44
Inadequate facilities provided	33
Loss of village 'community feeling'	31
Rural landscape spoilt	20
Loss of scarce agricultural land	7
Other	33

Source: 1971 Ringmer Survey

N.B. Some respondents gave more than one reason.

reasons set out. The main emphasis was therefore on visual considerations, concerning both the village and the surrounding landscape, with a rather lesser concern for 'community feeling'. The urban background of the large majority of the sample is evident from the relative lack of concern over the loss of farmland. Finally, all respondents were asked:

'Have you an opinion about the population size at which the growth should be stopped?'

The distribution of opinion between the three pre-coded categories was:

	%
Present size	29
Larger size	40
Already too many in the village	6
No opinion/not sure	25
	100

Surprisingly few felt that the village had grown too large and a much larger proportion were clearly prepared to see further growth.

Opinion on these issues was analysed by length of residence but since so few respondents gave each of the reasons on which objections to the growth were based, the results were not statistically significant. However there were some indications that regret over the loss of visual village character was felt more strongly by arrivals in the period seven to ten years ago, in the first wave of village expansion, than by any others. This seems to support the idea that those who come to a village at an early stage of growth, perhaps expecting rural peace and seclusion, are among the loudest objectors to continuance of the growth.

Opinions on Facilities Needed

Respondents were asked (without any prompting):

'What new facilities should be added to the village?'

The pattern of replies is shown in Table 9.4 overleaf. As in many other villages, street lighting is a key issue around which opinions tend to crystallise and latent conflicts to become manifest. Lamp standards are a visible expression of urbanism. To adopt them is to take an irrevocable step away from rural, and towards urban, living. The expectation was that ex-urban newcomers, many with young children who may come home after dark, will wish to have lighting while older country folk will be content to make their way around the village after dark with a torch as they have always done. This expectation was not borne out. There was no length of residence bias at all in the group that mentioned street lighting as a required facility. Some other variable must be operating to produce the two opposing camps which are evident from time to time on this issue.

Public transport services from Ringmer have been declining, as they have in most rural areas. This is a matter for concern in a number of ways. It clearly limits opportunities for employment, shopping and recreation for those who have no car (19% of the village households)[2] and especially for older people living fairly isolated lives. Beyond that, it is one of the contributory factors leading to the spatial segregation of people of different status levels (see Chapter 13). The issue of a children's playground also raises questions of social planning. Ringmer is bisected by a main road which carries, at peak periods, a vehicle every 3 seconds travelling at an average speed of 50 m.p.h. (the posted limit is 40 m.p.h.).[3] Much of the new development is on the south side of this road and many children have to cross it to reach the swings,

Table 9.4 Opinions on Facilities Needed

Facility	Percentage mentioning
Street lighting	21
Better transport services	19
Barber/hairdresser	18
Fish-and-chip shop	17
Children's playground	13
More shops	13
Tennis courts	9
Swimming pool	8
More frequent refuse collection	6
Café/teashop	4
More facilities for teenagers	2
Public conveniences	2
Dentist	1
Other	28

Source: 1971 Ringmer Survey
N.B. Some respondents mentioned several facilities; others mentioned none

roundabout and other facilities on the village green. Clearly, this is an undesirable situation in terms both of modern planning standards and of sheer common sense (see Chapter 10 for a selection of children's views on the situation). The Parish Council's current claim is that neither traffic lights nor a zebra crossing is possible, apparently because of bureaucratic obstacles. But they also, following a heated episode in 1971 involving a petition signed by a large number of worried parents, somehow argued that a zebra crossing would be more dangerous than the present situation. One obvious answer to the problem would be to set up a children's playground on the other side of the main road and this is probably what most people mentioning this facility had in mind. The Parish Council appear lukewarm, to say the least, on this issue too. There, for the moment, the matter rests and a large number of children remain at serious risk.

By and large, the shopping facilities appear to be reasonably adequate for a population of 3500–4000, although a price comparison would undoubtedly reveal that price levels for food are generally higher than in the Lewes supermarkets (accessibility to which depends partly on whether or not one can afford a car). The need for a barber's and for a fish-and-chip shop is still unsatisfied but a coffee shop has opened since the survey. Refuse collection, currently fortnightly, is a frequently voiced issue. Of all the needs listed this was the only one subject to a length of residence bias, since it was mentioned almost exclusively by residents of fewer than six years' standing. Older village residents are less squeamish, since the practice in earlier days was either to bury rubbish in the garden (see Chapter 3) or to throw it over the fence or in the pond. But then they did not have the present excesses of the packaging industry to deal with.

ATTITUDES TOWARDS VILLAGE LIFE

The survey contained the question:

> 'In general, apart from relations with immediate neighbours, do you find the village . . .?' (there followed five possible friendliness categories plus a 'don't know').

The intention was to get a generalised view of village friendliness rather than one based upon, say, very close friendships with one or two neighbours. The pattern of response reflected a high degree of satisfaction as shown below:

	%
Over-friendly (too much 'dropping in' or 'gossip')	1
Very friendly	26
Quite friendly	57
Not very friendly	8
Unfriendly	1
Don't know	7
	100

One suspects that a similar question put to an urban suburb of 3700 people, nearly half of them recent arrivals, would reveal a less satisfactory situation.

Cross-tabulation with a range of other variables indicated that most factors tested had little significant effect on the general pattern of response. Households with children who, before coming to the village, had lived as a married couple with no children in a town perceived the village as marginally more friendly than did others, but here two influences are probably confused – the fact of making new friends via the children and the fact of moving from town to village. Length of residence affected the results hardly at all, although there was a tendency for the opinions of very long-standing residents to be more polarised than those of other groups. Age had some biasing effect in that a rather high proportion of people over 51 found the village 'very friendly' – a curious result in view of the spatial and social isolation of some elderly people indicated by other findings in the research. The analysis of life-cycle stage showed that very few of the childless married couples were impressed with the friendliness of the village compared to those with children, whether the children were still at home or had left. Educational level had no systematic effect, but significantly fewer members of Social Classes IV and V found the village 'very friendly' compared to other groups. Church attendance had no effect on the results, but membership of clubs and societies, and especially committee memberships, was positively related to the degree of friendliness perceived. Other factors which failed to bias the results included the number of close relatives in the village, the location of the household, the estimate of the number of people known, and the place of work.

By and large the attempt to identify factors that might be associated with high or low estimations of the friendliness of the village was none too impressive. One can conclude either that the hypotheses were ill-conceived and that other factors are at work to affect people's perceptions of their social environment or else, more comfortingly, that the village is capable of making people feel reasonably assimilated regardless of the other factors that frequently bias such responses. Perhaps the village environment, if not 'all things to all men' is at least 'some things to most men (and women)'.

Comparison of the subjective evaluations of village friendliness with the more objectively derived integration scores discussed in the last chapter showed that there was a significant relationship between the two. The average household integration scores for the four main categories of response were as follows:

Reaction to village	Average integration score of the group
Very friendly	38
Quite friendly	29
Not very friendly	21
Unfriendly	15

This provides useful independent evidence that the integration scores, although produced by a limited and arbitrary procedure, do coincide broadly with what people say they feel about the village.

When husbands' and wives' evaluations of friendliness were cross-tabulated, 76% of couples were found to give an identical rating. Of the remainder, the tendency was for wives to give a higher rating than husbands. A partial explanation of this is perhaps to be found in Table 9.5. Disregarding the non-applicables (households not headed by a married couple) it is clear that it is more common for the wife to have a high proportion of her friends in the village compared to her husband than it is for the reverse situation to apply (there are 29 cases below the diagonal compared to 11 above). This corroborates the evidence in the previous chapter indicating that wives have a more localised set of friends and this might naturally lead to some conjugal differences in evaluations of the friendliness of the village.

In an attempt to gauge levels of satisfaction in relation to other environments residents may have experienced, the survey included the question:

'Compared to living in a town, is living in Ringmer . . . ?' (there followed five possible categories of 'pleasantness' plus a 'don't know').

Table 9·5 *Husbands' and Wives' Percentages of Friends in the Village*

		Husbands' percentages of friends in the village					
		0–19	20–39	40–59	60–79	80 and over	N/A	Total
Wives'	0–19	26	2	2	—	1	5	36
percentages of	20–39	3	10	1	—	—	2	16
friends in the	40–59	6	6	17	3	1	—	33
village	60–79	—	2	3	12	1	2	20
	80 and over	—	—	4	5	17	3	29
	N/A	2	1	3	2	5	3	16
	Total	37	21	30	22	25	15	150

Source: 1971 Ringmer Survey

Responses were:

	%
Much more pleasant	64
Slightly more pleasant	7
About the same	7
Slightly less pleasant	1
Much less pleasant	2
Don't know	1
Not applicable (no urban experience)	18
	100

This is a striking vindication, from the residents' point of view, of the policy of village expansion. Of those able to judge, respondents who preferred the village to living in a town outnumbered those who did not in the ratio 71:3. This is consistent with the findings of the Suffolk villages survey where 89% felt that village life was preferable to town life, especially for bringing up children,[4] and with those in the Hampshire study.[5] Further analysis of the pattern of response showed that it was virtually identical for husbands and wives and that it was not significantly biased by age, educational level, previous place of residence, life-cycle stage or location in the village. The household integration score showed some relationship, the group with very low scores containing rather more negative evaluations than other groups.

As an independent check on the previous two questions, respondents who had arrived since 1961 were asked:

'Do you feel you have 'fitted in' to the life of the village . . . ?' (there followed three possible categories of response plus a 'no opinion').

Responses were:

	%
As fully as one wished	74
Not as fully as one wished	20
Much less than one wished	2
No opinion	4
	100

This, again, reflects the capacity of the village to assimilate newcomers to their general satisfaction. Comparison to responses in a suburban situation would, once again, be instructive so long as the question made sense and that there was a 'life of the suburb' to fit into. The response pattern was almost identical for husbands and wives. Distance from village centre had, in this case, some biasing effect. Those farthest away tended to give the second or third answer rather more frequently than other groups. This raises the issue of village layout and development patterns which will be discussed more fully in Part IV.

One final question related to the idea of 'the village in the mind' developed by Pahl and others. Respondents were asked:

'Do you think that when people come to live in a village they feel they ought to make more effort to be friendly?'

The intention was to see whether people had any clear conception of the social norms of village life and of any possibly appropriate changes in the new-comer's behaviour pattern. Responses were:

	%
Yes	48
No	24
Don't know	28
	100

Thus those who felt that one should respond to village life in this way out-numbered those who did not by 2:1. This must surely help to explain the very satisfactory pattern of responses concerning friendliness and pleasantness shown earlier in this chapter since the mental association between 'village' and 'friendliness' probably underlies the response pattern to both questions. However, an analysis of the integration scores of the two groups showed the two means to be virtually identical. So whether or not people *feel* it is appro-priate to act in a more friendly manner appears not to affect the extent to which they actually *do* participate in village social life.

PERCEPTIONS OF SOCIAL STRATIFICATION AND TENSIONS

This section seeks to examine questions complementary to those of the previous two sections. Presumably attitudes towards the friendliness or pleasantness of the village as a place to live in are coloured by the extent to which it appears hierarchically structured which, in turn, bears upon the question of how easily one can move into, and take part in, a wide range of social activities. Apart from this factor there is the natural desire to be part of a unified, rather than a divided, social environment.

It was established in Chapter 4 that a surprisingly small proportion (43%) saw signs that the village was divided into groups of different social standing and that the strength of this perception was biased by the age and occupational status of the household head (see Table 4.7). The only other variable to have some biasing effect on the general pattern was length of residence. People who arrived in the period three to ten years ago tended to feel the divisions more strongly than others. It is not surprising that very recent arrivals are unsure about the social hierarchy since they may not yet have formed firm opi-nions on the question. But it was not expected that long-standing residents would be less conscious of divisions. Many of them lived through a period of much clearer social structuring in the village (see Chapter 3). Possibly they see the arrival of a large number of well-educated but not necessarily moneyed newcomers as a factor dissolving, or at least making less clear cut, the old social order based on land-ownership and 'connection'.

In view of the growing literature on conflict in expanding villages, all respondents were also asked:

'Do you feel there are any signs of tensions or resentments between long-standing residents and recent arrivals?'

The overall pattern of response was:

	%
Clear signs	5
Some signs	18
No signs	63
Don't know	14
	100

If the 'don't knows' are, in this case, counted as a negative result it seems that fewer than a quarter of the sample consider that tensions or resentments occur – an encouraging result for those who advocate growth on this scale.

Further analysis showed that opinion appeared not to be biased by educational level, social status, or life-cycle stage, nor were there any marked conjugal differences (spouses gave identical answers in 70% of cases). Two groups gave answers at variance with the general pattern. Of those who arrived seven to ten years previously, 41% detected signs of tension and of those in the 31–40 age group, 37%. There is some consistency here with the findings set out earlier that the under-40s and those who arrived in the first phase of expansion see much clearer signs of social divisions than others. Location in the village seemed to have no effect except that the percentage of 'don't knows' rose rapidly (to 40%) with increasing distance from the centre. This shows a lack of knowledge concerning the social atmosphere amongst those in outlying areas. There was no clear relationship between perception of tensions and integration levels, so opinion appears not to be divided along 'insiders' versus 'outsiders' lines.

In all, this section will probably read disappointingly to those thirsting for evidence of 'conflict' and 'mediation'. In view of the literature,[6] the survey found an unexpectedly small minority willing to declare that, in their view, tensions or resentments exist and those that did could not be clearly characterised in any other way. There are several possible explanations. Perhaps this type of survey is a poor means of analysing such delicate issues. Possibly a succession of evenings spent in *The Anchor* or attending committee meetings would have uncovered feuds, scandals and conflicts galore. Alternatively it could be that some previous researchers, keen to develop a theory about 'conflict', may have put into that category events and attitudes which those who participate in them and hold them would not regard in so serious a light. The fact remains that in this survey only one in twenty respondents saw 'clear signs' of tensions or resentments between 'newcomers' and the rest. This finding is tolerably well in line with the Suffolk villages survey where it was found that 80% of respondents felt that newcomers fitted in at least 'quite easily' with local people.[7]

Attitudes towards the 'gentry' were examined in Chapter 4 where it was found that opinion depended to some extent on the respondents' occupational status. Certain other factors had no bearing on opinion. These included length of residence, the degree of integration and whether the household was of urban or rural origin. It was noteworthy that the group in privately rented accommodation, some of whom must still be in 'tied' cottages, ascribed no special significance to the gentry. This is a rather dramatic change from the situation 100, or even 40, years ago when those renting privately, the majority of the population, would have had a much more deferential view of the gentry whose tenants, in most cases, they were.

The accuracy of the perception that the gentry have very little residual political power (see Table 4.9) would need to be tested by a more thorough analysis of the part played by this group (the identification of which might be difficult) in such matters as education, planning and development, and the general allocation of local government expenditure.

GENERAL COMMENTS MADE BY RESIDENTS

During the interview, and at the end, respondents were encouraged to elaborate on their replies to the pre-coded questions. This now enables the rather soulless discussions of percentages and cross-tabulations to be en-livened with more direct expressions of opinion. An effort has been made to make a fair selection of comment and to include mainly quotations that have a bearing on village planning generally rather than on Ringmer in parti-cular.

Comments on the Friendliness or Pleasantness of the Village

'. . . the prime value of village life is that people care and don't pass by on the other side . . .' (from a resident who was stressing the need for newcomers to be approached by older residents).

'. . . we don't want it to become a dormitory town; there is no friendly feeling at all in a town such as Harlow . . .' (where the daughter had lived: this comment was from a household that rated Ringmer as 'very friendly').

'. . . we are able to walk in the country without having to get into a car and drive . . .'

Several respondents valued the relatively free and easy nature of life in so large a village:

'. . . we are not watched all the time as we were in . . .'

'. . . you are left to please yourself about what you want to do in this village, which we like . . .'

and another welcomed the reduction in the amount of social control:

'. . . I can remember the time when I was a boy; if a worker wasn't at church on a Sunday his boss (the estate owner or gentry) would want to know why; so things have changed for the better . . .'

One comment reflects the importance of children to one's social life.

'. . . I'm not invited to coffee mornings any more now I no longer have any toddlers . . .'

Comments on the Sources of Resentment and Conflict

Many of these comments were introduced with the rather human disclaimer that 'I have heard . . .' rather than 'I think . . .'.

'. . . the shifting population give no stability to the village'.

'. . . there are new folks behaving as if they own the place . . .'

'. . . there's another new one come in; they get more than what I get . . .'

'. . . I resent newcomers being elected to committees . . .'

'. . . people in the new estates think they are better than those in council houses–can't think why they should . . .'

'. . . we have a go at the CTs (council tenants) and they have a go at us . . .'

'. . . there's the "cultured" group; at least that's what they think they are, I wouldn't call them that . . .'

'. . . the farmer resented it because they built on the grazing land he used to rent . . .'

'. . . one gets a feeling people look at you a bit sideways . . .' (from the wife of a company director who moved to the 'select' end of the village recently).

Despite the range and acidity of these comments it must be remembered that they come from the minority of only 23% of respondents in the survey who said they saw signs of tensions or resentments between established residents and newcomers.

Comments on Facilities Required

Many people elaborated on the need for street lights (an issue which faces many expanding villages):

'. . . one thing that is badly needed is street lighting. It's definitely dangerous for both the young and the elderly in the village. People just won't go out in the evenings in winter without a car . . .'

On the other hand:

'. . . the rates would go up and we do not approve of it . . .' (from a resident who arrived in 1903).

A large number stressed the need for more shops, hoping that competition would reduce prices. There was feeling, however, that supermarkets were not appropriate ('urban things'). One man made the point that small village shops were much more friendly and pleasant only to be contradicted by his wife who preferred the convenience of the supermarket.

By far the most frequent unprompted comment, made by at least half the sample, concerned the need for either a street-crossing or a children's playground on the south side of the main road, or for both. Concern was expressed by all sorts of people from professional planners (who no doubt are aware of the planning principle of separating wheels and legs, especially young ones) to those using simply their common sense judgment. This, again, is an issue current in many villages and one which frequently arouses informal community groups to press for action as happened, unsuccessfully, in Ringmer in 1971.

Comments on Village Development and Planning

There were several comments approving the relative lack of intrusion of the new development on the older part of the village (including the green). But there the compliments ended. Very many people felt the insensitivity and mediocrity of the new development (see Plates 5a–8a):

'. . . there is a complete lack of a rural planning policy . . .'

'. . . architecturally, the new buildings are appalling; either very ugly with no personality or character or else pseudo-Regency which just isn't in place here at all . . .'

'. . . Springett Avenue is an *urban* development, bleak, cold and out of character with a village . . .'

'. . . we fear rows and rows of houses without any planning . . .'

'. . . Springett Avenue is very bad, no thought has been given to retaining village character; and the other estates are bad. I am not saying expansion itself is bad, only the character of the present development . . .' (from a respondent who added modestly, but pertinently, '. . . but then, of course, I am an architect . . .').

'. . . I feel strongly that there is no sort of planning over new houses; they keep building suburban types, uninteresting houses, all similar, instead of retaining village atmosphere with carefully planned buildings . . .'

Concern about the quality of the new developments was not at all confined to professional practitioners; one does not need to be an architect to sense what is appropriate and what is not. In order to be fair (although the author agrees heartily with all the above) a careful and lengthy search was made for complimentary comments. Only one was found:

'. . . Springett Avenue is very tasteful and pleasant.'

These objections were not simply cries from out and out preservationists; there was a widespread acceptance that 'people have to live somewhere'. But clearly people are unhappy about the way things are done and perhaps question whether the developers are interested or competent enough to add sensitively to the village.

There was also widespread concern about the scale of the growth and its pattern and social mix:

'. . . the village is becoming more suburban, it is almost a minor town . . .'

'. . . there's not enough council housing, there should be the same number as the private houses . . .'

'. . . it is a mistake to develop the Broyle . . .' (this is the detached section of the village–see Map 2).

'. . . we are becoming a suburb of Lewes . . .' (this was a very frequently voiced comment).

There seemed a near-consensus that if the village grew much beyond the figure of 4000 some threshold would have been passed and it would be a village no longer. Obviously this threshold cannot be closely defined either in physical or social terms but it seemed very much present in many people's minds. As one person expressed it:

'. . . this size would be a "human" limit; you want to be able to walk comfortably from one end of a village to the other . . .'

Only one man wanted to see the village grow to a larger figure (9000) but since he manages a food shop he can hardly be called disinterested.

Comments Concerning Social Stratification

'. . . there was formerly the "martini" set and the "council" lot, now the new people have tended to integrate the two groups and bring them together . . .'

'. . . there's the university lot, the football club lot and the cricket club lot . . .' (if only social science were so simple, P.J.A.).

'. . . the church group are snobbish . . .'

'. . . there is some cliquiness among very long-standing residents . . .'

'. . . there are still people who will go to church gloved, hatted and dressed to kill while others prefer to go without any ceremony . . .'

Of the 'gentry':

'. . . all village societies have a local bigwig as president and so forth, always good for a big donation . . .'

'. . . the village needs someone to look up to . . .'

'. . . the gentry have power to veto things, but I'm not sure what . . .'

'. . . time, money and true altruism enable them to be of great importance still . . .'

'. . . I think a little bit of the "feudal past" adds to the character of a village . . . otherwise everyone is exactly the same . . .'

On the other hand:

'. . . the days of charity and benevolence are over . . .'
and, gratifyingly,

'. . . nowadays many ordinary people do these things very well . . .'

Finally, there are two comments which stand in implicit opposition to each other and which raise important issues to be discussed in Part IV: One man, in answer to the question about groups of different social standings, said:

'. . . one gets the normal differences in socio-economic standing . . .'
Another respondent, in her twenties, said:

'. . . expensive houses and cheap houses are never built in the same area, therefore social divisions are created . . .'

One comment is conventional and uncritical (what does 'normal' mean in this context?); the other reflects a perceptive, perhaps intuitive, grasp of a fundamental mechanism by which the 'normal' differences tend to come about. It is one aim of this book to show that the second comment is worth more than the first.

10 · What the Children Do and Think

As in mid-Victorian times, Ringmer contains a large number of children. These play a significant part in the social life of the village and especially in the processes by which recently arrived families become involved in village affairs (see Chapter 8). For this reason, because they are an important element in themselves, and because for many of them this is the first taste of rural life, it was decided to carry out a study analysing their reactions to village life, their friendship patterns and the way they use their recreational time.

THE SURVEY DESIGN

After discussion with the headmaster of the village primary school[1] it was decided that the study would take two complementary forms, a self-completed survey form and an essay. The survey aimed at gathering information on what children get up to in their spare time, where they get up to it and where their friends live. The essay, under the non-directive title 'Living in Ringmer' was designed to obtain more informal and spontaneously expressed opinions about village life. It was agreed that the study should be directed at the top year of the junior school (10/11-year-olds of the full ability range) since children at this age should have reasonably developed and partly independent views on village life and, unlike many teenagers, they probably spend most of their recreational time in the village. The survey was carried out in October (1971). While it is obvious that activities vary seasonally, it was hoped that the pattern revealed would be reasonably representative of the pattern for the year as a whole.

THE SAMPLE POPULATION

Altogether, 46 children took part in the survey, 23 each of boys and girls. The response rate was 100% of those approached but since the work was done under supervision in a lesson period this was hardly surprising. The survey was anonymous although naturally it might not have been perceived as such by some of the children. The distribution of family size was as follows (the figures relate to the number of children, including the respondent, still living at home in the sample household):

	Number of children at home						Total
	1	2	3	4	5	6	
Number of households	1	18	20	5	1	1	46

The distribution of length of residence of the respondent children was as follows:

					Years in Ringmer						
1	2	3	4	5	6	7	8	9	10	All life	Total
5	5	3	7	4	2	4	2	1	1	12	46

Thus over half of the sample had arrived in the last five years and only about a quarter had been born in the village. The source areas of the 34 children who had migrated into the village were as follows:

Previous residence	Number
Lewes	3
Brighton	4
Elsewhere in Sussex	13
London	—
Rest of the South-East	1
Rest of the British Isles	6
Elsewhere	1
Don't know/difficult to decipher	6
	34
	—

This is broadly consistent with the pattern of source areas in the main survey (see Chapter 7). The 'don't know' category consists partly of (presumably) vague children and partly of not very good writers.

The distribution of parents', mostly fathers', occupations is worth reproducing in full (as written by the children):

Teachers	2	Designer	1	Driver	1
Carpenters	7	Chemist	1	Lecturer	1
Shop managers	2	Coalman	1	Clerk	1
Railway worker	1	Farmers	2	Professor	1
Prison officer	1	Engineer	1	Garage manager	1
Traveller	1	Nurse	1	Not stated/Don't know	7
Gardeners	3	Shopworkers	2		
Bank Assistant Manager	1	Architect	1		
Insurance agent	1	Bricklayer	1		
Astronomer	1	Naturalist	1		
Machine operator	1	Lollypop man	1		

The main point about this list is its heterogeneity compared both to a similar listing for 40 or 100 years ago and, perhaps more significantly, compared to the lists that would result in many urban suburbs or housing estates. The mixture of high- and low-status jobs, of agricultural and industrial, and of manual and professional reflects an essential distinguishing feature of village life; the spatial proximity, within a primary school catchment area, of families with an enormously wide range of backgrounds. The social mixing among adults which occurs in the clubs and societies of the village, and in the informal social networks, is echoed and reinforced by the mixing occurring in a more encapsulated form in the classroom.

In view of the number of working wives in the village (see Chapter 4) the children were asked:

'Is your mother nearly always home when you get home from school?'

Replies were as follows:

Yes	40
No	5
Not stated	1
	——
	46
	——

This is perhaps a more satisfactory result than might have been expected.

RECREATIONAL ACTIVITIES

The analysis of recreational activities was in two parts relating respectively to more, and less, formal activities. The children were asked which, if any, of five formally organised activities they were involved in. Responses were as follows:

Activity	Percentage of sample involved
Swimming sessions (organised by the school out of school hours)	54
Sunday School	35
Cubs/Brownies	33
Junior St. John Ambulance	7
Church Choir	4

It is noteworthy that the proportion of the age group attending Sunday School is almost twice the proportion of adult households that include a regular church attender (18%–see Table 4.13). The survey also included the question:

'What do you do in your spare time when you are not with your parents and are free to choose what you do?'

The rather lengthy wording attempts to emphasise that it is the independent and unsupervised activities rather than, say, family outings in the car that the question is concerned with. The children could tick as many items as they wished from a long list (some children seemed astonishingly active in the recreational sphere) and they were finally asked to pick out the four activities they did most often. The responses are shown in Table 10.1.

Watching television heads the list both in terms of mentions and 'most frequent' mentions, followed by reading books. Boys tended to do more of the former and girls more of the latter. For the girls, the next most important

Table 10.1 Children's Play Activites

	Mentioned			Mentioned as most frequent		
	Boys	Girls	Total	Boys	Girls	Total
Watch television	23	20	43	14	10	24
Read books	21	20	41	6	13	19
Read comics	21	18	39	8	8	16
Play marbles	22	17	39	12	4	16
Play football	20	4	24	14	1	15
Play on your cycle	16	19	35	6	6	12
Play ball	14	19	33	1	7	8
Draw and paint	15	17	32	3	5	8
(C) Climb trees	18	8	26	3	3	6
Play with Lego, etc.	17	7	24	2	3	5
Write	11	16	27	2	2	4
Play on building sites	8	3	11	4	—	4
(C) Go for cycle rides (2 miles or more)	10	11	21	1	3	4
Other	5	5	10	1	3	4
Play with go-carts	10	4	14	2	—	2
Play on swings and roundabouts	15	13	28	—	2	2
(C) Ride horses	4	3	7	1	1	2
Go for walks along roads	14	11	25	1	1	2
(C) Go fishing	12	1	13	2	—	2
Play hide and seek	13	13	26	—	2	2
Play cricket	15	2	17	1	—	1
(C) Go for walks across fields and woods	14	15	29	—	1	1
Play with dolls and dollshouses	—	9	9	—	1	1
Play at hop-scotch	12	11	23	1	—	1
Skip	4	15	19	—	1	1
(C) Look for birds' nests	4	3	7	—	—	—
Play mothers and fathers	—	3	3	—	—	—
Play shops	1	3	4	—	—	—
Play dressing up	—	9	9	—	—	—
Play conkers	16	5	21	—	—	—

(C) = activities more closely associated with the country rather than with towns.

activities were reading comics, playing ball (shape and size unspecified) and cycling. For the boys football ranked almost equal with television, marbles enjoyed considerable support and comics were marginally more popular than books (for the girls the latter priority was decidedly reversed). Girls showed an understandable monopoly in playing with dolls, dressing up, and in playing at mothers and fathers. This last is puzzling but a good authority pointed out that father is either played by a girl or is presumed to be away at work or dead. Boys were much more drawn to building sites and fishing, although a lone girl angler was discovered. Horses were unexpectedly low in the ranking, although one girl was overwhelmed to see them on the list and marked them with three ticks rather than one. There was an 'other activities' category on the list which attracted an interesting miscellany including the response from one boy who stated bleakly 'war'.

The author lived in the country between the ages of six and twelve. He spent his spare time in a gang which hunted squirrels (grey ones) with catapults, dammed up streams, knew precisely which trees were climbable and which were not, and which learned never to take more than one egg from a bird's nest. He did, in brief, 'country' things. What of Ringmer children? The activities in Table 10.1 are divided into two groups; the more obviously 'country' things which are marked with a (C) and the rest. The distribution of recreational time between these two groups is as follows:

	(C)	Other	Total
Mentions	16%	84%	100%
Most frequent mentions	9%	91%	100%

In approximate terms, only a tenth or so of the total recreational activity of Ringmer children is spent on the more specifically rural pursuits and nine-tenths is spent on activities to which suburban, or indeed city centre, children have equal access. In fact most of the children, most of the time, might just as well be living in a town so far as their patterns of play are concerned.[2] Those with memories of a country childhood may feel a little regretful.

Linked with this issue is the question of where children play. The survey asked:

'If you are just playing out of doors with friends, do you play . . .' (there followed seven alternatives and an 'Other').

From the alternatives ticked, it was requested that two be selected as the most frequent locations. Responses were as shown in Table 10.2. The general pattern seems very home-based. Only 14% of the 'most frequent' mentions related to the village green and only 9% to playing in fields. The remaining 77% of mentions concerned locations that would also be available to urban children. So there is very little that is specifically 'rural' about the location of play either. Sadly, one reason for this is that many parents fear that children may be abducted if they stray too far from home. The frequency of play in roads is a matter of some concern. Nearly 50 years after the invention of 'Radburn' type layouts, where cars are segregated from people in residential estates,[3] and after numerous examples of this principle in new towns and elsewhere,[4] the layout of Ringmer's new estates still lead to a high proportion of playtime being spent on roads which are, furthermore, not subject to a speed limit (see Plate 5b).

Table 10.2 Location of Children's Play

	Mentioned	Mentioned as most frequent
In the garden (or a friend's garden)	42	33
In the road near the house	27	18
On the village green	24	10
On some other piece of grass near the house	19	8
In the fields near the house	16	7
On a building site	7	2
Around the shops and car park	7	—
Elsewhere	5	—

PATTERNS OF FRIENDSHIP

Concern had been expressed informally by a number of parents that the layout of the village, and particularly the gap between its two parts, was in some cases affecting patterns of friendship. In other words, close friendships formed in school could not be carried over into play after school because of the distances between the respective houses and possibly because of the barrier effect of the main road. To examine this idea, each boy or girl was asked to list the roads in which their best friends lived. They were also asked to list the roads in which their three most frequent playmates lived. The degrees to which these sets of addresses are different may be interpreted as the degree to which children are prevented by distance or some other obstacle from playing with their best friends. This cannot, however, be accepted without question. In children's friendships, as in those of adults, distance no doubt sometimes lends enchantment to the view and close friendships might become less close with more frequent contact.

Despite this reservation, the results are instructive. There were 54 differences (in a total of 138) between the addresses given. So in nearly 40% of cases a most frequent playmate was not one of the declared three best friends. It was noticeable that whereas in many cases close friendships existed across the village/Broyle divide, in nearly all cases the most frequent playmates were within the respective areas. It seems, therefore, that there are valid grounds for parents' concern and the obvious planning point can be made that for this reason, as for others, it is not socially desirable to have a ¾-mile gap between the two parts of a village.

Perhaps an even more significant issue is the extent to which children's friendship patterns bridge the council house/private house divide. Although, as has been pointed out earlier, the local authority and private developments do occur in very visible 'blocs', each is substantially represented in both the central and the Broyle areas of the village. It would therefore be possible for friendship patterns to be largely unbiased by house tenure. From an analysis of friends' addresses, the following pattern emerged:

| | | Close friend's tenure type | | |
		Private	Council	Total
Respondent's	Private	68	12	80
tenure type	Council	9	21	30
	Total	77	33	110

N.B. The figures relate to cases where both members in the friendship were in either private or council housing (not in privately rented accommodation).

Thus only 19% of friendships (21 out of 110) cross the tenure division while 81% exist within tenure types. One may see this as encouraging evidence that village schools act as social mixers (19% is probably higher than the corresponding figure for more socially homogeneous urban catchment areas) or as a distressing sign of the potency of tenure type as a continuing divisive influence. It rather depends whether one follows the pessimistic Bishop who says 'The churches are half empty' or the optimistic one who says 'The churches are half full.' Comparative evidence from a range of other settlement and estate types would give further invaluable insights.

PERCEPTIONS OF THE VILLAGE

The essays written by the children on the subject of 'Living in Ringmer' were examined from two points of view. First, in order to see which aspects of the village came most readily to mind under this general heading, a count was made of the frequency of mention of various locations and facilities. This distribution is shown in Table 10.3. From this table it is clear that the village green is a very important feature for children and that, together with the shopping parade built in 1968–69, it is more frequently mentioned even than the school which they were attending. If the mentions of the cricket pitch, which is on the village green, are added in its significance becomes even greater. Youth-oriented facilities are mentioned comparatively rarely compared to, say, the football ground whose use is normally restricted to adults. A few differences emerged between boys' and girls' responses. Predictably more boys mentioned the football and cricket grounds, and more girls the swimming pool, housing estates and the church. But by and large the general pattern of perception was not biased by sex. From the essays it was possible to discern what the children liked and disliked about the village. Various comments have been abstracted and arranged under headings. Some of these headings are used elsewhere in the book so comparison can be made between the views of adults and children on certain issues. In some cases amendments have been made to the spelling but the syntax has not been changed.

Table 10.3 Frequency with which Locations and Facilities were Mentioned

	Number of mentions	Percentage of total number of essays (46)
The green/the swings, etc.	31	67
Shops	27	59
Schools	21	45
Football ground	12	26
Church	9	20
Cricket pitch	8	18
Housing estates	7	15
Swimming pool (at the school)	5	11
Pub	4	9
Youth club	4	9
Cubs/Brownies	4	9
Hotel	3	7
Disco	3	7
Filling stations	3	7
Delves House (old people's home)	3	7
Other (Sunday School, etc.)	16	35

On the Pattern and Rate of Development

'Ringmer is larger than some people think it is, if you go up on the downs you will agree with me. You could say Ringmer *looks* old but in some cases it is quite new.'

'Ringmer is near the country, it is in the country really but it is rather busy to call it in the country.'

These two quotations neatly incorporate much of the essence of a rapidly developing village. Another writer referred to a specific development problem:

'Ringmer is getting too packed. I think the school will overflow.'

While the street light issue was mentioned several times:

'When I go to the Youth Club at night it is dark and there is no lights in Ringmer and I wish there was lights.'

The separation of the two parts of the village was often referred to:

'A few of my friends live near me but some live the other end of Ringmer.'

'I live down the bottom end of Ringmer. I don't like it down the bottom end because there are no swings I can play on.'

The new houses were criticised:

> 'On the way to Norlington Lane is a lot of new houses which I dislike.'

but the shops and services were warmly praised by several writers:

> 'There are some shops and a launderette which is very good I think.'

One essay captured so accurately the combination of regret, resignation and acceptance that it seemed worth quoting in full:

> 'I think Ringmer is a nice little village. Now they are making it big with houses. I have a field which I can see. In about three years time the field will have houses on it. There is a cow shed; this has to go. I don't like the idea of this. There are some shops which I go to. I think they are alright but there was a field there once. I go out riding on the lanes. They are very nice but soon they will not be there. There are some very nice trees around but they will have to go as well. But on the whole Ringmer is a very nice village.'

On the Friendliness and Pleasantness of the Village

A large number of essays referred to the friendliness and pleasantness of the village and it seems that the young find it generally as congenial as their elders (see Chapter 9):

> 'The people in Ringmer are very friendly.'

> 'I think Ringmer is a nice place to live in, it is good enough for me.'

however (from the same essay):

> 'Sometimes I get a bit bored of Ringmer and feel as if I want to get away to some other county like Surrey or Essex.'

Nearer to the bright lights of London, perhaps.

> 'What I like about Ringmer is that it has lots of things that boys and girls, men and ladies can join and have lots of fun at, for example – stoolball, football clubs, a cricket club, a band, cubs, scouts and brownies and guides organisations.'

> 'I think living in Ringmer is very nice because you can always go to the shopping centre. On Sundays you can go out into the countryside and Dad can wash his car.'

The village is thought to be equally congenial to dogs;

> 'We have got a dog and she likes the fields. She goes and disturbs the cows.'

but less so, unfortunately, to budgerigars:

> '. . . we also have a budgie but he can't see much of Ringmer.'

On Rural Pursuits

A number of the essays referred to aspects which are largely specific to rural life:

'The farm is quite near to our house so we have not got very far to go to get eggs.'

'In the winter we go up on the downs with our sledges.'

'I have lots of friends which I go conker picking with.'

'I think it is nice living here because there is a lot of green country.'

'The lanes around Ringmer are very pleasant to go blackberrying.'

One boy, however, was less enamoured of country life:

'One thing that smells is all the farms that there are. These make an awful smell and I hate it.'

On Traffic Dangers

The danger from the volume of traffic passing through the village elicited more spontaneous comment than almost any other topic. This no doubt reflects parental anxieties and very active road safety work at the school. While it is clearly desirable that children should be so aware of the dangers, the underlying cause of them, poor design and planning, can only be deplored:

'I often go up to the green in Ringmer and I think it is not the best place to play because it is near a main road and little children may get run over.'

'I don't like the main road much in the evening when it is busy.'

'. . . and Mummy hates me crossing it (the road) when it is that busy.'

'The green is across the main road and lots of children get run over.'

'I like the swings but I think that having to cross the main road to get to them is rather dangerous.'

'Ringmer is a nice place but people get run over.'

'The Lewes road is hard to cross and as my mother won't allow me to cross it separates me from the shops and most of my friends.'

(This last comment bears upon the patterns of friendship discussed in the previous section.)

The survey of children's attitudes and activities was useful in giving an alternative insight, usually in refreshingly direct language, into the life of the village. It might be helpful to give a brief review of the findings. It seems that only a small minority of children's activities and play locations reflect the fact that they are living in a village (although rural aspects of village life are often mentioned). They spend most time watching television, reading books and comics and playing ball games, most frequently in the garden or the road. They could hardly look back on a 'country' upbringing. Friendships exist across the private/council tenure division but they are relatively infrequent; and the actual friendship pattern differs considerably from the 'ideal' largely because of the layout of the village but also partly because of the barrier effect of the road. Children, by and large, find the village a friendly and pleasant place. To most of them the green, the shops and the school are the things that come most readily to mind when writing about it. Many of them recall wistfully that 'there was a field there once', but they tolerate the growth with instinctive generosity. A large number of them dislike, and fear, the main road.

PART FOUR

REFLECTIONS

11 · On Community and Social Systems

LOCAL SOCIAL SYSTEMS

This chapter is concerned with the nature of the village society and particularly with some aspects of the idea of 'community'. Community is one of those words which, by over-use and over-definition, has become virtually useless for any serious analytical purpose. In fact '. . . the analysis of the various definitions was at one time quite a thriving sociological industry'.[1] One end-product of this industry, Hillery's paper analysing 94 different meanings,[2] demonstrates the way in which social science has, at times, been over-concerned with the definition of some of its central concepts. It seems that the most sensible course, when confronted with this situation, is not to dream up a 95th definition but to drop the word altogether and to use a suitable alternative concept (preferably in ways strictly consistent with the meaning given by its originator). It might thus be possible to add a little to the admittedly low level of comparability between different case studies. Stacey has developed such an idea. Following a discussion of the word community, during which she makes the point that '. . . as a concept "community" is not useful for serious sociological analysis . . .' she offers the alternative concept of a *local social system*.[3]

> A *social system* is here used for a set of inter-related social institutions covering all aspects of social life, familial, religious, juridical, etc. and the associated belief systems of each. This is what many sociologists have called 'social organisation' and bears some resemblance to what Parsons calls the 'societal community'. Each of the aspects mentioned, familial, political, etc., can be considered as systems themselves and are parts of any social system. A *local social system* occurs when such a set of inter-relations exists in a geographically defined locality. If there are *no* connections between the major social institutions in the locality, that is connections which are specific to the locality, there is *no* local social system.

Thus is offered, in relatively plain language an apparently precise concept to replace that of 'community'. The same idea has subsequently been referred to by Pahl as a 'locality social system',[4] which seems a quite unnecessary change in terminology. Stacey goes on to discuss certain characteristics of a local social system and particularly the significance of process and time:

> The concept of a local social system in mind here involves *structure* and *process*. It involves not only what institutions are present, but the

165

processes of their operation . . . Processes take *time* and the dimension of time is therefore, as was shown above, essential to the conceptualisation of any social system.

She then suggests a set of 31 'tentative propositions about local social systems'. These propositions arise out of her general appreciation of the field of 'community studies' and they are an admirable framework for thinking and research. But inevitably, in the paper in which they are set out, they are not supported by any empirical research findings or data.

RINGMER AS A LOCAL SOCIAL SYSTEM

The data from Ringmer is directly relevant to various of the ideas put forward and the historical depth of the study meets Stacey's insistence on the importance of process and time. Because the propositions seem to have been accepted as a useful step forward (for example by Bell and Newby),[5] because they and the Ringmer data might illuminate each other, and because social science is full of promising conceptual schemes which nobody has subsequently bothered to clothe with empirical findings, it has been decided to organise this discussion of the village as a local social system around certain of the propositions. These are numbered according to the scheme used by Stacey in her paper.

1. Certain conditions are necessary for the initial development of a local social system:

(*a*) the minimum condition is that the majority of the local population should have been present together in the locality for some period of time

(*b*) the longer is this period the more likely is there to be a local social system present

(*c*) where the majority of the population have been born and bred in the locality it is highly likely there will be some sort of local social system present. E.g. Old Banbury, Winston Parva, Zones I and II [the references are to various case studies].

But unless this condition 1(*c*) applies,

2. It does not necessarily follow that because a majority of the local population have been present in the locality for some period of time that a local social system will develop. E.g. Winston Parva Zone III (see propositions 21 and 22 below).

(The empirical relationship between the development of a local social system and the passing of time is not at all clearly known).

One can immediately see the difficulty inherent in all attempts to make social scientific analysis more quantitative and rigorous. What do 'some period of time', 'highly likely' and 'some sort of' mean?

Despite these uncertainties of meaning the ideas are helpful, especially in relation to the Ringmer data. The percentage of the population born in the locality, in this case the parish, fell from 53% in 1871 to 33% in 1921 to 9%

in 1971 (see Table 5.7). The mean number of years length of residence, while not precisely ascertainable for the two earlier dates, must be declining drastically over time since nearly 60% of the 1971 sample households and over 70% of the respondents in the children's survey had been in the village fewer than ten years. It appears that, on any reasonable definitions, proposition 1 is no longer satisfied and that with the passing of time, far from a local social system developing, the village is getting further and further from this condition.

3. Following from proposition 1, in a situation where there has been a local social system in existence one may deduce that:

(a) When the number of migrants into a locality increases, there must be a critical point at which the increase will place such a strain upon the system as to prevent its previous operation. In this case if the system continues to exist it will be in an altered state. The critical point will be determined by the number and/or type of migrants in relation to the host population.

(The empirical conditions under which this may occur are not known at all accurately).

(b) There must be a further critical point when such an influx would destroy the system altogether, that is to say social relationship in the locality would become dominated by institutions other than those of the erstwhile local social system. In view of the inter-penetration of systems considered in propositions 16–18 and 20 below, it seems more likely that change of the kind indicated in 3(a) above will occur, except in extreme conditions such as conquest.

There are a number of points to be made here in the light of the Ringmer data. The village has expanded by over 50% in ten years so we would expect 3(a) and/or 3(b) to apply. The second of these is only partially true. Some systems, for example social security and political control, have undoubtedly passed almost entirely from the local to the national sphere; others, for example institutions of employment, are now two-thirds external to the village and one-third internal (as measured by the spread of work locations set out in Table 4.2); others again, for example the system of social organisations, still seem largely specific to the village. The football club is not a branch of a larger football club. It is impossible to generalise, but the destruction referred to in 3(b) has by no means been total and the critical point referred to must occur either on a steeper growth curve or further up the present one. Proposition 3(a) may well hold good. The scale of the increase has been considerable and no doubt the operation of the system has been altered; Chapter 5 tried to show specifically in what ways this had happened.

One suspects, however, that the transition from 'closed cell' to 'open system' documented in Chapter 5 stems from technological change not from village expansion. Much the same developments could probably be identified in villages that have not grown at all.

The reference to '. . . the number and/or type of the migrants in relation to the host population' and the admission in parentheses that we know little empirically of the relationship between growth and change raise crucially important issues for the social planning of expanding villages. Following consideration of the Ringmer data two observations are offered:

(i) The success with which a local social system, as defined, survives a mass influx may be as much related to the *size* of the original host village as to percentage rates of increase. One suspects that, other things being equal, more of the original social organisation will remain in a village expanded from 2000 to 3000 in a given time period than in one expanded from 200 to 300. In the first case the social 'fabric', the organisations, the facilities and so on, were more robust to start with and the sheer variety of people and institutions will make it easier for newcomers to find congenial friends/clubs/services, etc.

(ii) While the social complexion of the newcomers in relation to that of the older established is doubtless important, so too is the *physical layout* and arrangement of the new estates. If these are spatially segregated and visually distinctive the original system is likely to alter more than if the additions are integrated into, and in harmony with, existing development.[6]

> 7. The presence or absence of certain institutions produce critical differences in the type of local social system which may be found. Thus, in a locality which is entirely residential, only sub-systems connected with neighbouring and with familial and kin relations can develop. The addition of workplaces to the locality not only increases the number of available roles, but may alter the characteristics of the relations between people and make possible, through the development of new institutions, a different type of social system.

It seems likely that a large village may have more variety in the institutions present than most other settlement forms of comparable population size and certainly more than many suburban estates. Ringmer, with nearly one-third of the employed population working in the village, with nearly all the children going to school there, with a varied and flourishing range of formal social organisations and with satisfactory informal social relationships (to judge by the 'friendliness' ratings in Chapter 9) would appear to match up well to proposition 7. But in this respect, as in many others, no firm conclusions can be drawn concerning the validity of this proposition until comparative studies examining a wide variety of settlement types, with different ranges of sub-systems, have been carried out.

> 8. Where any substantial institutions are removed the system is modified. E.g. in Pentrediwaith where the local social system was modified by the removal of work from the locality.

The chances of modification in this particular way in a large, diverse and growing village are clearly slim.

> 9. Where any substantial institutions are greatly changed the system cannot work as it did previously, as in Banbury where new economic relations were introduced.

Over the 100-year perspective of the study, it can be seen that at least three 'institutions' have changed a great deal. One hundred years ago it seems likely that the majority of employees were dependent upon perhaps a dozen members of the local landowning and farming group for their livelihood. Today the employment dependency pattern is enormously more complicated and in the great majority of cases the 'employer', whom it is sometimes difficult to identify, is some person or organisation outside the village. This change has clear implications for the formal and informal power structure of the village (as discussed in Chapter 5). Another fundamental change, closely connected with the first, is in the fading of deference to 'authority', as embodied by the gentry and the church. This is just one aspect of the general weakening of status barriers (as discussed in Chapters 5 and 9). Finally, there have been fundamental changes in the role and status of women in village society, especially in the last 50 years. It is more likely now that a man, especially one who works elsewhere, will be known in the village as 'Mrs. X's husband' rather than, as previously, the woman be known as an adjunct to her husband. These three exemplifications of the changes referred to in proposition 9 have each had far-reaching effects and together substantiate the idea that when changes of this magnitude occur, 'the system cannot work as it did previously'.

14. As with any social system, a local social system will have a system of beliefs associated with it. In a locality where there is a local social system these beliefs will be shared by many members of the populations to which the system relates. The mechanism of this sharing operates through the multiplex role-playing and the over-lapping group membership of the local population.

It is less easy to see how this proposition applies in the case of Ringmer. There is no doubt that, as in many villages, multiplex role-playing occurs – the solicitor known both professionally and as publicity officer of the village hall appeal fund and so on. Group membership also overlaps, although the degree and direction of overlap has not been researched in this study. But it seems unlikely that any 'system of beliefs' occurs that is in any way locality specific. If some large external threat were to be posed, for example a proposal to bisect the village with a motorway, no doubt there would be a whole-hearted, if transitory, acquiescence to a system of beliefs about the desirability of the project. But in more normal circumstances, social, political or religious beliefs transcend the village and align with national trends of thought. One need look no further than the development of the media (see Chapter 1) as an explanation of this circumstance.

Although no communality of beliefs was detected, the Ringmer survey did gather some data on a related issue as a result of the question:

'Can you think of any events and issues in the past few years that have concerned most people in the village?'

The question was asked since what has been termed 'community sentiment' is generally held to be one component of the total concept of 'community'.[7] In fact in Hillery's analysis of the content of various definitions of the word,[8] the idea 'possession of common ends, norms, means' occurs more regularly than any other. Frankenberg, in a useful aside when discussing methods of community study, wrote of a Sheffield housing estate:

'. . . there are no activities which concern the estate as a whole.'[9]

Are there activities which concern Ringmer as a whole? The responses to the survey question were as follows:

Event or issue	Percentage of sample mentioning
Ringmer Football Club	34
Village fête	24
Street lighting	19
Refuse collection	6
Village Hall Extension	1
Church Bells Fund	1
Glyndebourne Opera	1

It should be pointed out that Ringmer F.C. is no ordinary village club. In 1970/71 they reached the 1st Round proper of the F.A. Cup and were finally beaten, but not disgraced, by a 4th Division team. Leeds United would have been the next step but one. This unprecedented cup run clearly had an important cohesive effect on the village. Pahl was strangely prescient when he wrote: '. . . the football team may help to foster more locality consciousness than anything. . . .'[10] Apart from this sporting event, the pattern of responses is probably unremarkable for a village. The insignificance of the Glyndebourne Opera as a perceived focal point of village feeling is hardly surprising. Apart from providing a handful of jobs and a number of musical lodgers in the larger houses during the summer, the main impact seems to be the stream of Bentleys, Mercedes and Jaguars that glide impressively, but as curtain time approaches ever less sedately, through the village.

15. Where a majority of the population of a locality do not share to any considerable extent common groups, institutions, beliefs and expectations there can be no *one* local social system for that locality [various examples are then given].

(The empirical meaning of 'majority', and 'considerable extent' are at present not at all clearly known.)

Under this proposition, as under several others, Ringmer has been shown not to rate as a local social system. But perhaps the study has helped a little towards reducing the lack of understanding referred to in parentheses. Perhaps the 'majority' threshold condition depends upon the size of the settlement. In a village of 200 it might be reasonable to expect 100 or more people to be knowledgeable and united about some beliefs or expectations. In a village of 3700 perhaps the result that as large a proportion as 34% view the same event as a unifying factor is surprising. The football team's achievement did, after all, gain press and television publicity at national level. Few village events anywhere make more of a stir. Yet the 'majority' stipulation was not reached. In proposition 15 at least, therefore, perhaps allowance has to be made for the scale effect and the size of the settlement. Or else one concludes that no settlement of 3700 is remotely likely to qualify as a local social system under the criteria contained in the proposition.

16. In any locality in Britain, not all the residents of a locality will be involved in the institutions which are components of the local social system, e.g. some may work, worship or play outside the locality, these being governed by institutions which may or may not be the same as specifically local institutions.

The integration analysis carried out in Chapter 8 sheds some light on this proposition, although the index used in that chapter did not contain any element reflecting workplace. It was shown that residents were involved to different extents (not either 'involved' or 'not involved' as the proposition implies) and that certain systematic biases were evident in the degree of local involvement. For example length of residence had some effects, not all of them predictable, wives were generally more involved than husbands (especially in the early years of residence) and highly educated/high-status people, and especially husbands in these categories, tended to be less locally involved. So the proposition as it stands needs refinement in the light of further research.

21. Some structural and cultural features of a local social system will render some individuals socially invisible to each other [an example is given]. Therefore

22. Physical proximity does not always lead to the establishment of social relations.

Several exemplifications of these ideas can be given. There are 600–700 people over retirement age in the village.[11] But it was found that a large number of them live in outlying cottages as retired farm workers, and sometimes as widows or widowers. Another group live in the recently developed local authority bungalows for old people at the extreme end of the village, one mile from the centre. Others live in Delves House, an old people's home, from where they have to venture across the main road to reach the shops and services. All these circumstances, plus the natural reduction in mobility and sociability which often comes with old age, help to render this group 'socially invisible'. Unfortunately the features which bring this about are not so much 'structural and cultural' as matters of bad village planning and design.

Proposition 22 is clearly true in a strict interpretation although the data in Chapter 8 show that proximity *very often*, and more than any other mechanism, leads to the establishment of social relations. It can also lead to tensions: '. . . we have a go at the CTs (council tenants) and they have a go at us . . .' (see Chapter 9). The question whether conflict between 'CTs' and houseowners is a divinely ordained fact of life or whether it might be some function of the visual and spatial distinctiveness of the two housing forms will be taken up in later chapters (see Plate 6b).

28. Where a local social system is present there tends to be a convergence of the élites within the system, that is, a tendency to the development of a total social status in the locality.

This appears not to be the case in Ringmer. The analysis of trends in status over a 100-year period shows strong signs of a *divergence* of élites. The mid-Victorian situation could have left little doubt about which group constituted the élite. A set of people were concurrently the land (capital) owners, the chief employers, the dispensers of justice via the bench and of social security via the poor law agencies and the private charities. Today those functions are spread among a wide variety of individuals or, more frequently, impersonal agencies. At the same time many other avenues to the achievement of high local status have opened up, for example via the Parish Council, via prowess in a sports club, via energetic activity in some other club or society or as the leader of some informal campaign. As a result very few residents ascribe much significance to the 'gentry' (Chapter 9) or, to judge by attendance rates, subscribe to the authority of the church. Ringmer, in short, cannot be regarded as a local social system under the criterion set out in proposition 28; the trends are in the reverse direction.

31. Given that in any one locality there are persons not involved in the local social system (proposition 16) and that elements of other systems will be present (proposition 18) the local social system will be sensitive to any changes which take place in these social systems outside itself. This sensitivity is increased because of the connection of parts of the local social system with parts of wider social systems (proposition 20).

The issue here relates to one of the central concerns of this book—the extent to which changes in village life are sensitive to, and mirror, changes in the social organisation of society at large. This has been the central concern of several other studies notably those by Bensman and Vidich,[12] Warren[13] and Stein.[14] Much of this recent empirical work stems in one way or another from some original concepts developed by Tönnies[15] in the 1880s. A systematic attempt will be made in the next section to review the extent to which national and local social systems reflect each other.

This close examination of some of Stacey's propositions in the light of empirical findings seems to show that the village cannot be regarded as a local social system under any strict interpretation of that term. Nevertheless many of the ideas are thought-provoking, and matching analyses of them based on data from other settlements would probably add a great deal to the degree of comparability between case studies. Before leaving her paper it will be as well to reproduce one other passage:

. . . locality studies cannot stand on their own. They must be compared not only with each other, but with data gathered in other ways in other fields. Statistical generalisations about the whole country are important to place the locality in a national pattern. A local study equally shows some of the limitations of such overall generalisations. Non-statistical national studies on particular topics are also needed to illuminate the local incidence. These methods of data collection and analysis are not alternatives. All are needed to inform each other.

The organisation and design of the Ringmer study reflect complete agreement with these views.

RELATIONSHIPS TO NATIONAL SOCIAL SYSTEMS

It is notoriously difficult to describe any precise meaning to the word 'system'. The various comparisons that follow stem directly from the points raised in proposition 31 and in the last quotation. . . . Whether they deal with 'systems' specifically or simply with trends in social organisation seems less important than any light they may throw on the local/national sensitivity referred to in the proposition. A selection of aspects will be examined and in each case the national changes for the period 1871–1971 will be compared to village changes. The data will be derived chiefly from Chapter 1 (national) and Chapters 2–5 local).

Employment

Table 1.1 shows that, nationally, employment in the agricultural sector has fallen from over one-sixth of the total to something like one-thirtieth, the manufacturing sector has not quite doubled, and the tertiary sector has more than quadrupled. In the village, agriculture occupied a majority of the male workers in 1871 (see Table 2.1); it now appears to employ perhaps 1% to judge by the employment pattern of the households surveyed. The manual component has dropped from 83 to 34% and the non-manual has increased from 15 to 62% (Table 5.5). The data are not precisely comparable but the experience can be seen to be broadly similar. For women (see Table 1.2) there has been a vast increase in commercial and professional employment. This has been mirrored in the village. Such work was probably unknown in 1871, relatively rare in the 1920s (see Chapter 3 '. . . there were just not the jobs for married women in those days'), and commonplace now (see Chapter 4). Employment in domestic service fell nationally from over 15% in 1871 to about 2% in 1951 (Table 1.3). In Victorian Ringmer it was the normal fate of girls on leaving school; now it is virtually unknown in the village except as an extra part-time source of income for a limited number of housewives.

Hours of Work and Holidays

A comparison of the admittedly sketchy data in Table 5.6 with that in Table 1.4 shows that changes in hours of work locally have been generally similar to those nationally. Hours of work, like holidays, have for long been settled mainly by national legislation and negotiating systems so one would expect little that is locality specific in price levels and conditions for labour.

Education Systems

Here, since the very outset of the century under review, there has been a close relationship between the development of the education system as prescribed by national legislation and the administration of the system locally. It is clear from the early School Board minutes that every local matter of any importance at all was referred to the Ministry in Whitehall for a decision. Questions relating to the syllabus, hours of work, sanctions, holidays and so on were all dealt with centrally and the inspectorate ensured that local deviations were kept within statutory bounds. For all practical purposes the system has, since 1871, been a national one administered locally.

Social Security System

The operation of the national system and the local system has converged more or less completely over the 100-year period. Although in mid-Victorian times there was a nationally legislated poor-law system, its local administration varied widely depending upon the view of the local Guardians concerning, for example, the relative merits of in- and out-relief. This system was, in any case, complemented by a wide variety of village-specific agencies whose policies were controlled locally, either by the gentry or by the participants (see Chapter 2). There was, therefore, only a weak structural relationship between national and local systems and the latter was by no means perfectly sensitive to changes in the former. Today's welfare systems, whether public or private, function nationally. The pensioner receives a standard amount by way of a standardised mechanism; he does not depend upon soup dispensed by the vicar and Cousin Lucy. The unemployed man draws his benefit as a right; he does not attempt to sell his labour as a 'Michaelmasser' and depend upon the vagaries of the local economy. Those wishing to insure against adversity use one of the national insurance companies, with nationally applied rates of benefit; they do not invest in the Anchor Inn Benefit Society. In short, access to social security does not vary with locality; it is a-spatial. The local and national systems are not merely connected; they are identical.

Information Systems

Daily radio broadcasts by the BBC began in November 1922. A village resident, speaking of life in the 1920s, recalls (see Chapter 3):

> '. . . wireless was beginning to have tremendous effects on people's understanding of national events . . . they became personally involved on Cup Final Day and Boat Race Day.'

The circulation of daily papers in 1920 was only about a quarter of today's total (see Table 1.9). Another village resident recalls:

> '. . . there was no radio or TV when we were younger (in the early 1920s). I don't think we took a daily paper so there was no way of keeping in touch with national events as we do now.'

The explosive growth of television coverage is shown in Table 1.11. The results have been far-reaching, especially on the activities of children. The most frequently recalled activities between the wars were cycling, birds'-nesting, fishing, swimming in a nearby river, skating on dewponds, looking for meteorites and fossils in chalkpits (and inducing small landslides) and tobogganing, either on grass or on snow. Table 10.1 shows a different pattern:

Activity	Number of times mentioned as among the most frequent
Watching television	24
Reading books	19
Reading comics	16
Playing marbles	16
Playing football	15

The 'country children' have become the 'media children'.

In all, in so far as national events are concerned, there is no local information system so there is no question of sensitivity of the local to the national. There remains the very important word of mouth 'gossip', system, an essential characteristic of village life. But since, by its nature, the elements in this system are local personalities and the 'flows' along it concern local events and relationships there is fortunately no risk of a takeover by the national system.

It would be possible, by examining various other aspects of life, to show that proposition 31 is correct; there is almost total sensitivity at the local level to national events, decisions and trends of thought. This is really the same as saying, as almost everybody does, that regional and local 'cultures' are weakening over time and that we are all converging into some sort of 'metropolitan man'. This convergence stems from technological development and particularly from the two inventions singled out at the end of Chapter 5; the internal combustion engine and the electronic media of communication. Without them the centralisation of records, the promulgation of decisions, the growth of non-agricultural employment, the diffusion of new political and social trends of thought to a mass audience, and the daily importation of new ideas from extra-parochial sources by word of mouth could hardly have been possible. And without these developments the five systems discussed, and others, would still be largely local in orientation and administration. These 'mobility' inventions are the chief technological underpinnings of the national/local connections which were referred to in Stacey's proposition 31 and which were substantiated by the Ringmer examples.

12 · On Local Social Networks

NETWORKS IN SOCIAL SCIENCE

It has been pointed out by various recent works that valuable insights might be obtained into the nature of social organisation by using the idea of *networks* of relationships[1] rather than the idea of community. The discussion of local social systems, and particularly Stacey's proposition 31 concerning the relationship to national systems, supports this approach. It is clear that the people and organisations with whom we interact, and the sources of information upon which we base our actions, are by no means all close to us in space; many are hundreds of miles away. We do not have equally close interaction with *all* the people and organisations that lie closer than the farthermost point of our 'network'. It therefore follows that our social, economic and political relationships follow specifically defined 'channels' which can be mapped. When the mapping has been done it will be seen that our interaction pattern can more easily be conceived as a star-shaped pattern of radiating lines than as an area enclosed by some roughly circular line centred on our home.

This spatial arrangement of interaction patterns is not new. Pahl, following the quotation of a passage from *Pride and Prejudice*, points out:

> It is clear that the characters in Jane Austen's world lived in social *networks*, not communities. They moved about the country, staying in each other's houses, wintering in London or spending the season in Bath. The so-called 'rural communities' in which their friends' houses were located were rustic prisons only for those without the means to escape them.[2]

The data in Chapter 2 substantiate this view of previous rural life-styles. Now, however, various of the 'mobility' inventions referred to in the previous chapter have transferred Jane Austen's patterns of social and economic interaction to a much larger segment of society, although one can still see examples of people living in 'rustic prisons'–those without access to the personal mobility which now seems to be assumed by many planning decisions.

Some powerful techniques to analyse networks exist in the branch of mathematics known as graph theory.[3] A handful of social scientists have attempted the difficult task of applying these elegant and precise notions to their own rather more messy field. One of these is the mathematical anthropologist Barnes, who wrote a seminal paper on a Norwegian parish.[4] In a more recent technical review of the social applications of graph theory, he draws attention to the confused terminology of various 'borrowers', and adds the invaluable warning: 'It is laudable to try to give to social science that quantitative and logical rigour we admire in the natural sciences, but we should not forget that good intentions alone are not enough: he who would be numerate must keep his wits about him.'[5] Barnes' Norwegian work has been followed by interesting work by Bott,[6] Udry and Hall,[7] Turner[8] and

176

others on social networks and conjugal roles, by Garrison[9] and Kansky[10] on transportation networks, and by Mitchell and others on social relationships in African towns.[11] Haggett and Chorley[12] have reviewed the growing body of geographical applications and Pitts[13] has applied network notions to the analysis of trading relationships in thirteenth-century Russia. This frame of thinking has, in fact, been extremely fruitful in a number of situations.

The present purpose is not to add any new theoretical ideas nor to test existing ones with empirical data. It has been pointed out by various researchers that it is extremely difficult to get sufficiently precise and detailed field data to satisfy many of the ideas currently being explored. The present aim is to give further insights into differences between 'suburban', 'growth village' and 'traditional village' life-styles by means of a number of simple network ideas. It has been suggested that expanding villages are no more than 'discontinuous suburbs' – that they are socially indistinguishable from suburbs and just happen to be surrounded by fields not by other suburbs. One point of this analysis is to undermine that view.

SOME NETWORK INDICES

Figure 12.1 shows a friendship network consisting of six people, each one shown as a point. The lines linking any two points represent 'friendships' and are referred to subsequently as 'links'. An immediate definitional problem arises. At what level of social interaction between two people does a 'friendship' arise? And might the relationship not be asymmetrical (for example, 4

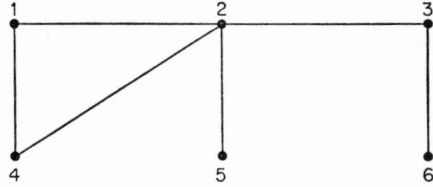

Fig. 12.1

may claim 5 as a friend but this may be denied by 5)? These problems must for the moment simply be sidestepped; it is assumed that some objectively verifiable threshold for 'friendship' exists and that all relationships are reciprocal. One other point to note is that the length and orientation of the links, and the particular location of the six points, are irrelevant to the analysis; the representation is purely diagrammatic. If a line links two points (2–4) a friendship exists, if it does not (3–4) there is no friendship between the two people specified. Note however that 4 and 2 are friendly and so are 2 and 3. So 4 has a route to 3 that is two links in length. Routes of this sort will be referred to as 'paths'; a path therefore consists of two or more links. They always follow the *shortest* possible route. Paths exist between *all* pairs of points that are connected to the network.

On the basis of these ideas we can develop a number of indices which describe either the network as a whole or the component parts of it (the points, links and paths). It is important to remember that these deal simply with the topological properties or *structure* of the network and not with the frequency, strength or content of the social 'flows' along specified links; in other words all 'friendships' are undifferentiated. The first such index is the *degree of connectivity* of the network (as Barnes[14] points out, the terminology varies so much in the literature that it is impossible to be perfectly consistent with previous studies; at least the present work resists the temptation to invent any new terms). The network as a whole is less than perfectly connected, for example, 4 does not have a friendship with 3, 5 or 6. The maximum possible number of friendships if six people are involved is found by calculating:

$$\frac{n(n-1)}{2}$$

where n is the number of people. Thus 15 *possible* friendships could exist but the *actual* number of friendships is six (the number of links in the network). The degree of connectivity is:

$$\frac{\text{Actual friendships}}{\text{Possible friendships}} \times 100 \quad \text{or} \quad \frac{6}{15} \times 100 \quad \text{or} \quad 40\%$$

The friendship network is 40% connected. The addition, or termination, of any friendship would change this value. The frequently repeated claim of old Ringmer residents that 'everybody knew everybody' between the wars[15] can, in theory, be tested. If the population were 2000 this would require

$$\frac{2000\,(1999)}{2} \quad \text{or} \quad 1{,}999{,}000 \text{ friendships}$$

The actual number, of course, must have been far less than this. But then the word 'knew' would need to be more precisely defined; it might mean 'had heard of' or something similar.

The relationships in Figure 12.1 can equally be represented by a table or *matrix* where a link between two points is signified by 1, and no link by 0:

	1	2	3	4	5	6	Total
1	–	1	0	1	0	0	2
2	1	–	1	1	1	0	4
3	0	1	–	0	0	1	2
4	1	1	0	–	0	0	2
5	0	1	0	–	–	0	1
6	0	0	1	0	0	–	1

Since it was specified earlier that no 'one-way' friendships exist the matrix is symmetrical about its diagonal. The 'total' column shows that point 2 is linked to four other points and points 5 and 6 to only one each; this can be verified from the diagram. A second matrix can express the path lengths from each point to every other point (by the shortest possible route as specified earlier):

	1	2	3	4	5	6	Total
1	–	1	2	1	2	3	9
2	1	–	1	1	1	2	6
3	2	1	–	2	2	1	8
4	1	1	2	–	2	3	9
5	2	1	2	2	–	3	10
6	3	2	1	3	3	–	12
							54

For example, 6 is friendly with someone (3) who is friendly with someone (2) who is friendly with 5. This is the closest relationship between 6 and 5. As the old music-hall song has it 'I danced with a boy who's danced with a girl who's danced with the Prince of Wales'.

This second matrix gives us five more indices concerning the network or points on it. We can compare the relative *accessibility* of the points on the network, accessibility that is between each point and all other points on the network. This index is expressed as:

$$\sum_{j} d_{ij} \quad ^{16}$$

where d_{ij} is the length of the path in links from 'home' point i to 'distant' point j. These values are given for each point in the final column. The lowest of the set of values shows the most accessible point. This is point 2, which has a value of 6. The least accessible is point 6 with a value of 12. In other words, if you wanted to go from point 6 to all other points (in separate journeys) you would have to traverse a total of 12 links. Another way of comparing accessibility is by means of the *associated number* of each point. This is the length of the path from that point to the farthest point in the network. The second matrix shows that the associated number of points 2 and 3 is two and of points 1, 4, 5 and 6 is three. The lower the associated number, the more accessible the point.

The *diameter* of the network is simply the largest associated number in the matrix. In other words, it is the length of the path between the two most widely separated points. In the example given, paths 1–6, 4–6, and 5–6 are all equally long in terms of links and the diameter of the network is three. The *shape* of the network is specified by the ratio

$$\frac{\text{Diameter}}{\text{Total number of links}}$$

in this case $\frac{3}{6}$ or 0·5. The lower this value, the more compact the network shape. The extreme value of 1·0 would mean that the diameter equalled the number of links and that the network was entirely linear with no lateral development at all; rather like the mainline railway system in Chile. The final index to be derived from the path matrix is the *dispersion* value of the network. This is the sum of the accessibility values:

$$\sum_i \sum_j d_{ij}$$

As can be seen in the matrix, the value is 54.

This brief review has by no means exhausted the possibilities. By various manipulations it is possible to show the *number* of paths of any specified length between all pairs of points but this would lead to unnecessary complications. As new friendships occur, or existing ones terminate, the values of the various indices change. For example if 2 became linked with 6 the degree of connectivity, diameter, shape and dispersion of the network would change; so would certain of the associated number and accessibility values. One of the most powerful aspects of the network approach is that one can make informed guesses about future developments given certain hypothetical changes in relationships.

SOME SOCIAL PROPERTIES OF NETWORKS

So far attention has been focused on the *structure* of the network and on its mathematical properties. The frequency, social character, permanence and intensity of the flow along each link has been assumed constant between links. But one can speculate about these aspects of the 'traffic' along the network. For example, if all the paths between all pairs of points in the system are of equal social significance, some links are carrying more social traffic than others. There are 15 paths in the system (since there are 15 pairs of points). Link 2–3 is on eight paths between points while link 3–6 is on only five. Similarly, by virtue of its previously established accessibility, point 2 handles a bigger flow of 'traffic' than points 1, 4, 5 and 6, which have no 'through' traffic at all. He, or she, is obviously the person to go to in the village if you want to find something out or get something done.

The social character, permanence and intensity of the various flows raise issues of great complexity which have been discussed by Southall[17] and others but which cannot be developed here. Links can be based upon kinship ties, in which case they exist permanently (although their traffic may fluctuate) and have a content culturally consistent with blood or marriage relationships. One area of analysis would be to compare the kinship structure of a group with its observed social network. The percentage of links that are kin-based would vary widely between, say, a small remote 'traditional' village largely untouched by immigration and a large fast-growing village in the south-east. This distinction has, of course, been discussed qualitatively in numerous studies[18] but it appears not to have been explored in network analytic terms.

The stability over time of the components in a locality's network also varies greatly. This variation is a function of the rate of population replacement, either by natural causes or by in- and out-migration. Clearly, the degree of component stability will affect not simply the degree of connectivity at any point in time but also the character and intensity of the flows along the links. Link 2–3 may be a newly formed relationship with a purely social content. In time it may become like link 1–4 which combines, say, ties of friendship and business, or even like link 3–6 which combines friendship, common involvement in a sports club and a work relationship. This question of the 'multiplex' nature[19] of some relationships has been intensively discussed in the literature by a range of social analysts from Merton to Frankenberg.[20] But, so far as is known, there is no research on the plausible hypothesis that the degree to which multiplex relationships exist in a network may be, *ceteris paribus*, a direct function of the degree of connectivity value of the network. Moreover, it will be argued in the next section that this key aspect of the network, its connectivity, may well reflect a number of physical characteristics of the settlement – size, design layout and growth rate – which are themselves a result of conscious (one hopes) planning policy. Thus population turnover, connectivity, multiplex relationships, village design and planning policy may all be closely inter-related.

RELATIONSHIP OF NETWORK CHARACTERISTICS TO SETTLEMENT FORM

It is reasonable to believe that there is an intimate relationship between network characteristics, both topological and social, and settlement form. Villages are different from suburbs in that they are contained by the visible, if often convoluted, line where the houses stop and the fields begin; they have a physical perimeter. Suburbs have no such advantage. Their limits may sometimes be marked by a physical feature such as a railway embankment but more often they are purely administrative and invisible.

This difference is vitally important for an understanding of the social networks likely to occur in the respective settlement forms. Given that the time and money cost of making journeys does have some effect, and especially where a good spread of social facilities, services and employment is available within the settlement, the tangible perimeter of the village is likely to act like the cushion on a billiard table; social and economic interactions that would otherwise be lost over the side 'bounce back' into play. This must lead to an increase in the degree of connectivity since the proportion of links that are 'intra-village' (rather than between a villager and an outsider) is probably higher than would be the case without any effective perimeter.

Some fragmentary data on this question in so far as the purely social interactions of Ringmer residents is concerned were gained in the 1971 survey. Respondents were asked:

> 'Can you say very roughly what proportion of your present friends and acquaintances live *within* the village?'

Surprisingly few (about 3%) said they did not know or could make no estimate. The remainder answered as follows:

Percentage of friends within village	Percentage of sample
0–19	27
20–39	14
40–59	23
60–79	16
80 and over	20
	100

Unfortunately the figures mean little in isolation. Comparative data from other settlement types would be required to substantiate the hypothesised reflective effect of the village perimeter. But it may be significant that nearly one-half of the total of all friendship sets are intra-village, despite the recency of arrival of a very large proportion of residents who presumably still have well-developed friendship networks elsewhere.

But perhaps more fundamental than the suggested 'reflective' effect is the relationship between a visible and effective perimeter and the vexed problem of network definition. Nearly all network studies have the weakness that the values calculated for the indices depend upon how the network is delimited on the ground, or rather, the map. Garrison's[21] use of a subset of the total U.S. interstate highway network to show certain index values can be criticised on the obvious grounds that if he had defined the sub-network differently the values would have been different. It is argued now, despite the discussion centred around Stacey's proposition 31 in the last chapter, that the physical limits of the village at least give some logical justification for delimiting a village social network. Delimiting a suburban social network on the map is likely to be much more difficult and would, in many cases, be meaningless.

If one cannot specify the network spatially, then it could be argued that all attempts to carry out an analysis in graph theoretic terms also become meaningless. Not only does the degree of connectivity mean little or nothing; so too do the concepts of accessibility, associated number, diameter, shape and dispersion, all of which depend upon the unambiguous specification of a socially meaningful and finite network. If the suburb of a large city is defined, in administrative boundary terms, as an object for network analysis a large proportion of social links, and not simply among those living near the boundaries, will be with people outside the administrative area. This means that the diameter will either have to be arbitrarily curtailed by ignoring a large number of trans-boundary links or else it will be almost infinitely large by allowing these links; the first solution has little meaning in social terms, the latter means one has immediately abandoned the network definition adopted. The same general arguments apply to all the indices discussed. Because one cannot, in any socially meaningful way, delimit a network of manageable size one cannot calculate the associated number or accessibility of any point on the network. Nor can one assess the connectivity, diameter, shape or dispersion of the network as a whole. The suburbs of a large city are not only (very often) environmentally shapeless, incoherent and centreless, they also exhibit these qualities from a strictly graph theoretic consideration of their social network characteristics.

There are, of course, said to be 'urban villages';[22] and there is Bethnal Green.[23] Nothing written here is intended to diminish such inspired and respected work. But studies claiming that 'villages' exist set in the urban fabric of a large town take intuition, not measurement, as their premise. For all we know the number of trans-boundary links of Bethnal Green residents may have been as great, in relation to total population, as would have been the case, say, in Neasden or Abbey Wood. It seems unlikely, but the research did not demonstrate otherwise.

One other relationship remains to be explored; that between the shape of development in a small settlement and its network characteristics. Let us assume that the residents are less than perfectly mobile as they move around in the village. Some are old people with no car, some are housewives with perambulators to push; in either case a one-mile walk for a visit to a friend seems about the desirable limit. This gives a radius for one's social 'action space' of one half mile. It is not suggested that this is the *invariable* limit of social movements but rather that distance may well inhibit social interaction at a greater range and that some social links which would otherwise exist are prevented from occurring (see the data on children's friendships in Chapter 10). Next we can insert a hypothetical and simplified social network into two alternative village forms. Figure 12.2 shows the two villages; one roughly circular and one irregular but showing some resemblance to Ringmer (see Map 2). The villages are equal in area. It is assumed that population density is constant within and between the two and that some constant rate of friendship selectivity applies (based on the proportion of a total population one envisages as potentially congenial). Given these, and a few other simplifying assumptions, the two social networks between eight randomly spaced people might look like this:

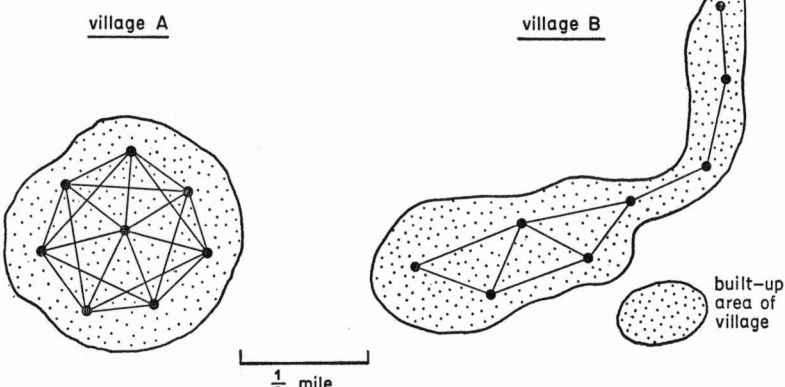

Fig. 12.2 Social Networks in Alternative Village Forms.

Using the half-mile distance constraint, the degree of connectivity in Village A is:

$$\frac{21}{8(7) \div 2} \quad \text{or} \quad 75 \cdot 0\%$$

In Village B it is:

$$\frac{10}{8(7) \div 2} \quad \text{or} \quad 35 \cdot 7\%$$

This difference is purely a function of shape; no other conditions have been varied. The three other network indices, diameter, shape and dispersion, also vary between the two cases. For example, the diameter of A is 2 and of B is 5. And in relation to the individual points on the network, the average of the associated numbers and of the accessibility values is much higher for B than for A. This denotes potential or actual impoverishment of social interaction possibilities.

It is not simply the structural qualities of the network that are affected by varying the settlement shape. Although as Mitchell[24] points out the relationship between network connectivity and the incidence of multiplex role-playing, in other words diversity of link content, has not fully been explored, it appears reasonable to assume that some positive relationship exists. It follows that the *character*, as well as the density, of social links may hinge partly upon village shape and that the development of multiplex role relationships, recognised as a typically rural social phenomenon by many observers,[25] may be inhibited by the elongation of the village layout.

The arguments in this chapter, with the exception of those concerning village shape, are summarised in Table 12.3 which sets out the likely network

Table 12.3 Network Characteristics of Alternative Residential Environments

	Traditional village	Growth village	Suburb
Network components	Stable over time	High turnover of population	High turnover of population
Social basis	More kin-based	Less kin-based	Less kin-based
Connectivity	High	Medium	Low (no 'perimeter' effect)
Accessibility	Most accessible point identifiable	Most accessible point identifiable	Calculation socially meaningless
Diameter/Associated number	Calculable	Calculable	Calculation socially meaningless
Dispersion	Low	Medium	Calculation socially meaningless
Shape	Calculable	Calculable	Not calculable/ amorphous

characteristics of three alternative residential environments; a suburb of a large city, a rapidly expanding village and a 'traditional' village of roughly similar size. 'Traditional' here means largely untouched by manufacturing industry, immigration or commuting influences. Obviously exceptions can be found to all these generalisations but the table is intended to show loose characterisations of the various forms.[26] From this table it is clear that villages of both types cannot be regarded as 'discontinuous suburbs'. They have different networks, both topologically and socially, from suburbs. In fact the problem of network delimitation makes graph theoretic analysis of the latter either difficult or meaningless.

There are perhaps two main objections to this general approach to social analysis. One is that the content of the links/relationships is infinitely variable and extremely difficult to ascertain in the field. The other is that network analyses like the one just carried out simply restate in more rigorous ways truths which are self evident to anyone with half an eye. But since both objections can be applied to virtually the whole of social science, one soldiers on.

13 · On the Development Process

THE PLANNING FRAMEWORK

Virtually all development in Britain is subject to statutory control. The growth of planning legislation up to and including the important measures of the 1945–51 Labour Government are usefully dealt with by Ashworth.[1] The 1947 Town and Country Planning Act, with various subsequent legislation, formed the main framework of planning until the 1968 act and the consolidating 1971 act were passed. These recent acts make far-reaching changes to the framework. But since the 'structure plans' and 'local plans' which they call for will not be finalised for the study area till the mid-1970s, and since Ringmer has grown under the preceding framework, this brief discussion will relate to the pre-1968 procedures.

Proposals for development, either by the landowner or others, are submitted to the local planning authority. The county, the statutory authority, normally delegates powers to the next tier down, the district councils and municipal boroughs. The agreements by which powers are delegated vary widely from case to case. But generally, if the application received is in line with the development plan prepared by the county, then approval rests primarily with the planning committee of the lower authority, following advice from its appointed officials and those of the county. If the application is at variance with this plan, or of particularly wide significance, or an initiative of the lower authority itself (for example public housing), or in various other circumstances, the decision rests with the county.

Applications can take one of two forms, 'outline' followed by 'detailed', or the two combined in a complete application. 'Outline' simply applies for approval for a category of development, for example, residential. The detailed application must specify the location, size and elevation of each building, the density of dwellings or habitable rooms, materials, roads and paths, in fact every detail. The authority does not have to publicise the application unless it relates to noxious or unpleasant uses, for example, a refuse dump, or is a major departure from an existing development plan. It may, however, inform residents or others who may be directly affected by noise, infringement of 'ancient lights', or in other ways by the development. If public notification is judged to be necessary, notices must be posted at the site and an advertisement inserted in the local newspaper. *All* applications are kept in a file in the planning authority offices and can be inspected on demand by anybody.

The application may be accepted, accepted subject to certain conditions and changes, or refused. If the application is refused or if the conditions are unacceptable the applicant can appeal to the Secretary of State for the Environment. If the matter is one of public concern the appeal will probably take the form of a public enquiry conducted by a department inspector. If the matter is one between the applicant and the authority, the appeal and subsequent decision can be dealt with entirely in writing. The inspector himself can, in certain circumstances, make a decision on small disputes but if a development of more than a few houses is involved he will report to the Secretary of State and the decision rests nominally with the minister. It is evident from this outline that the room density, internal layout, house style, building materials, estate layout and size, circulation system, and housing 'mix' of new private developments result generally from the developers' initiative. As Green has pointed out: 'Whichever form of village plan is adopted, the result will depend largely on the ability of the developer's architect.'[2] Planning policies concerning densities, layout or amenity, on the other hand: '. . . exist in a vacuum until the developer decides to take positive action.'[3] This is not to say that the expertise of the planning authority's staff is not available to the developer, as he prepares his application, should he seek it. There is, however, no obligation on him to consult.

The road and footpath systems of the proposed development must meet the standards applied by the county surveyor's department. This sometimes raises problems for 'Radburn'-type developments involving separation of the vehicle and pedestrian networks.[4] Unless the footpaths run alongside the roads in conventional fashion the county surveyor may not automatically take over the maintenance of the roads and paths. And if the planning authority rejects an application on the grounds that it would like to see a segregated circulation plan rather than a conventional one, it appears that the county surveyor's known attitude would increase the applicant's chance of winning an appeal. In practice, much prior consultation between the planning office, the surveyor's office and the developer may be required before an estate incorporating the extra safety of a segregated system is approved.

Tree preservation is another matter of some consequence to the appearance of the completed estate. Anyone can ask for a tree-preservation order on a tree, given that it is in sound condition and meets certain other conditions concerning safety and so on. If, however, a detailed application is approved which incorporates the removal of the tree, then this approval naturally cancels the order. It will be appreciated that a tree once felled and cut up cannot be re-erected, that the soundness of its condition is difficult to determine once it has been burned, and that a prosecution for felling a preserved tree (the maximum fine is £250) is difficult to obtain and does not restore the tree. Judging by local events it seems to be a fact of life that developers like trees the way postmen like dogs (see Plate 7c). It might well be, also, that planning authorities are too lax in ensuring the preservation of trees on new estates.

Public participation in planning is an issue about which there has been considerable recent discussion. The 1969 report of the Skeffington committee on this topic[5] proposes a wide range of new devices to involve the public more closely, and at an earlier stage, in the preparation of structure and local plans under the 1968 Act. These include better publicity via the local media, specified stages in the sequence of events for public comment, the convening of meetings and forums, the appointment of community development officers and the involvement of the public in the survey work upon which planning is based.

These proposals are beginning to have considerable effect. A local plan being developed for Heathfield, a settlement near Ringmer, is currently going through the stages of public exhibition, public comment, official consideration of the comment, amendment and presentation to the relevant planning committee. A total of 266 written observations was received from a population of 4000, a much higher rate of public response than has been normal. The increased public involvement is not without its cost since the final approval of the plan will probably take longer than under the previous system. But since the plan will influence the pattern of the settlement for perhaps a century or more the cost in delay seems worth while. Had the Ringmer developments been subject to the same procedure it seems likely that something very different and better might have emerged.

PRIVATE DEVELOPMENT

The crucial significance of the private developer in both urban and rural residential growth has been pointed out by various writers. In the south-east region, in particular, there has been a preponderance of private development over recent years as the following figures show:

Table 13.1 Dwellings Started, South-East Region, 1962–71

	Public	Private	Total
1962	37,321	62,358	99,679
1963	44,779	67,498	112,277
1964	50,990	83,387	134,377
1965	54,240	69,013	123,253
1966	52,763	59,561	112,324
1967	65,710	73,769	139,479
1968	55,921	55,684	111,605
1969	49,619	47,500	97,119
1970	45,009	49,283	94,292
1971	44,019	58,399	102,418
	500,371	626,452	1,126,823

Sources: M.H.L.G. Housing Statistics, Great Britain, 8 January 1968, and D.O.E. Housing and Construction Statistics, 1, 1st Quarter, 1972, both H.M.S.O.

A survey of residential development in Kent, an adjacent county to East Sussex, showed that the percentage of new development in the county carried out privately varied from 68 to 78% over the period 1961–6. This compared with 33% over the period 1951–5.[6] It was further pointed out by Craven that in the process of 'natural' growth of existing settlements (which will be far more significant numerically for the foreseeable future than, for example, new town growth) private developers will continue to play a predominant role.[7]

In these circumstances it is surprising how little is known about the private developer's mode of operation, social and economic assumptions, capabilities and basic aims, although the latter may be fairly predictable.

Craven's study gives a few insights into these questions. His view is that: '. . . the developer is a catalyst who interprets, albeit inaccurately, major forces in the urban environment; an initiator of action based on this interpretation and a challenger of public policies which obstruct such action.'[8] Furthermore: 'Public control over land use, however advanced our planning machinery, presents a framework within which the developer must act. This framework has wide limits which allows the developer considerable scope for initiative.'[9] Much of the discussion in this chapter and the next will be concerned with an identification of the 'major forces', the situation upon which the 'public policies' are based and upon the poor results which have, in at least one case, stemmed from the initiatory role of the private developer.

There is a clear relationship, in the Kent study at least, between the size of a developer, his area of operation and the type of development produced. American research shows that the larger the developer, the larger the individual estates produced.[10] The Kent data shows a rapid increase in the size of developments such that whereas in 1956 53·6% of new dwellings occurred in estates of five or fewer houses and estates of 76 houses or more were unknown, by 1964, the relative percentages in the two size categories were 17·6% and 39·2%.[11] Since also it was established that large estates tend to be relatively homogeneous in house type[12] and to be dominated by three-bedroomed semi-detached and terraced housing, while smaller developments were more varied in type, it can be seen that all the trends converge in one direction; a move towards greater similarity and homogeneity of development types. This movement is reinforced by the increasing significance of non-local developers who tend to build large, rather than small estates. In particular, London-based developers accounted for 7% of new houses in 1956, 26% in 1959 and 42% in 1964,[13] a surprisingly rapid change which possibly owes something to takeovers of local builders by larger national concerns.

Discussion with various estate agents confirmed this general picture in relation to the area in which Ringmer is situated. Developments of up to 20 houses are often carried out by small local firms and they frequently concentrate on low density, detached houses or some other 'non-standard' type. Larger developments tend to be carried out by one of half a dozen large national development companies. As will be seen, Ringmer itself constitutes an exception to this generalisation. Each developer seeks to acquire and maintain a 'land bank', or reserve of land for future operations. This is built up either by approaching landowners direct, or through their estate agents, or by bidding for plots at auction or by tender. Often developers arrange to hold options to purchase land subject to its being granted development approval. Since, however, the value of the land depends upon the density and type of development that will be allowed on it, a price is not agreed until at least outline planning permission is obtained.

In practice, a developer tends to be influenced in the detailed plan he puts forward by a variety of considerations. His perception of the state of the market and the specific needs of prospective purchasers is a vital consideration although it appears that few developers, apart from one or two notable exceptions, do much market research.[14] He will also tend to confine himself to the sort of development which he has carried out in the past and which, therefore, is within his capabilities. Clearly in a seller's market, as the south-east has been for some time, there is little point in experimenting with non-standard designs and materials when it is cheaper and safer to build conventional houses. He is also considerably influenced, in each development, by the size, shape and physical characteristics of the plot. The developer handles all aspects of the work, financial, administrative, architectural and constructional except that the estate roads, and the wiring, heating and plumbing of the houses are normally sub-contracted out to specialist firms. It is evident that the developer is generally the most important influence on the built environment that finally emerges, especially in small settlements.

The company responsible for most of the recent and future building in Ringmer is locally based but has interests elsewhere, mostly in Sussex. It was started soon after the first world war and expanded in the early 1930s, partly as an initiative to provide work in a period of high unemployment (see Chapter 3). The local family who founded the company still maintains an interest in its management but no longer owns it. The company employs roughly 100 staff and its operations involve something like 200 others in the sub-contracting. They expect to build approximately 50 new units per year up to at least 1976 primarily by adding to a large estate they have already built and on land already approved for development.[15] Much of the building is on areas previously owned by the family which founded the company, so there is little mystery about how the land was acquired for development. They have also carried out a scheme directed by a housing association for the 'middle-income' elderly and have extended the local hotel. In a literal sense they are building the village and the results of the growth process depend very largely on their expertise, or lack of it.

LOCAL AUTHORITY DEVELOPMENT

Under the 1957 Housing Act, and subsequent amendments, the local housing authority is empowered to provide and manage publicly owned housing. It is charged to consider the housing needs, and particularly to survey the existing stock, the degree of obsolescence, and the spread of present and future needs in the light of trends in household size.[16] On the basis of these surveys the authority should prepare schemes for new housing, or for the improvement of old, and submit them to the Secretary of State for the Environment. The list of those waiting to be allocated accommodation serves as a useful, but not exclusive, guide in assessing future policy. It is perhaps noteworthy that every act up to 1949 specified that local authority housing was for 'the working classes' but that subsequently this reference has been dropped.

Central government subsidises the development and exerts certain controls. The subsidy system is currently undergoing change as a result of the 1971 Housing Finance Act. But for the period of growth covered by this study the subsidy assumes that the 'approved' capital cost has been raised by a loan over 60 years. The amount granted is the difference between the loan charges at some average rate specified annually by the minister and the charges that would have been incurred had the rate of interest been 4%. The rate specified by the minister will be based on average rates actually paid in the previous financial year. This will be considerably higher than 4% (it was 6·19% in 1965–6 and 9·23% in 1970–1).[17] The 'approved cost' is the estimated or tender cost at the time of acceptance. This cost must meet a ministry 'yardstick'. A 10% tolerance in actual cost is allowed above this yardstick but the excess above the yardstick figure does not attract a subsidy. If schemes cost more than 110% of the yardstick figure they attract no subsidy at all.

Since 1969, all new local authority housing has had to conform to standards laid down in the 1961 report of a sub-committee of the Central Housing Advisory Committee (the 'Parker Morris' report and standards).[18] These standards were based not simply on internal density criteria but on an analysis of user patterns within the house. As Smith pointed out: 'The Parker Morris committee recommended that housing standards generally should be expressed in terms of the activity of the occupants rather than the number and size of rooms. . . .'[19] The standards cover such matters as the provision of a second W.C. in larger houses, adequate storage space and kitchen fittings, play space for children, heating standards, the supply of electric sockets, and storage space for household durables. The ministry cost yardsticks take account of these standards and of other considerations, such as sound insulation and the location of houses in relation to vehicle traffic flows and play areas. The yardsticks are increased from time to time to allow for rising costs and they vary from region to region, and from one scheme to another (for example, schemes specifically for old people attracted a larger increase in 1971 than others). In all, the Parker Morris standards represent a sound basis for the internal design of housing and for the production of enlightened environmental standards and layouts. It has been claimed, however, that the need to meet both these standards and the cost yardsticks has led to the use of inferior materials and standards of construction and, possibly, to standardised and unimaginative designs.[20] Despite this, a wide variety exists in the schemes produced and since some look much more exciting than others it is clear that imagination can rise above financial yardsticks.

One other significant feature of local authority housing finance should be made clear. Each authority's housing revenue account has to be balanced every year. The largest single expenditure in the average authority's account relates to interest on previously raised loans.[21] If an authority happens to have undertaken a great deal of building in some previous period of high interest charges (for example, the late 1960s), then the continuing cost of those operations will reduce the amount of new building that can currently be carried out by a greater amount than if the previous loans had been raised in a period of low interest rates (for example the period 1946–53). Thus the ability of an authority to build reflects quite strongly its previous building sequence, and thus its accumulated pattern of debts, rather than current needs in the locality.

It was estimated by Lord Fiske[22] that during 1969–70 the subsidy per household for local authority and housing association tenants was roughly £30, and for owner occupiers it was roughly £22 (as a result of tax concessions on mortgage interest). The 1972 housing legislation aims to make the local authority sector largely self-financing, by means of rent increases, by the mid-1970s. This will mean that the exchequer subsidy to local authority tenants will cease while the subsidy to owner occupiers will, presumably, continue. The net effect will be to redistribute wealth upwards even more effectively than at present (the argument that the system is redistributive upwards will be made in the next chapter).

The housing authority for Ringmer is Chailey Rural District Council. The larger district council which will supersede Chailey after the 1974 local government reorganisation will continue to act in that capacity. The authority has over 500 families on its list and the trend is rising. It is building at a rate of roughly 60 units per year to add to its total stock of about 1300 units.[23] A committee meets annually to assess the pattern of demand, the land available to the authority for development, the state of obsolescence of existing stock and the existing state of provision in each part of the local authority area. On this analysis a programme for two to three years ahead is worked out.

Each authority devises its own allocation system, subject to various central government directives.[24] For example there is a statutory obligation to favour large families and those living in unsanitary, overcrowded or otherwise unsatisfactory conditions. Similarly, central government has recently been strongly opposed to the use of residential qualification in the allocation procedure. In practice, not only do schemes vary widely but so does the willingness of local authorities to discuss them with other interested parties (for example voluntary housing agencies).

The Chailey authority shares with those of other rural areas the legacy of the 'tied cottage' system of housing. With the decrease in labour needs on the land and the sale of farms, many ex-farm workers, or their widows, are forced to leave cottage accommodation and have to be added to the housing list. It is clearly very difficult to assess their claim, and that of, for example, ex-servicemen, against the claims of young couples or families. The same problem occurs when domestic servants who previously lived in at a 'big-house' are made redundant.

The housing authority will also have regard to the need to provide accommodation in all parts of its area. Should the county planning authority develop a 'key village' policy by which certain villages only are designated for growth, this may not be compatible with the rural district's aim to provide accommodation in all villages. Discussion will then be necessary between the two authorities. In practice, however, in view of the rapid decline in rural public transport services, district housing managers are often reluctant to allocate houses in less accessible villages to those without cars since they are aware, from experience, of the problems of isolation that may ensue.

The rate at which the local authority can build is constrained by a number of factors. Land has to be acquired, whether by compulsory purchase or not, at full development values according to the market at the time. Thus the full

Part of the new shopping centre; with the 'urban' ~rmarket and a flourishing children's goods shop. ld be surburban anywhere. The three-storey buildings quite out of scale with the immediate surroundings page 195).

5b The main road on a new estate; brisk traffic flow, 'village variegated' architecture, and functionless patches of front garden (see page 195).

Haphazard grouping, no focus, variations without a ne, '. . . the aesthetics of the suburb' (see page 197).

5d The density of new development seems to increase all the time. The amount of privacy in these back gardens can be imagined – 'isolated yet on view' (see page 195).

6a '... architecturally pretentious "neo" features, such as small-paned windows (difficult to paint and clean), functionless ironwork and over-elaborate door arches' (see page 194).

6b A better solution; simple, clean lines, tile-hung and weather-boarded finish (see Plate 2c). This is one of the few points in the village where council and private houses abut on the same road. Why need it happen so rarely? The illustration also shows that there need not be the usual marked differences in appearance between the two.

increment in value following development approval, an increment which arguably results from the collective needs of the whole community expressed via its elected and appointed agents, accrues to the landowner at the time of sale. The issue of a levy on betterment, as the increment is termed, has a long and complex history.[25] Between 1947 and 1954 some charge was made on this profit. Subsequently, between 1967 and 1970, the Land Commission sought to operate a betterment levy, to encourage the flow of land on to the market for a variety of needs and to reduce the effect of land scarcity in inflating prices in growth regions such as the south-east. In 1970 the incoming government abolished the commission and returned to the system of encouraging planning authorities and landowners to release or sell sufficient land for development needs.[26] Since this policy, and perhaps most previous ones, has been less than totally successful in ensuring an adequate supply of development land, a local authority is partly conditioned in the extent to which it can build by the size of its 'land bank'; land which was previously purchased and held against future needs.

Chailey, in common with a number of other authorities, is now tending to build more two-bedroomed than three-bedroomed houses. This is partly to redress the existing imbalance in the stock, since for many years it was customary for local authorities to build three-bedroomed houses without much close analysis of needs, and partly because the smaller houses are more flexible in their range of possible uses. For example they can provide appropriate accommodation for young married couples, either childless or with up to two children, or older couples whose children have left home. The authority is well aware that the easiest way to keep to the ministry cost yardsticks is to use the same rather limited range of designs in its various development schemes. Despite this, however, architects have been involved, efforts have been made to use materials sympathetic to the particular local environment, and the most recent development in Ringmer looks refreshingly un-council-like (see Plate 6b).

SOME SHORTCOMINGS OF THE OUTCOME

During the course of the research, a wide variety of opinions on village development was expressed by residents. Apart from the comments made in response to the more open-ended parts of the questionnaire by the 150 households in the survey, and the opinions given in the children's survey, discussions were held with a number of long-standing residents (see Chapter 3) and with various other people including the doctor, the vicar, the district nurse, the health visitor and the local authority housing manager. In order to preserve anonymity, views expressed by any member of the latter group will be referred to as 'professional opinion'. Apart from these sources of opinion, the author has discussed the issues dealt with in the book with a wide range of friends and acquaintances in the village. From these processes, and from seven years residence, one might reasonably hope to get a fairly balanced view of the collective village reaction to the very rapid growth that has occurred.

By and large, as can be seen from Chapters 8, 9 and 10, a quite high degree of overall satisfaction exists. The village is undeniably a pleasant, healthy and friendly environment in which to live. There is obviously none of the squalor which has been shockingly exposed by a number of studies of inner urban suburbs (for example by Coates and Silburn)[27] nor is the village socially dichotomised, as are some in the Surrey 'stockbroker belt'.[28] But this does not mean that things are as good as they might be. This section will deal with a number of specific points of criticism, in roughly ascending order of scale and social significance, raised by one or other of the sources of opinion outlined in the previous paragraph.

The internal design and external appearance of many of the privately developed houses leave much to be desired. The small terraced houses near the shops have tiny third 'bedrooms' of an almost impossible shape, too much wasted space on the landing, inconvenient cupboards and excessively long thin 'through' reception rooms.[29] Too frequently there are bay windows, which are difficult to curtain, carpet and furnish, and fireplaces located so that it is difficult to arrange comfortable seating in a focused group around them. No doubt it is difficult in any small house to design an area specifically for young children to play, but it should not be impossibly expensive to incorporate an area, say 10 ft. by 6 ft. leading off the kitchen and with access to the garden. This would greatly reduce the conflict of uses in the one main living area, obviate the daily burden of clearing up toys and cut down tension all round. With high-level shelving it could also enormously increase storage space, while for childless couples the whole area would be 'utility space'. Possibly one of the most stress-inducing aspects of tiny modern houses and flats is that there is nowhere one can be creatively messy (with paint, woodwork, models, etc.) and happily leave the mess overnight.

The external appearance of the new estates is generally felt to be at best uninspired and at worst, awful (see Chapters 9 and 10 or just come and look at the village). There are long rows of 'standard' semis which could equally appropriately be found in a new suburb or new town; architecturally pretentious 'neo' features such as small-paned windows (difficult to paint and clean), functionless ironwork, and over-elaborate door arches (see Plate 6a); and semi-detached houses laid out to look like detached. One is tempted to assess how far the money spent on such useless features might have gone towards the cost of providing the invaluable extra 60 square feet of internal space argued for above.

The layout of most of the new development follows the hackneyed procedure of placing houses in long lines along roads. The arguments against this in terms of safety and social 'focus' are obvious, especially in a village where some sense of small scale and enclosure is presumably appropriate. Ironically enough, cogent arguments were put forward in a paper in 1965 for the 'cluster planning' of village development in Sussex.[30] This involved building small groups of houses around communal green spaces. Reference was also made to a 'cellular' village structure with pedestrian walkways focused on the village green and school. These concepts were guided by the need to keep 'village scale'. The paper was written by three members of the county planning department ultimately responsible for the development of

Ringmer. What has actually happened in the village could hardly be more different. One wonders what went wrong along the way.

Various people were critical of other aspects of the estate layouts. It was pointed out that the unfenced patches of front garden in many of the homes were quite wasted; they were not very practical for children's play and one could hardly picnic or sunbathe on them (see Plate 5b). It would be better to combine the space into communal play areas. Also one case was mentioned where a housewife hanging our her washing in the back garden could be overlooked by more than 100 people. It was felt that in some situations this can induce considerable stress. Coupled with the loneliness and insecurity that some new residents feel, it led to 'being isolated yet on view' (see Plate 5d). Other professional opinion felt that there was a relationship between the 'bleak' design of much of the development and a relatively high incidence of mild psychological illness, but in this situation it is clearly extremely difficult to separate design factors from other influences that may be at work.[31]

Much of the bleakness of the estates results from the removal of pre-existing mature trees. In one recent case in the village a line of Lombardy poplars was cut down despite various previous assurances by the developers that they would be preserved. The particular species normally grows for 70–100 years and the felled trees were known to be only about 40 years old and in good condition.[32] Many village residents were angry at this 'act of vandalism'.[33] Clearly profits come before trees.

Criticisms were also made of the shopping centre on both architectural and social grounds. The three-storey buildings are quite out of scale with the village and their immediate environment, and they cut the skyline of the downs as seen from the village green (see Plates 5a and 8a). It is difficult to see why they should not have been of more appropriate scale and laid out around three sides of a small square, enclosing a pedestrian precinct. This could have been more imaginatively softened with greenery, could have incorporated distant views of the church, and would probably have been more socially effective than the existing rather odd layout. As it stands, shopping 'paths' appear to work along the shops from one end to the other. A more enclosed format would have led to more criss-crossing of the central space and would have, as Mumford once put it, 'multiplied the accidents of human contact'.

The general shape of the village has already been delineated and certain implications of the 'two-cell' structure identified (see Chapters 8, 9, 10 and 12). Various professional opinions support the generally held view that the growth of the smaller detached section is an unfortunate planning error. It was felt that newcomers on the peripheral estates suffer from all the usual problems of integrating into an area plus the added problem of isolation. Old people on these estates were felt to be particularly disadvantaged. As was pointed out earlier, new local authority bungalows for old people have been built on the extreme periphery in the last few years. A responsible official described this decision as resulting from 'Hobson's choice' since there was no other land that the local authority could purchase at the time.

The channelling of many thousands of vehicles a day through the village, many of them heavy lorries, was the subject of criticisms and fears (see Chapters 9 and 10) by people of all ages. There is an intimate historical link between the growth of a settlement and the growth of its means of access to other settlements, In other words one expects villages to be on roads; that is part of their rationale. But under today's conditions, with the volume of both originating and through traffic, the close juxtaposition of people and vehicles found in most villages and towns, including Ringmer, is perhaps more than just unpleasant or inconvenient; it is dangerous, uncivilised and insupportable. This is not an indictment of any particular local or national authority, or even of the vehicle-manufacturing industry; we are all, to varying degrees, to blame. But at some stage in the gradual pushing back of the limit of what is environmentally acceptable, objectors have to stand up and be counted, as they frequently are at planning enquiries and on demonstrations.

Partial solutions exist at various scales. Some of them, for example the increased subsidisation of railways, and the inclusion of an element of 'environmental' cost in the taxation of road-haulage operations, are matters for national legislation. Others, for example the reduction of parking facilities in town centres to encourage the use of public transport, are matters for more localised decisions. For villages, in particular, the demand for road space generated by numerous private car movements with one or two passengers could be drastically reduced by the development of frequent and regular subsidised bus services and/or, for late at night, 'limousine' services partway between present bus and taxi services. Clearly, for many current rural needs, standard-size buses are uneconomically large and run three-quarters empty. Possibly 10- to 15-seat vehicles could replace them for certain hours of the day. The overall result of such measures might well be a reduction in vehicle movements through villages, less danger, less pollution, less noise, better transport facilities for non-car-owners (and especially the elderly) and less wear on roads following a reduction in the 'metal to people ratio' in the total weight of traffic using the roads. Unfortunately, due to the primitive state of public accountancy procedures, these benefits cannot be quantified as exactly as the costs involved in the necessary subsidies.

At the level of the individual village, decisions on parking restrictions, street lighting, speed limits and street crossings can be made or influenced. Ringmer clearly needs a 30-m.p.h. limit. It also badly needs a street crossing. The arguments against one, for example that it would be more dangerous to have a crossing than not to have one, seem on the face of it feeble in the extreme. No doubt there are bureaucratic and technical problems involved in making a street crossing. But if it is beyond the wit of administrative man to provide a crossing, especially in the face of the evidence presented in Chapters 9 and 10 of this book, then that itself is grounds for condemnation. In the end the appeal is on humanitarian and common-sense grounds. A child is killed and the grief is beyond cost; an 80-year-old lady forces herself painfully to run to avoid the lorry bearing down. It should not, and need not, happen. The intellect that produced the technology must be capable of managing it in a more humane fashion.

SOME RELEVANT QUESTIONS

On the basis of the viewpoints presented in the previous section, one feels entitled to raise a number of questions about the current operation of the development process as it has affected the village. It is of course true that nothing that has gone wrong in the village is remotely as serious or socially damaging as the things that are chronically wrong with the housing situation in many urban areas. But the existence of big problems elsewhere does not render the discussion of smaller local problems irrelevant. By and large the system that produces the one produces the other.

It seems clear that the visually uninspired, hackneyed and socially unsympathetic nature of most of the recent private development in the village stems from a combination of causes. The developers, as argued previously, must be primarily responsible. The present author agrees strongly with the sentiments (if not with the punctuation) of R. J. Green when he wrote of: '. . . the relatively poor quality of new residential building, and in particular, the introduction of estate development, breaking up the scale of the old village, and introducing into it the aesthetics of the suburb.'[34] The recent developments in Ringmer fall far short of many developments elsewhere, of the ideas in the 1965 paper by the County Planning Officer and others,[35] of the environmental standards suggested by Parker Morris, of the principles of pedestrian/vehicle separation which have been current for half a century or more and, perhaps more important, of the ideals of many residents.

There are a number of reasons for these poor standards of development. The company concerned is in business to make money. This is entirely blameless; that is the whole rationale of private enterprise. If research directed towards the social implications of various estate layouts is undertaken, if as a result slightly more expensive solutions involving 'cluster planning' and vehicle segregation are carried out, and if, in a seller's market, these operations cost more than is recouped in slightly higher selling prices, then the shareholders, confronted with reduced profits on their investment, will want to know why. And the argument that such operations were thought to be *socially*, as opposed to financially, desirable will not be well received. Private business concerns are not social welfare agencies. It would be fruitless to try to make them so.

Another reason for poor private developments is that while the planning authorities responsible for approving schemes have powers to refuse them on a large number of grounds, they are not able, at present, to use these powers to the full. It was the opinion of one senior, and socially very aware, planning official that in a situation of great housing scarcity to refuse a proposed scheme on purely social grounds would be pointless. In his own words: '. . . one would get cut to pieces at the appeal stage.'

Perhaps this is partly the fault of researchers, academic or otherwise. It has not yet been sufficiently well demonstrated to the public, including prospective purchasers, that there *is* a relationship between good design and a decent lifestyle, and between bad design and various sorts of stress.[36] Everybody believes this in a general sort of way but when the time comes to design or approve a specific scheme the intangibles come second to the hard realities of finance. Nobody has yet demonstrated the savings (in the reduced use of doctors, ambulances, social service officers and policemen) which one suspects must be inherent in good and socially sensitive housing and house layouts. Only the extra costs are calculable. If the savings had been adequately quantified, planning authorities could act with greater confidence in rejecting socially undesirable proposals. At present they hardly dare.

Not only is the incentive to produce socially sensitive environment lacking in most development companies, so too is the expertise. Very few development companies choose to run a research department, or employ first-class architects and landscape designers. Those that do frequently produce interesting and valuable reports and often base their developments upon them.[37] In fact, in the opinion of a director of one of these companies,[38] socially effective and visually interesting developments need *not* cost more. And even if they do, within reason, the extra quality of the design can be a selling point and can increase sales revenue. In other words, a socially satisfactory outcome is as much a question of imagination, research and expertise as of extra cost.

A final point can be made which relates to the two previous ones. In the process of private speculative building, the developer plays the creative and initiatory role and the planning authority the regulatory and passive one. It seems likely that the latter, headed by officials who are professionally qualified and who carry a public and countywide responsibility, may often be in a much better position to assess and propose what is required than are the former. And apart from this question of expertise it may be that the rather negative role which the present system assigns to the planners is resented by developers who in many cases may perceive the planning staff as one more obstacle to overcome rather than as a source of potentially valuable information and expertise. This point was made by a government white paper which observed that: '. . . the system (of land use planning) has been better as a negative control on undesirable development than as a positive stimulus to the creation of a good environment',[39] while Pahl observed of planners and developers that: 'Very little consultation or discussion is found between the two, at the local level in particular, and contact is only made when disputing proposals for development.'[40]

The public authority housing system avoids certain of the defects apparent in private development. The system operates on the basis of public service, not private gain, and it appears from a comparison of the two that the local authority procedures to assess housing need are more thorough than any carried out locally by commercial concerns. Public authority housing must, in addition, conform to Parker Morris standards whereas private development need not and this increases the risk of poor design in privately built houses and estates. Proposals for new public developments must also normally be approved by the county planning authority, whereas most private development proposals can be dealt with under delegated powers by the district council or municipal borough planning committee, under advice from the county staff. Normally one expects a rather greater spread of expertise in the higher level authority, better discrimination between good and bad schemes, and a wider range of professional advice from appointed officials.

New local authority housing schemes in some areas, including Ringmer, are however tending to exhibit some of the same overall design defects as those noted in a number of private developments. Estates are tending to be large and socially homogeneous and at least one social services fieldworker consulted felt that these design characteristics were likely, ultimately, to lead to a greater charge on the social service agencies. But, as in the case of internal house design and layout, research has not yet adequately demonstrated the relationship between social homogeneity and standards of physical and mental health. Research into such complex issues costs money. Developers, except for a few of the very largest, will not underwrite the cost since they have little incentive to do so. Housing authorities, in a situation of almost universal shortage, are hardly likely to be able to allocate money for this purpose. And, as Pahl and Craven have pointed out:

> Some planning departments collect 'facts' and describe patterns, even though they, as yet, have little knowledge of the processes behind them; indeed, with the acute shortage of planners, it is less likely that research without immediate pay-off can be attempted.[41]

One is left at the end of this study of the development process and its results in Ringmer and elsewhere with a number of questions:

– is the production of new private housing too important socially and environmentally to be left to market forces operating under their present degree of freedom?[42]

– should identical design standards and planning approval procedures apply to private as to public developments?

– should planning departments be given more 'muscle', in the shape of central government support, to reject socially doubtful schemes?

– should they play a more initiatory and less passive role in the development process?

– should more consultation occur between planning authorities, social service departments and developers before schemes are approved?

– in view of the complexity of the issues, is it wise to move most decision-making in planning down to the district council and municipal borough level where professional expertise will clearly be scarcer? (This will happen under the 1974 reorganisation of local Government.)

–should more be known about the effect of the design of the built environment on life-styles, patterns of interaction and pathologies;[43] and if so whose job is it to pay for the fundamental research involved?

The first of these questions seems the most important because it underlies a number of others. It will be examined more closely in the following chapter.

14 · On Housing – A Critique

The detailed process of analysing social change in the village over the past century, and especially in the last decade, leads one to question the present organisation of housing provision. This last chapter seeks to present four arguments against the existing system. In several cases a Ringmer example is given and the argument is then generalised. Implicit in the criticisms are some radical notions concerning, for example, the underlying bases upon which housing should be provided and development should occur. It would be unwise to dismiss these implicit ideas as utopian or politically impossible. The first two parts of this book document the revolutionary changes, all based ultimately on technological change, that have occurred in social organisation over the past century. It would be rash to assert that our technology shows signs of stagnation. It appears, on the contrary, to be evolving at a rapid rate. Man will contrive, as he always has, to develop his attitudes and institutions in a manner consistent with the problems presented by his technological developments. The adjustments may be 10 or 20 years late (as they were, for example, in relation to the testing of nuclear weapons or to the confidentiality of computer-stored personal data) but they will occur; it cannot be otherwise.

It would be equally shortsighted to reject the arguments as politically un-realistic. At given points in time so were the arguments in favour of universal suffrage, free education, a national health service, the right to strike and much else we take for granted. If the situation which underlies and perpetuates the present housing crisis is seen to be a damaging one, and if it can be presented as such to the electorate, then sooner or later radical measures to change it will become part of an election-winning platform. Policies to meet the criticisms advanced have, after all, been put into operation by other nations[1] and have been discussed from time to time here.[2] Further change will have to come because each of the criticisms offered has serious social implications; together they constitute an indictment.

THE FIRST ARGUMENT: THE SYSTEM IS SPATIALLY DIVISIVE

This argument operates at various scales. At the local scale, in Ringmer and almost everywhere else, the local authority housing and the private housing exist on separate estates. Nearly all new housing is of one of these two types and most estates are visibly one or the other. This arrangement is quite obviously socially divisive (see Chapters 9 and 10, innumerable studies of council estates and Collison's absorbing book on the Cutteslowe Wall).[3] In many local villages the local authority housing is conspicuously off-centre; in others the council houses are adjacent to the private ones. Very rarely are the two types intermixed.

There are, of course, good practical and financial reasons for these patterns. The agency, public or private, that develops the estate has to arrange for the services to be laid and no doubt the unit cost of drains and so on reduces with increasing size of estate. No doubt, too, it would make no commercial sense at all, given prevailing attitudes, to build small groups of houses for sale interspersed with local authority developments for renting. It is also frequent practice, within private estates, to separate out the 'standard' two/three-bedroomed houses from the more prestigious four/five-bedroomed units. The latter will thus achieve a higher selling price and appreciate more quickly. At the same time, certain areas of some council estates are used as repositories for 'problem' families; official denials of this practice will be met with ironic smiles by social workers and others who know it happens. Thus social segregation is operating *within* both the public and the private estates as well as between them.

At the inter-settlement scale, it seems likely that other segregating processes are at work. The spectrum of housing need is a wide one, conditioned by a combination of each individual household's requirements and its ability to pay. One can discern rough groupings of households. These are based on general observation rather than empirical data but they seem to fit reality, as least so far as the region studied in this book is concerned:

(i) those who have capital, can afford a house of 'character' and can run two cars

(ii) those who can afford a four-bedroomed house and can run a car

(iii) those who can afford a three- or two-bedroomed 'semi' (or could until the 1972 price rises) and can run a car

(iv) those in a similar situation but who cannot run a car

(v) those who cannot afford to purchase but whose situation enables them to gain a council house and who can run a car

(vi) those in a similar situation but who cannot run a car

(vii) those who cannot afford to purchase, cannot get a council house and who live in privately rented accommodation

Increasingly, by the operation of the market, the unimaginative pattern of development, and the decline of rural public transport, a powerful self-selection mechanism is at work. This mechanism can be clearly seen in Ringmer and similar villages. They are filling up primarily with households in categories (iii) and (v), especially the former.

Category (i) tend to buy and modernise large old houses, often former farmhouses, outside the villages. The second car renders the housewife independent of the need for facilities within perambulator range. And once one has the capital, know-how and professional contacts to help plan the conversion, one's good fortune is powerfully supported by generous local authority grants (non-repayable). The result is a comfortable, pleasantly situated house and a very large capital appreciation.

Category (ii) are surprisingly ill-served within the local villages. There appears to be a chronic shortage of four-bedroomed houses on new estates, both private and public. So affluent larger families frequently opt for an old house in a near-by town since there are not many suitable large old houses in the villages. The ones outside the villages will have been pre-empted by category (i) who can afford the cost of their 'character' and isolation.

Categories (iv) and (vi) are increasingly being discouraged by the decline in rural bus services and by the closure of branch railway lines. It is, as was noted earlier, the policy of at least one housing manager not to allocate houses in the less well-served villages to those without a car. The penalties of being car-less in a village are quite severe since one cannot lead any sort of social life involving a late night return to the village from, say, theatre or cinema. And as a result of lack of competition, village food prices are high and the cost of living is higher than in an urban situation. Pahl has usefully reminded us that car-ownership is not universal, nor ever could be, and that: '. . . too often figures for the mobile middle class [sic] are held to be representative for the population as a whole.'[4]

Category (vii) families are also largely excluded from village life except on the objectionable, and fortunately declining, basis of 'tied' or 'service' tenancies. There are very few large older houses which have been subdivided for private tenants, and no new one or two-bedroomed flats or bed-sitters. Households who, for one reason or another, need accommodation of this type normally find it in the inner suburbs of a near-by large town. This includes not only families but the large number of young single people who have left their parents' home and moved away, often involuntarily, because the village or suburb they lived in does not provide the accommodation they require.

The result of this spatial sorting process is that villages like Ringmer tend to consist, to a larger and larger extent, of households in categories (iii) and (v) who are mutually similar in their life-cycle stage, and their access to private transport, but who differ in the crucial respect of tenure. Because they are only two groups from a possible seven, and because their polarity is not softened and blurred by significant representation from the other five groups, the differences stemming from the variation in tenure are perhaps more obvious and more socially divisive than they might otherwise be. And the two-car affluent are less aware of the life-style of local authority tenants, and both are less aware of the problems inherent in a furnished tenancy, than they would be if village development patterns supplied the needs of all seven categories listed. The importance of using the full social catalytic potential of village life should not be under-estimated. Too much uninformed nonsense is written about council tenants with expensive cars and colour televisions who waste their money on drink and gambling. Whether or not it is desirable that growing villages should develop a relatively narrow social and life-style base is, in the end, a matter of opinion; that it is actually happening is not, as the evidence of Chapter 7 makes clear for Ringmer.

These long-term and potentially damaging trends can to some extent be countered at the stage of planning approval if the officials and committees concerned are socially aware and sufficiently powerful to counteract 'natural' pressures. It is generally known that applications have been referred back on the grounds that they would aggravate existing *age* balance problems in an area. In principle, similar action could be taken over proposals which threatened to produce *social* imbalance. But, from the evidence, it seems that this second step is difficult to take in the face of the economic and political forces that would oppose it.

As it stands at present, the operation of the housing system undeniably leads to the spatial sorting of individuals and families, like with like. From the evidence in Chapter 8 concerning how close friends are first met (the category 'very near neighbour' attracted by far the largest response) this cannot possibly be dismissed as socially insignificant. It appears, on the contrary, to be a powerful mechanism for limiting the aggregate level of knowledge about the assumptions, backgrounds, preoccupations and life-styles of people in different situations from oneself.[5] The only justification one can see for this mechanism would be the assertion that different groups of the species man are inherently and intrinsically different; and that it is therefore ultimately appropriate they should live in different locations in partial ignorance of each other, perhaps to minimise the risk of conflict. This notion of 'social apartheid' seems scientifically far-fetched and unnecessarily pessimistic. If, as one hopes, it is an idea that most people would reject as strongly as they reject the other form of apartheid, why is the operation of the housing system allowed to reinforce it?

An extension of this argument, which has the effect of multiplying its ramifications, is that the environmental pleasantness and the level of provision of facilities in an area is often strongly and positively related to the quality of the housing. It has been established, for example, that the inhabitants of areas such as St. Ann's, Nottingham, experience more than bad housing.[6] They suffer from 'the public health hazards of overcrowding',[7] from inadequate play areas for children, increased noise and pollution, lack of privacy, poorer provision of youth facilities, a high turnover rate of teachers in the schools, possibly adverse discrimination in applying for hire purchases and a hundred other disadvantages. Schorr[8] has even demonstrated the link between poor environment and poor performance on strictly physiological grounds and Douglas has substantiated the same relationship on largely cultural and environmental bases: '. . . when housing conditions are unsatisfactory, children make relatively low scores in the tests.'[9]

The general conclusion to be drawn is that where large, relatively homogeneous, spreads of housing occur the differences between good and bad housing conditions will be *reinforced cumulatively* by the quality of the neighbourhood environment and facilities; advantage will pile up upon advantage in the one case and deprivation upon deprivation in the other. The tendencies are deep-seated, vicious and difficult to break. The best answer would be not to allow differences of this sort to occur on this scale in the first place, but rather to ensure that rented and owner-occupied housing of various sizes and types are intermixed to form heterogeneous residential areas.

THE SECOND ARGUMENT: THE SYSTEM IS SOCIALLY DIVISIVE

No use has been made in this book of the terms 'upper class' ,'middle class' and 'working class'. In fact the word 'class' has not been used at all except in quotations or when using the Registrar-General's divisions for the purpose of certain analyses. This may seem strange since the idea of social class has tended to dominate analyses of society for the last 100 years or more, not just among Marxists but among all commentators, academic, lay and journalistic, on social organisation. It is neither appropriate nor possible to review here the many currents of thinking on this theme. Bottomore's useful book[10] is a brief and authoritative survey of some of the main ideas of Marx, Weber, Ossowski, Mallet, Tawney, Dahrendorf, Goldthorpe and Lockwood, among others. It is quite beyond the present author to add anything of substance to this literature. But, for the purpose of developing the arguments concerning housing, a fresh approach to the whole issue is offered, based upon a deeply felt suspicion that much of what has been written, and indeed 99% of current discussion on the subject in the mass media,[11] does not relate to the facts of society and is, in fact, a damaging, self-perpetuating nonsense.

One has to accept that there are two distinct facets to the question of social stratification. There is the question whether or not most people *think* that different social clases exist and that they belong to one of them. And there is the separate question whether, on the basis of all relevant ascertainable objective data, they actually *do* exist. For the purposes of this brief analysis the first idea will be referred to as 'subjective' differentiation and the latter as 'objective' differentiation. Naturally one's belief in the former hinges powerfully on what one reads and is told about the way society is structured, both in academic literature and in the mass media. To be convinced that the differentiations are objectively verifiable, that they exist on a basis of fact, is another matter altogether.

The subjective categories exist because Marx, and a host of earlier and later analysts, found some grouping scheme to be useful analytically and, indeed, to appear in accord with the facts at the time; because this scheme, involving such concepts as the bourgeoisie, the middle class and the proletariat, was based in a logical manner on the relationship of defined groups to the means of production; and because revolutions could be based upon 'class solidarity'. None of what follows would presume to question the greatness of these insights or the immense benefits they have brought in terms of social justice. It is, however, interesting (as numerous others have observed) that volume III of *Capital* breaks off on a crucial empirical question; given that there are three classes, wage-labourers, capitalists and landlords, what precisely sorts any given individual into one class or another? Marx believed that the economically based class structure of mid-nineteenth-century England was the most highly developed in the world. Yet, he points out: 'Middle and transition stages obliterate even here all definite boundaries, although much less in the rural districts than in the cities.'[12] This and other comments by the greatest analyst of all show that he grasped the immense complexity of the reality far better than the myriad subsequent commentators who daily use such meaningless terms as 'the workers', 'the middle class' and so on.

It should be relatively easy to verify whether or not objectively based class divisions exist in society. The first step is to disaggregate the components which, collectively, make up the idea of 'class' to most people. The following seem to be some of the relevant variables. (It will be noticed that they go some way beyond Marx's idea that the divisions might be primarily based on an individual's relationship to the prevailing means of production.)[13]

1. *Income level*

2. *Educational level* (number of years of full-time education)

3. *Occupational status, etc.*
     i whether a manual worker or not
     ii whether a manager (boss) or not
     iii whether a capitalist or not
     iv whether in a trade union or not
     v whether salaried or not

4. *Property tenure type*
     i whether a house owner or not
     ii whether a landlord or not

5. *Behaviour pattern*
     i choice of newspaper, TV programmes, etc.
     ii leisure activity patterns

No doubt many other variables could be adduced but the more there are, the more difficult it would be to demonstrate the objective existence of class divisions.

The next step is to define the conditions under which an objectively validated division of society could be said to exist. Since the most commonly used terms for the supposed categories are 'middle class' and 'working class', and since this must pre-suppose an 'upper class', we are looking for empirical evidence of a three-fold division. The conditions for a perfectly verified division would be as follows:

1. The *n* million households in Britain, when ordered hierarchically upon each of these variables, must exhibit a discretely arranged, not a continuously arranged, distribution. There must be a three-fold grouping with two gaps to distinguish the groups.

2. Each household must fall consistently across the various scales, that is, households must not fall in the high category on some variables, the middle on others, and the lower on yet others.

These points are illustrated in Fig. 14·1 overleaf (using only nine households). Society A meets the conditions. The nine households fall in discrete groups on each variable and are fairly 'status consistent' across the variables;[14] no family crosses group boundaries. This society would be characterised by clear class divisions, consistency between social and economic status, and probably by low social mobility. One could correctly speak of upper, middle and lower classes.

The present-day reality in Britain may be much closer to society B. The values on most variables are ordered more nearly continuously than discretely, and the 'path' of a given family across the scales is less consistent than in A. For example, household 5 is headed by a self-made, relatively

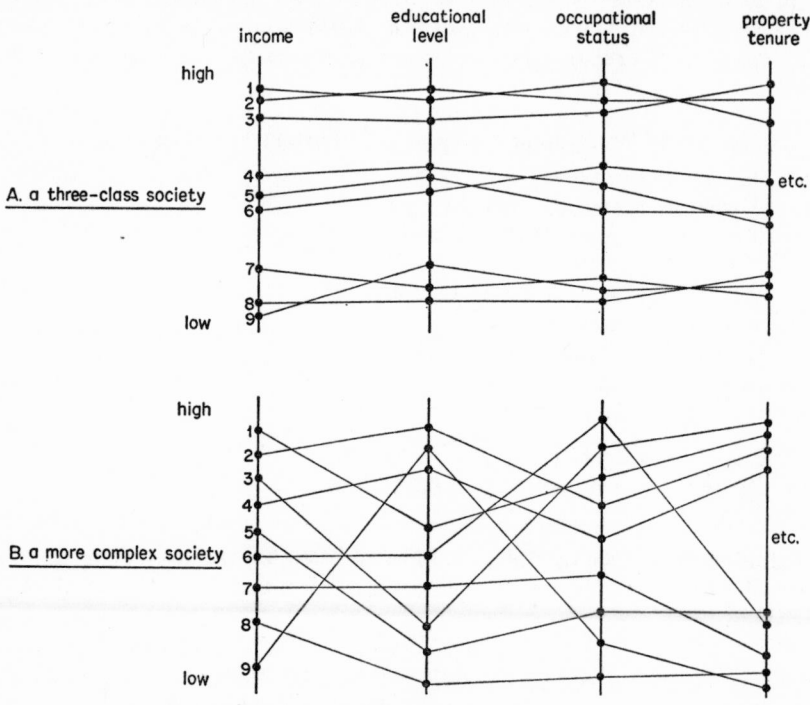

Fig. 14.1 Two Alternative Societies.

affluent shopkeeper, household 6 is a priest who joined the ministry late in life, household 9 is headed by a graduate who has, perhaps temporarily, opted out of the rat race, and so on. This pattern seems a much more plausible representation of current reality than diagram A. And on the basis of B, it is quite simply meaningless to envisage the existence of three classes.

It may be objected that many of the variables *would* show a discrete distribution. It is conceded in diagram B that the education level distribution has discrete tendencies. This is because we are still living to some extent with the outworn legacy of the 11+ and of the separation of children into two broad systems of clearly differing status. But this curious procedure is currently disappearing and in a generation's time the ordering will be more nearly a continuous one. Of the other variables identified earlier it is evident that 5(i) and 5(ii) are non-quantifiable and therefore cannot possibly be discretely ordered. Variable 3(i) looks discrete, and its apparent discreteness is reinforced by the Registrar-General's over-neat classification of occupations.[15] But do warehousemen (nominally manual) never write things down, do bank clerks (non-manual) never lift heavy books and boxes, do dentists (non-manual) never use their strength and do building workers (manual) never stop to make sketches or calculations? When we stop to look at the *content* of jobs, is not the ratio of cerebral–clerical input to strength–manipulative input not perhaps continuously ordered rather than ordered in the discrete fashion that the simple, and socially far-reaching, idea of manual versus non-manual would imply? The same sort of argument could be developed for variables 3(ii) and 3(iii). The term 'boss' must always be a relative one. Every boss has a bigger boss to whom he is answerable. The chain looks continuous, not discrete. And who, precisely, is a capitalist? Everybody who owns a £1 unit trust; or £100 worth of shares; or a shop? Where are the natural breaks in this distribution?

These arguments have been sketched, but not fully developed, for four main reasons. First, it seems that our subjective image of society is based on a model, projected by academics and by the media, that may be objectively very unsound. In subscribing to the notion of a 'middle class' and a 'working class' we may all be victims of the biggest example of collective self-deception since the episode of the emperor's clothes.

Second, by hanging so much of our research on such theories as the 'embourgeoisement of the working class' or on defining in close detail the characteristics of 'the middle class' we may be neglecting much more fruitful fields. For example, how discrete *is* the ordering on the specified variables; what characteristic 'paths' exist across them; what is the incidence of inter-generational movement up and down each of the scales; do some families have a high standard deviation in their scores across the scales and some a low; and what other qualities characterise high/low standard deviation families? The list of questions is endless. Some of them have, of course, been quite fully researched. Others have not – because the notion of a three-class society does not lead one to think about them. It seems, as a general principle, that the degree of insight obtained in any field of scientific enquiry may depend heavily on the validity of the categorisation scheme adopted. If our understanding of society appears not to match up to the effort put into researching it, might the cause lie in our use of a classificatory framework which is, to say the least, inadequately verified in terms of hard data (as opposed to theory and dogma)?

Third, might it not be socially reprehensible and perhaps arrogant for one set of people (writers and commentators) to categorise others, and thus to foster self-categorisation; all the more so of course if they use a doubtful and poorly verified categorisation scheme. Who precisely are 'the workers' to whom all economic ills can be ascribed? Anyone who works (and very few do not)? Not really. Anyone who works mainly with his or her hands? The whole idea is socially divisive, insulting and reflects an uncritical and stereotyped view of society.

Fourth, the analysis highlights those variables on which the values *do* fall relatively discretely. There is no doubt that 3(iv) and 3(v) are discrete variables. But trade union membership need not be apparent to one's friends so it carries no real divisive consequence for the individual (unless he or she wants it to). In any case one can normally vary one's position on this variable. Being salaried carries with it other implications concerning security of tenure, status at work and so on. The discrete difference in the mode of paying for labour is regrettable but could easily be remedied (the Giro system could be used for all payments for labour if the recipient had no bank account). The rather pointless distinction between 'staff' and 'payroll' need not last indefinitely.

But variable 4(i) is a vastly different matter. The households of this country are discretely ordered on the scale. A natural break occurs between house-owners and non-house-owners. For most people it is difficult to move 'up' across this break. As one respondent said in a recent survey: '. . . the amount required for a deposit is growing faster than I can save.'[16] And property ownership carries with it a host of other advantages, social, financial and psychological.[17] In short, the tenure division stands out in bold relief as the last great divisive variable. If the tenure differences were removed, or even made less obvious and far-reaching, the weaknesses of our present stereotyped perception of 'classes' would be more clearly apparent. This assertion constitutes the second argument against the current operation of the housing system. Its power to perpetuate 'demarcation lines' between people persists at a time when, in most other respects, the lines are weakening or have disappeared.

THE THIRD ARGUMENT: THE SYSTEM REDISTRIBUTES WEALTH UPWARDS

There has been a great deal of discussion, especially since the publication of *The Poor and the Poorest*[18] concerning the stability over time of the distribution of income and wealth in Britain. This study found that nearly 2 million people were living below the government's own 'poverty line' (National Assistance level) and that the situation had worsened since the early 1950s.[19] The main issue, whether inequalities have been reduced or have increased, is an extremely complex one. It is more emotive, more sensitive to changes in definition, and more prone to measurement problems than almost any other in social science.

Nevertheless, there seems to be some kind of consensus that, by and large, both income and wealth inequalities have remained remarkably persistent, at least since the turn of the century. As Titmuss[20] has shown, income is not simply a matter of wage or salary levels. There are a whole range of 'fringe' benefits, for example expenses, assistance with house purchase, subsidised cars, educational benefits, ability to purchase the services of an accountant and so on, to which richer people have more ready access than the poor. As he concludes: 'Ancient inequalities have assumed new and more subtle forms . . .'[21] Similarly, Bottomore observes:

> We must conclude that the general advance in the material conditions of the British working class, in recent decades, has been due over-

7a 'I think living in Ringmer is very nice because . . . you can go out into the countryside and Dad can wash his car' (see page 162). Of the 'newcomer' households interviewed, 90% had some form of private transport (see page 118).

7b '. . . bleak, cold and out of character with a village . . .' (see page 151).

7c A new estate adjoining the Green on an area that was formerly well wooded. A thin inadequate screen has been left. '. . . it seems to be a fact of life that developers like trees the way postmen like dogs' (see page 187).

8a Back view of the shopping centre from the Green. The village pub is dwarfed and the Downs no longer visible.

8b The symbols of change – old building, new shop front; tile-hanging and television aerial; bicycle and perambulator; the 'established' and the 'newcomer'. Cf. Plate 4a.

whelmingly to the rapid growth of national income, which has also
made possible the expansion of the social services, and not to any radical
redistribution of wealth or income between classes.[22]

In case these two commentators should be thought unduly biased, a Department of Employment and Productivity report of 1969 also commented on
the remarkable stability of manual wage distributions, measured by deciles,
over the past 100 years.[23]

Clearly, certain factors are working in favour of reducing inequalities. The
income tax system, for example, is reputed to be progressive in its impact.
There is, however, increasing doubt about this. Taken in conjunction with
means-tested benefits, its effect is frequently the reverse. Relatively small
wage increases can mean not only increased tax but also the loss of certain
income related benefits (for example Family Income Supplement) so that the
marginal rate of taxation becomes higher than the surtax rate. This recently
discovered phenomenon is known as the 'poverty trap'.[24] Indeed a recent
study has shown that during the 1960s tax rates rose far faster on low incomes
than high, that the net real income of an average wage earner has risen far
less than gross wages have risen and that larger families have suffered more
from changes in the income tax system than smaller.[25]

Against the apparently partly illusory downward redistributive effects of
fiscal policies must be set a number of influences which tend to lead to an
upward redistributive effect over time. These include marriage, assuming that
mating is not random but tends to occur between pairs relatively close on
the income scale, the well-known tendency of money to make money (the
first million is the most difficult to make), the environmental and educational
advantages inherent in a wealthy home, and the 'fringe' benefits listed above.
But most relevantly for this chapter, and perhaps most importantly overall,
one suspects that powerful upward redistributions of wealth flow from the
ownership of a house.

From personal knowledge, the average cost of a three-bedroomed semi-
detached house in Ringmer rose as follows:

1966	£4,500
1968	£5,500
1970	£6,500
1971 (Dec)	£8,500
1972 (Dec)	£11,500[26]

Virtually all home-owners in Ringmer, that is, those who were relatively
better off to start with, have got £5000 richer in the past two years; some have
got richer still. One doubts whether many local authority tenants have saved
£5000 over the same period. Nationally, the growth in house values has far
outstripped income rises in the past three years[27] and the inflation of values
in the south-east has meant that a first purchaser, unless he has capital, needs
an income well above the national average to buy an average 'semi'. This
situation has a number of alarming side effects. Many teachers for example,
have declined to take up jobs in the region because they cannot afford to buy

a house. But the issue is raised now largely in relation to the question of wealth distribution.

It is often argued that appreciation in the value of one's house is meaningless since, having sold, one needs to buy again in the same market. Both Willis[28] and Harrington[29] have shown the weakness of this argument. People often choose to move from the south-east to some less expensive part of the country especially if, as at present, they could treat themselves to a new Aston Martin with the resultant profit. In any case the capital gain is realised eventually, perhaps by the children on the death of the parents.

The crucial point has been made by Corry: 'If property prices rise more than in proportion (to incomes) then, given the unequal distribution of property ownership, there will be an increase in the degree of income and wealth inequality',[30] and: 'The distribution of wealth, unless offsetting forces are put in motion, must move secularly in favour of the owners of property.'[31]

Willis has provided a plausible example (see Figure 14.2) based on a set of realistic assumptions.[32] The purchase of a house for £4208 in 1972 would, if one 'trades up' three times, lead to the ownership of a house worth over £45,000 21 years later. In each trade-up a mortgage of two and a half times income is assumed. At present about half the population can take this route to family wealth and half cannot. One would have to be very frugal as a tenant with increasing rent outgoings to save over £40,000 in 21 years.

As if this were not sufficiently inequitable, local authority improvement grant policies can add up to £1200 to the wealth of the relatively wealthy, that is, those with sufficient capital already to be able to buy and renovate an older house and to match the level of grant provided by the authority. One Ringmer resident, already well-off, has received at least two local authority grants to improve properties which she is not using and one of which she has sold. Examples of this sort of abuse by developers, large and small, are no doubt commonplace. The minister responsible maintained recently that abuses occur only in 'very exceptional cases'. It was left to a voluntary organisation to provide the evidence, which the department should have been able to obtain, to prove that abuses were, on the contrary, very common in London.[33]

But as Wishlade[34] has pointed out, the advantages of owning a house do not end with the capital gain. The house provides almost complete security of tenure and can be used as collateral for a loan. One can be sure that the mortgage repayments will constitute a declining proportion of income while for tenants rents are likely to increase at least proportionately with income. Owners have a disposable asset which they can sell at any time if they wish to move and buy elsewhere. Those with mortgages, the majority, benefit from valuable tax concessions on the interest payments. And apart from these tangible advantages there is the pride of ownership.

Small wonder that the official policy of both major political parties (and of course the building societies who stand to do ever-increasing business) is that we should become a property-owning democracy. This would be an admirable policy if it could be 100% achieved in the foreseeable future. Unfortunately such a situation would be unlikely before the turn of the century,

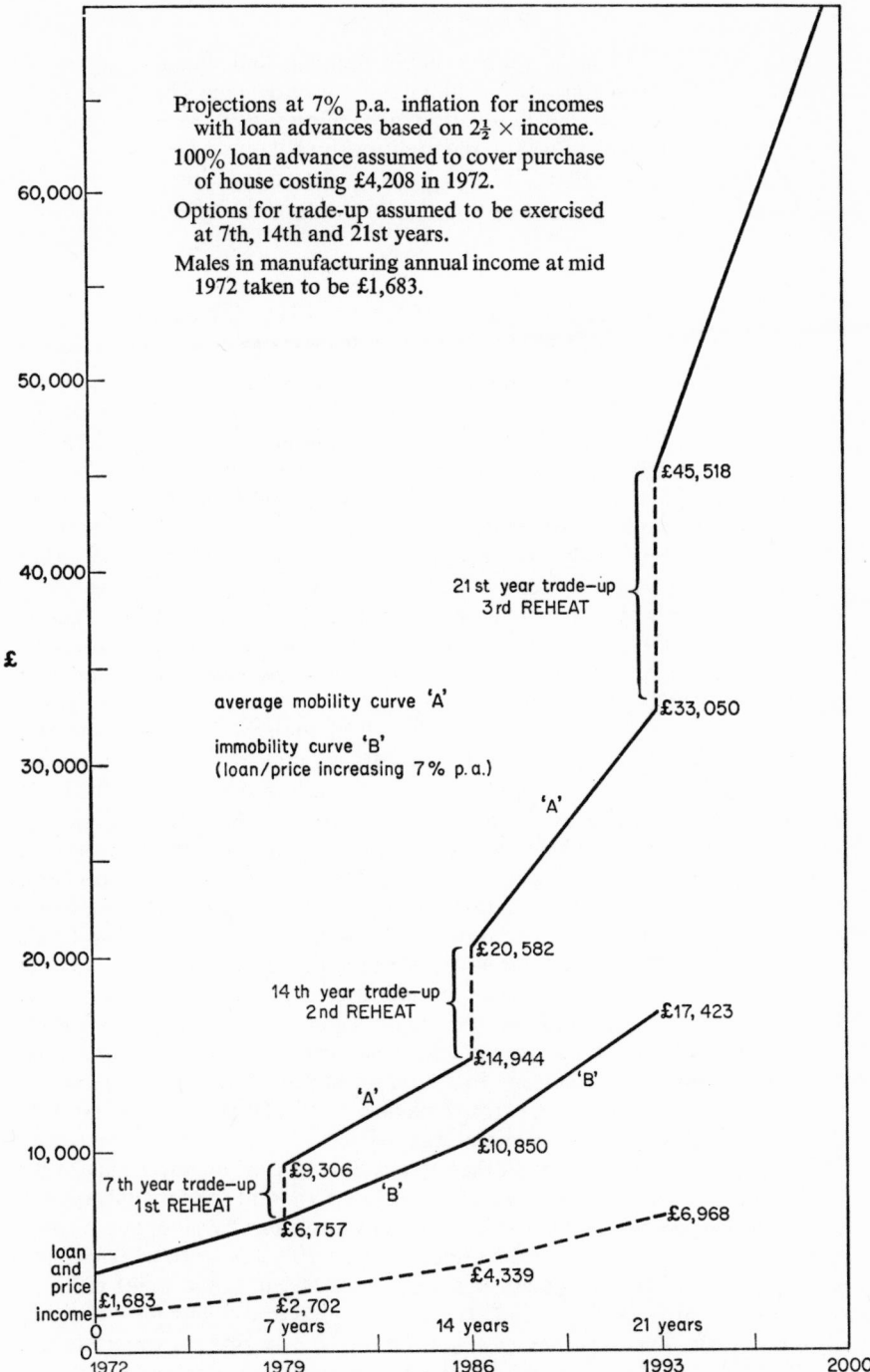

Fig. 14.2 Shelter's Prospect of House Price Inflation, 1972–2000.
Source: J. Willis, *The Social Consequences of House Price Inflation*, Shelter 1972.

if then. In the meantime the social, environmental and financial chips are stacked very heavily against tenants and in favour of owners. This gross social injustice to nearly half the population, which may well be an important factor in the persistence of wealth inequalities since it could be redistributing wealth upwards faster than the 'progressive' direct taxation system is redistributing it downwards, constitutes the third argument against the existing housing system.

THE FOURTH ARGUMENT: THE SYSTEM FAILS TO SATISFY NEED

This argument, like some of the others, can be substantiated at both the local and national scale. The local housing authority in which Ringmer falls has a waiting list for council housing of over 500 families and is building at the rate of about 60 units per year, which is insufficient to reduce the size of the list.[35] The rate of private building is also insufficient to satisfy all potential purchasers, although the recent drastic increase in house prices resulting from a heavy excess of demand over supply has had the effect of elevating prices to a level which few can afford. The local situation is thus in some sort of equilibrium, which apologists for market forces will no doubt say is a vindication of the system. The only problem is that the average price level now reached is beyond the resources of any first purchaser with an income below about £4000 per annum.

The shortage locally is being aggravated by at least two other factors. Evictions from 'tied' cottages in the county are running at a rate well in excess of 40 per year. This is the rate at which cases come to the notice of the local branch of the National Agricultural and Allied Workers Union.[36] Many more cases must occur where the evicted families are not union members. The chief causes of eviction occur where farmland is sold off for development, where a cottage is required for a domestic servant on a change of ownership, where redundancies occur, or where a farmer wishes to raise capital and sells a cottage, very often to a London businessman as a second home. In one notorious case a farm manager was evicted after over 20 years' service when the farm changed hands and the new owner wanted the house for his butler. In another case a man on a wage of about £80 per month was made redundant. He was offered the cottage in which he had lived at a purchase price which would have implied mortgage payments of £60 per month. He was unable to purchase at this price and was evicted.

The tied cottage system, and other associated 'service' tenancies, give very little security of tenure. Although many cottages are rent free, the farmer has a right to charge up to 50p per week. If he has not been charging, and if some dispute arises, he has only to threaten to collect 20 years or so of back payments at £26 per year to quell the tenant. This threat would be of dubious legality but that is not the point. It has been used and it has produced the required result. The same sanction can be invoked to prevent unionisation, to stifle complaints concerning conditions, or to induce workers to vote in a particular way. There is no doubt at all that these practices still occur. The system also perpetuates the extremely low wages in the industry, and, in all, constitutes an archaic and undesirable survival from an obsolete socio-economic structure.

Ageing property in nearby urban areas adds to local housing shortage. A recent survey in Lewes by the public health department revealed that between 500 and 600 houses, over one-tenth of the total stock, were to varying degrees substandard and over 200 of them were unfit for human habitation.[37] Thus in addition to those actually homeless, those whose tenure situation is highly precarious, and those who have found they cannot afford to live in the area at all although offered a job here, there is another sizeable minority who are living in conditions that are statutorily unfit for people. A great deal of other evidence concerning the local housing shortage could be offered, especially in relation to Brighton, but there would be little point. The existence of an acute shortage cannot reasonably be denied.

At the national level the evidence is, again, indisputable. There are those who argue that since in 1970 there was a stock of 18·6 million dwellings and a total of 18·3 million households there is therefore an overall housing surplus.[38] But, as many authors have pointed out, there is not just one housing market; there are several. And some of them, for example owner-occupancy and local authority tenancy, have entry conditions that many cannot meet. So certain sectors of the system show clear imbalances. There are also persistent regional imbalances stemming from the partial failure of successive governments to achieve a good balance between the supply of jobs and of complementary social capital, including housing, in the various regions. This is, admittedly, an extremely difficult task; the degree of enthusiasm and competence with which it is tackled has varied visibly over the years.

But perhaps the strongest refutation of the 'surplus' argument lies in the proportion of the total stock which is substandard and should be renewed. Buchanan estimated, on the basis of statutorily defined standards and official statistics, that in 1967 4·6 million dwellings could have been classified as un-inhabitable on grounds of either condition or the provision of basic amenities (hot water, inside toilet and bath).[39] This is one quarter of the total stock. One can hardly argue that a shortage does not exist when a quarter of the population live in conditions defined in law as unsatisfactory.

The human consequences of these figures have been fully documented elsewhere and the casualties of the housing system have spoken for themselves:[40]

> 'I have rats, bugs, everything. It's very damp. That's why I send the kids away from here.'

> 'All the bedrooms are leaking and the chairs have gone rotten.'

> 'I had to move my bed out of the bedroom because of the mice.'

> 'There's nowhere for the children to play . . . so they're getting on my nerves. So I row with my husband, then I take it out on the kids.'

> 'Once I just went out the front and when I came back in the baby was playing with a rat in the pram.'

'I had another little girl but the ceiling fell on her and she died.'

'I've always sympathised with the homeless but I never knew . . .'

Another report[41] challenges the official view that the 'homeless' can be defined as those in emergency accommodation as specified in Part III of the 1948 National Assistance Act. This would give a total of about 27,000 'homeless'. But this excludes thousands who cannot get into such accommodation because nearly all local authorities are defaulting on their statutory duty to provide sufficient of it.[42] It excludes families forced to live with in-laws or friends, families in caravans, families sleeping in cars and tents, families living at up to six people to a room, and single people 'sleeping rough' in all sorts of adverse situations. And it excludes the millions of people living in statutorily 'unfit' housing.

The report advances a definition of homelessness much more in accord with social expectations in the latter decades of the twentieth century: '. . . any family is actually homeless if it is split up because the home is too small, or if it is living in housing conditions so unfit or overcrowded that it cannot lead a civilised family life . . .'[43] Under this definition there could be no argument; *the number of homeless runs into millions*. To reject the contention that there is a housing shortage of crisis proportions is, quite simply, to reject the definition offered. It would be interesting to hear the arguments for rejecting this definition. The housing shortage constitutes the fourth argument against the current system.

HOUSING DEMAND OR HOUSING NEED?

The four arguments against the present housing system, all of them exemplifiable in Ringmer but all of them also operative elsewhere, lead to the most fundamental question. On what basis should housing be available? Is the requirement for adequate housing analogous to the *demand* for a substitutable and non-essential commodity, such as apples or a television set? If so, in a largely capitalist system, it seems inevitable that market mechanisms will operate to adjust the level of supply. Or is adequate housing an essential and non-substitutable *need*? If so, the degree to which market forces operate in the system must be closely constrained and public intervention must ensure that any shortfall in provision is quickly rectified. The degree of intervention must be adjusted in accordance with the efficiency of the system in meeting need.

In view of the great mass of evidence connecting housing conditions with other aspects of well-being, mental, physical and psychological, it can be argued that adequate housing is a human need, not an economic demand. It is surely similar in nature to the needs for education to a certain minimum level and for medical treatment. Most countries, including Britain, accept that a near-100% level of public intervention and subsidy is necessary in these two vital respects. We cannot have people waiting till they have saved up the money before having an appendix out. Nor, on grounds of national efficiency alone, could we afford to educate only those who can pay the economic cost of their schooling. But the housing system in Britain is left with a very large market component in the face of all the consequent demonstrable short comings.

The insistence that housing is a need echoes the view of many other writers. For example, Smith maintained:

> Our present use of existing housing agencies . . . is obviously not providing sufficient and appropriate housing where it is most needed. .... The housing needs of the community and finding the best ways of meeting them should be the starting point for this examination rather than preconceived ideas based on the present system.[44]

Similarly Howes in a PEP broadsheet (not a likely source for over-radical thinking):

> 'In Britain, housing policy has been confused by indecision as to whether the provision of houses should be regarded as a social service or as a commercial operation.'[45]

The main issue could hardly be more succinctly stated. The central paradox is this: while everybody seems to agree that decent housing is a social need, many people seem to acquiesce in the present market domination of the system. It is commonplace to talk of 'the housing market'. We long ago discarded the concept of the 'health market' or the 'education market'. Some economists, in particular, see the problem in quite the wrong terms:

> The one plea I make is that analysis should be based on fact, but not facts assembled to fit preconceptions or prejudice. This same plea should apply to all discussion in the housing field – more reliance on economics and less emotional involvement is a good recipe for unbiased investigation and sound policy formulation.[46]

And the same author's apparent panacea for the problem: '. . . better economic analysis and more of it.'[47] One hardly knows where to begin. This author apparently feels that 'facts' *can* be assembled objectively in social science, which is naïve; that emotional involvement is out of place, which, in the face of such shocking malfunctioning of the system, seems inhuman; and that the issues are economic not political, which is surely a fundamental misconception. The whole argument is about the *basis* on which housing resources are distributed among a population exhibiting differing abilities to pay. This is politics. To allow the discussion to be dominated by so-called 'objective' economic models is a nonsense. If, that is, one accepts that housing is a social need and not an economic demand. It seems massively illogical to call it one thing and treat it as the other.

THE FUTURE

What suggestions for future policy can one make on the basis of this serious questioning of the present system? The issues are technically very complex and emotionally very loaded. In a situation of majority owner-occupancy how, in political terms, might reforms be achieved? Perhaps by an appeal to morality and conscience. The homeless and badly housed constitute a not very vocal minority in: '. . . a society that pretends to prosperity while it countenances poverty; that professes opportunity while it permits deprivation.'[48] The minority stare at us from Shelter posters; but because of the situation outlined in the first argument in this chapter few people see the problem at first hand.

Or a political argument could be made in terms of national efficiency; similar to the argument made a century ago in favour of state-run education (see Chapter 1) or by the 1909 Report of the Royal Commission on the Poor Laws.[49] Most, if not all, social workers see the close relationship between the damp, dilapidated, overcrowded home and the poor health record, between the insecure tenancy and the neuroses, and between the inflated 'economic' rent and the resentment that shows itself in strong support for a necessary pay claim. As Octavia Hill pointed out: 'You cannot deal with people and their homes separately.' Multiplied up several million times these circumstances constitute an unknown, but enormous, cost to the economy. The departmental thinking and carefully prescribed limits of responsibility inherent in modern bureaucracy serve as a sop to conscience and as an excuse for inaction. Nobody in contemporary politics seems big enough to say 'the buck stops here'. But, on all logical and common-sense grounds, a relationship *must* exist between decent housing and national efficiency. It should be possible to show that the housing system is spatially, socially, and financially divisive; that it is failing to meet the level of need; and that the consequences impair not only levels of happiness *but also levels of economic efficiency*. After all, anyone can see that, in principle, preventive social medicine is better than picking up the pieces via the social security services. And it should be feasible to put these arguments together in a form appropriate for the electorate and to combine them with the powerful appeal on the grounds of conscience.

But the arguments would have to be clearly projected because the mainspring for reform would need to be greatly increased public intervention in the housing system, a consequent interference with property, and an overall increase in the resources allocated to housing at the expense of some other item of government expenditure. Any one, or combination, of a number of measures would be necessary. These might include development land being taken into public ownership (the last chapter showed how powerfully ownership influenced the outcome); a levy on betterment; increasing public ownership in the privately rented sector,[50] a tax on under-occupancy of existing accommodation; a stronger and more initiatory role for development control authorities so as to increase the degree of public answerability in the development process; the rationalisation of the building industry (which currently includes a large number of very small firms); the abolition of archaic forms of tenancy; and a reduction in the 'pampering of the owner-occupier'.[51] Obviously some of these would need great political skill to implement. Peels, Lloyd Georges and Attlees seem in short supply; or perhaps today's politicians, in the new mass media situation, have traded all sense of mission for the personality cult or, even more alarmingly, have come to believe in their own mass consumption rhetoric.

It is pointless to treat the symptoms (with legislation concerning land hoarding and 'fair rents' for example) and to ignore the disease. The disease is the over-prominence of market forces in a vital and sensitive area of social need. The philosophy must be '. . . to each according to his needs'. The trouble with allowing the housing market to stand on its own two feet is that too many people are standing on other people's feet. One can hardly blame some of the feet-tramplers. They are, by nature, good at it and anyway the system offers generous collusion. One final example may drive home the point. A house reserved by a purchaser in Swindon in September 1971 for £9740 was finally offered to him in November 1972 for £18,980 plus a possible addition for Value Added Tax. The price 'freeze' in operation at the time did not include land and property deals. The managing director of the development company (whose profits had doubled in the past year) was quoted as saying: 'I am sure our shareholders would not think the profit was scandalous.'[52] The candour is admirable; the shareholders hardly culpable; but the system that invites them to invest in the provision of a social need is lamentable.

Epilogue – The Quiet Revolution

A social revolution may be said to occur when radical and relatively rapid changes take place in social structures, living standards, access to opportunities and in the bases upon which authority and privilege are conferred and exercised. Changes of this nature have occurred in Ringmer, quietly but surely, primarily since the inter-war period and most of all in the last decade. The changes in social structure and living standards have been documented and it is clear that the information media, the vote, education and health care, personal mobility and a number of other factors have greatly increased the access to opportunities for personal advancement and fulfilment, especially over the last few decades.

But changes in the bases of *authority*, or power to influence the life situation of others, and of *privilege*, or access to advantages denied to others, have not been discussed. Both are probably a necessary part of any organised society. What distinguishes different societies, or a given society at different points in time, is the mechanisms by which these benefits are conferred and enjoyed. Two obvious possibilities are inheritance and democratic mandate. A third possibility exists; expert operation within a system which is nominally answerable to the electorate but which, in practice, is oligarchic or even autocratic in nature. This may result from the complexity of the decisions involved and the very limited technical knowledge of elected representatives. (During the course of this study it was incidentally discovered that no member of a near-by local authority planning committee was aware of the existence of the Strategic Plan for the South-East; the key policy document upon which the region's growth is reputedly based. This would seem to imply a rather worrying degree of dependence on the advice of non-elected permanent officials.) Or the democratic nature of decision-making may be impaired by the genuine difficulty of presenting a meaningful choice to the electorate in advance. Or the public may be apathetic towards the issue until it is too late to do much about it. The execution of a project like Concorde seems to fit into this last category.

In mid-Victorian Ringmer, as in the nation as a whole, a small, identifiable group enjoyed considerable authority and privilege; political, economic, social and juridical. They employed labour, set wages, owned and developed property, administered the law, dispensed charity and led opinion. Even between the wars the power of this group had only partially disappeared. A few landowners could (and fortunately did) create work. The 'gentry' dominated social life and village occasions, they had political influence locally and they owned many of the cottages. They sought to keep public health expenditure to a minimum and were baffled by the idea that some cottages might be unfit for habitation. Every summer they listened resplendently, just a few miles away, to international opera in the unique setting of a large country house. Meanwhile some of the less privileged lived in century-old

218

hovels, worked long hours, drew water laboriously from wells and kept quiet about any radical political views they might hold. It was the way of the time. Even after the war some members of the local squirearchy were uncertain about the benefits of the welfare state (the extract is from a letter setting out the conditions upon which help could be given from a private charity in the village):

> We are beginning the idea of the Welfare State. Its danger is that people will not be grateful for what they get, and that this practice will spread to include good works done by others without thanks, resulting in the disappearance of gratitude.
>
> When you come to collect your share each half-year you say 'thank you'.[1]

The old expectations of deference towards authority based on wealth, land and connection die hard in some cases, not altogether surprisingly.

It might be assumed in the 1970s, after nearly half a century of democracy in the form of universal suffrage, that authority and privilege, especially where the lives of others are vitally concerned, would be conferred by purely democratic processes and that the holders would be answerable to the public, either at an election or in some other way. In many respects the study of Ringmer shows that this assumption is correct. The hiatus of the 'super-imposed' growth phase, with its influx of articulate ex-urban newcomers, has loosened old structures of power and influence. National planning and public health legislation, and county-wide policies, have fashioned the growth of jobs, and of social and transport facilities. The local experience reflects the national more closely than ever; and the arbiters of both national and local conditions have to face the electors at regular intervals to have their powers over others confirmed or cancelled. And all the time more and more people are finding that political expression need not be confined to the ballot box; one can vote with one's feet at work, take to the streets, indulge in 'community action', and boycott the products of companies seen to be acting anti-socially.

Despite all this, important pockets of non-democratic authority and privilege remain. Land-ownership at the local level, as at the national, is still relatively concentrated and 'tied' and 'service' tenancies continue. The system of school managers and governors is non-elective, exhibits some curious features and seems to take the British cult of the amateur altogether too far. But perhaps the main lesson of the Ringmer study, which has in effect been a study of a century of emancipation from late-feudalism, is that the most striking contemporary example of anachronistic authority and privilege is provided by the housing system, and private property development in particular. It is here that the danger inherent in all capitalist economies, that profits will come before people, is most pervasively at work. It is here that the democratic process seems to be most comprehensively and damagingly confounded; and perhaps for all three of the reasons set out previously.

Constrained, but not too uncomfortably, by the planning machinery, the developer can double prices during a price freeze, serve only the most profitable areas of need, influence the social and age balance of whole villages and suburbs, perpetuate social divisions in patterns of bricks and mortar and produce, as in Ringmer, long-standing monuments to architectural mediocrity. When the criticism wells up, as it did quite spontaneously in this survey, he will be off developing the next estate. And all the time the soaring land prices hinder the efforts of public agencies to acquire sites and build more housing for those who, regardless of their needs, have been priced out.

This is not to blame all individual developers. Some are very aware of the social implications of their actions (and two companies showed this by helping to finance this research). Developers operate quite legally (mostly) in a very complex and technical field and perhaps few of them see the essential connection between their free market in land and the free market of others in misery; between the mounting profits and the mounting local authority waiting lists; between the prestige development and the child playing with a rat in his pram. They are not paid to see these connections. But something is terribly wrong when developers have the licence to produce villages as socially unbalanced and aesthetically insensitive as Ringmer and when, to take an extreme case, they can profit from millions of square feet of empty office space in London when countless men, women and children are homeless. So long as abuses such as these are possible, the quiet revolution is not yet complete.

Notes and References

Prologue

1. Population Census; various County Reports for Sussex.
2. Figures suggested by the County Planning Office on the basis of land already allocated for development.
3. T. Hardy, *The Mayor of Casterbridge* (1886), Macmillan Papermac, 1968, pp. 65–6.
4. See various recent regional plans for the south-east and especially M.H.L.G., *Strategic Plan for the South East*, H.M.S.O., 1970.
5. See Chapter 13 for an outline of these procedures.

Chapter 1

1. See almost any economic history textbook; the main source of contention is not whether real incomes have gone up but rather whether income inequalities have been reduced.
2. D. S. Landes in the *Cambridge Economic History of Europe*, Vol. VI, Cambridge U.P., 1965, p. 353 note.
3. See the examples of clerical salaries quoted in G. Best, *Mid-Victorian Britain*, Weidenfeld and Nicolson, 1971, p. 89.
4. This section, and various others in the chapter, draw heavily upon Best's readable and well-documented study (see previous note).
5. *ibid.*, p. 207.
6. *ibid.*, p. 117.
7. *ibid.*, p. 209.
8. See J. S. Maclure *Educational Documents, England and Wales 1816–1967*, 2nd edition, Chapman and Hall, 1968.
9. *ibid.*, p. 104.
10. R. L. Archer, *Secondary Education in the Nineteenth Century*, Cambridge U.P., 1921, p. 306.
11. *ibid.*, p. 318.
12. Report of the Committee of the Secondary Schools Examinations Council on the Curriculum and Examinations in Secondary Schools, H.M.S.O., 1943, p. 14.
13. J. G. Fitch, *Lectures on Teaching*, Cambridge U.P., 1881, p. 45.
14. P. Nunn, *Education: its Data and First Principles*, Arnold, 1922, p. 5.
15. Committee on Higher Education, *Higher Education*, H.M.S.O., 1963 (The 'Robbins Report').
16. Statistical Supplement to the 7th Annual UCCA Report, 1968/69.
17. See D. Butler and J. Freeman, *British Political Facts, 1900–1967*, Macmillan, 1968.
18. See D. C. Marsh, *The Changing Social Structure of England and Wales, 1871–1961*, Routledge, revised edition 1965, p. 182.

19. There are the 'man bites dog' definitions; or see D. A. N. Jones in *The Press We Deserve*, ed. R. Boston, Routledge, 1970.

20. See R. Williams, *The Long Revolution*, Chatto and Windus, 1961, upon which much of the discussion in this section is based.

21. W. A. Belson, *The Impact of Television*, Crosby Lockwood, 1967.

22. See various *Annual Abstracts of Statistics*, H.M.S.O.

23. R. Fletcher, *The Family and Marriage*, Penguin, 1962.

24. See the *Economist*, 20th July 1844, p. 1011.

25. T. C. Barker and M. Robbins, *A History of London Transport*, Vol. I, Allen and Unwin, 1963, p. 216.

26. J. R. Kellett, *The Impact of Railways on Victorian Cities*, Routledge, 1969, p. 95.

27. See, for example, Chapters 3, 4 and 5 in *Greater London*, eds. J. T. Coppock and H. C. Prince, Faber, 1964.

28. C. Buchanan, *Traffic in Towns*, H.M.S.O., 1963.

29. See any recent *Family Expenditure Survey* (published by H.M.S.O.).

30. See Best (note 3 above), p. 72.

31. R. M. Titmuss, *Income Distribution and Social Change*, Allen and Unwin, 1962.

32. See W. Ashworth, *The Genesis of Modern British Town Planning*, Routledge, 1954, for a useful review of legislation.

33. C. Booth, *In Darkest London and the Way Out*, Salvation Army, 1890.

34. B. Abel-Smith and P. Townsend, *The Poor and the Poorest*, Bell, 1965, p. 39.

35. See T. C. Barker *et al.*, *Our Changing Fare*, MacGibbon and Kee, 1966, upon which this dietary discussion is based.

36. See Booth (note 33 above).

Chapter 2

1. H. J. E. Peake, *The English Village: The Origin and Decay of its Community*, Benn, 1922.

2. *ibid.*, p. 214.

3. *ibid.*, p. 205.

4. F. M. L. Thompson, *English Landed Society in the Nineteenth Century*, Routledge, 1963.

5. 1871 Census, Enumerators' Returns for Ringmer.

6. See various Census County Reports for East Sussex.

7. A. C. Day, *Glimpses of Rural Life in Sussex During the Last Hundred Years*, 'The Countryman', *c.* 1929 (the recollections in this book relate mostly to Hadlow Down, a village about 10 miles from Ringmer).

8. *ibid.*, p. 52.

9. *ibid.*, p. 51.

10. See note 5.

11. Ringmer Parish Marriage Register.

12. See Day (note 7 above), pp. 13–14.

13. See Day (note 7 above), pp. 16–17.

14. J. Constable, unpublished diary entry 14th July 1851. The diary is a fragmentary but invaluable source. It is kept in the East Sussex County Record Office.

15. R. V. Kyrke, *History of East Sussex Police, 1840–1967*, duplicated, 1969, p. 53. This is another invaluable source of information available in the East Sussex C.R.O.

16. *ibid.*, p. 97.

17. *Sussex Express*, 23rd November 1869.

18. *Return of Owners of Land, 1873*, H.M.S.O., 1875, Vol. II.

19. *Valuation List for Ringmer*, 1867.

20. Various Census County Reports for East Sussex.

21. See H. E. Bracey, *People and the Countryside*, Routledge, 1970, Chapter 6.

22. *ibid.*, p. 89.

23. See also C. Arnold-Baker, *The New Law and Practice of Parish Administration*, Routledge, 1968, for a full review of parochial powers.

24. See, for example, T. Mackay, *History of the English Poor Law*, King, 1899.

25. See Best (see note 3 of Chapter 1), pp. 35–54, for a review of the complications arising from the tangled situation in mid-Victorian local government.

26. Chailey Union, Ringmer Parish, *Collectors' Monthly Statements*, 1862.

27. Chailey Union, *Board of Guardians' Minutes*, March 1866.

28. Best (see note 3 of Chapter 1), pp. 133–48.

29. *ibid.*, p. 142.

30. *Sussex Express*, 6th October 1866.

31. Ringmer Voluntary Rate Books (available in East Sussex C.R.O.).

32. See various *Reports of Visitors*, 1851–3 (in East Sussex C.R.O.).

33. See various committal orders (in East Sussex C.R.O.).

34. Various diary entries for 1825 and 1828.

35. Various entries for 1851.

36. *Sussex Express*, 29th January 1867.

37. Most of the following details were obtained from a current trustee.

38. See Day (note 7 above), p. 44.

39. *Sussex Express*, 11th June 1867.

40. *ibid.*, 13th June 1968.

41. *ibid.*, 12th June 1866.

42. See Day (note 7 above).

43. *ibid.*, p. 14.

44. *ibid.*, p. 47.

45. *ibid.*, p. 8.

46. Minutes of the School Board for Ringmer Parish (in East Sussex C.R.O.), 6th and 11th January 1876, and subsequent meetings.

47. See Kyrke (note 15 above), pp. 58–9.

48. *ibid.*, p. 61.

49. *ibid.*, p. 54.

50. *ibid.*, p. 104.

51. *Sussex Express*, 21st March 1868.

52. *ibid.*, 11th January 1868.

53. *ibid.*, 7th April 1866.

54. From an interview with Miss Martin (W. F. Martin's daughter).
55. See Constable (note 14 above), various entries.
56. See Kyrke (note 15 above), p. 62.
57. See Day (note 7 above), p. 34.
58. M. A. Lower, *History of Sussex*, Vol. II, Smith, 1870, p. 117.
59. *Sussex Express*, 21st January 1865.
60. *ibid.*, 9th September 1865.
61. *ibid.*, 16th September 1865.
62. *ibid.*, 29th August 1866.
63. *ibid.*, 24th June 1865.
64. *ibid.*, 16th June 1868.
65. *ibid.*, 21st March 1868.
66. *ibid.*, 6th June 1865.
67. *ibid.*, various entries during the late 1860s.
68. See note 54.
69. *ibid.*
70. *Sussex Express*, 1st June 1869.
71. See J. A. Banks, *Prosperity and Parenthood*, Routledge, 1954, for a thorough discussion of Victorian family life.
72. 1871 Census Enumerators' Returns for Ringmer. See also Banks, *ibid.*, Chapter V, for national data.
73. See Day (note 7 above), pp. 22–4.
74. See note 54.
75. See Constable (note 14 above), entry 3rd August 1851.

Chapter 3

1. G. Bourne, *Change in the Village*, Duckworth, 1912.
2. *ibid.*, p. 78.
3. *ibid.*, p. 86.
4. *ibid.*, p. 137.
5. *ibid.*, p. 198.
6. Peake (see note 1 of Chapter 2), p. 219.
7. *Sussex Express*, 18th April 1915.
8. 1921 Census, East Sussex County Report.
9. 1921 Census, unpublished material.
10. Ringmer Parish Marriage Register.
11. 1931 Census, East Sussex County Report.
12. *ibid.*
13. Miscellaneous Parish records.
14. C. Arnold Baker (see note 23 of Chapter 2), p. 5.
15. Letter dated 23rd May 1928 in Parish miscellaneous documents.
16. Various Parish Council minute books and accounts.
17. See, for example, M. Bruce, *The Coming of the Welfare State*, Batsford, 1961.

18. *ibid.*, 4th edition, 1968, p. 240.
19. Lewes Union Board of Guardians minutes, 3rd October 1924.
20. *ibid.*, 13th February 1925.
21. In the course of an interview.
22. Bruce (see note 18), p. 245.
23. *ibid.*, p. 254.
24. *ibid.*, p. 260.
25. J. J. Clarke, *The Local Government of the United Kingdom*, 12th edition, Pitman, 1939, p. 584.
26. Information given by one of them.
27. All records of this enquiry have unfortunately been lost.
28. Annual Report of the Chailey R.D.C. Medical Officer of Health, 1934.
29. *ibid.*
30. Ringmer School log books.
31. Report dated 1st June 1928.
32. As note 30, 19th October 1926.
33. 1921 Census, unpublished material.
34. As note 28.

Chapter 4

1. See Bruce (note 17 of Chapter 3), Chapter 7.
2. See Chapter 13 for an outline of this process.
3. The details set out in this paragraph come from the Ringmer 'War Book', at least one copy of which has fortunately survived.
4. See R. E. Pahl, *Patterns of Urban Life*, Longmans, 1970, p. 102.
5. Information from G. Self, then headmaster.
6. County Welfare Officer, *Survey and Report for the Period October 1944 to December 1945*, East Sussex County Council, 1946.
7. Annual Report of the Chailey R.D.C. Medical Officer of Health, 1945, pp. 12–13.
8. Chailey R.D.C. records.
9. *ibid.*
10. The interviews, which each lasted over one hour, were carried out by a small team of fully experienced professional interviewers. The interview form was appropriately piloted.
11. 1971 Census, County Report, Sussex, Part I.
12. Ringmer Parish Marriage Register.
13. Annual Report of the Chailey R.D.C. Medical Officer of Health, 1971, pp. 2–3.
14. Hants C.C., *Village Life in Hampshire*, 1966, p. 10.
15. Ringmer P.C. Chairman's Report to the annual Parish Meeting, 1972.
16. See note 13, p. 13.
17. *ibid.*
18. Obtainable from the local education authority.

19. East Sussex Association for the Advancement of State Education, Survey of Primary School Managers, J. Jacobs, 1969.

20. From an authoritative but obviously undisclosable source.

21. See note 13, p. 10.

22. *ibid.*, p. 12.

Chapter 5

1. But see R. Blythe, *Akenfield*, Allen Lane, 1969, which deals (quite beautifully) with about 50 years of change in a Suffolk village through the eyes of various inhabitants.

2. 1871 Census Enumerators' Returns for Ringmer.

3. Especially in relation to the concept of alienation. See D. McLellan, *The Thought of Karl Marx*, Macmillan, 1971, pp. 105–21, for a brief introductory review. See also Bourne (note 1 of Chapter 3), pp. 76–84.

4. But, from first-hand experience, try to avoid writing a book at the same time.

5. Personal recollection of an elderly resident.

6. See note 19 of Chapter 1.

7. 'Status', like many words in social science, has a much defined 'technical' meaning as well as the meaning given to it in everyday speech. See the useful introductory review by J. Tunstall on social stratification (Unit 17 of the Open University foundation course, Understanding Society) which briefly discusses the seminal work of Max Weber. The word is used here in the sense in which most laymen would understand it.

8. See Chapter 3 for various other similar comments.

9. 1871 Census Enumerators' Returns for Ringmer.

10. See, for example, the minutes of Chailey R.D.C. meetings in this period.

11. Information from a builder/developer in a near-by town.

12. From personal knowledge of members.

13. See Bruce (note 18 of Chapter 3) for a readable account of the changes.

14. *ibid.*, p. 241.

15. See, for example, various issues of *Poverty*, the journal of the Child Poverty Action Group.

16. D.E.P., A National Minimum Wage; report of a government committee working party 1969. See also R. M. Titmuss, *Income Distribution and Social Change*, Allen and Unwin, 1962, for a thorough analysis of income inequalities. Also A. B. Atkinson, *Unequal Shares*, Allen Lane, 1972.

17. As in the case of 'status', it is recognised that a large body of literature exists in political science on the precise meaning of 'power' and the problems of measuring it; see R. A. Dahl, *Who Governs? Democracy and Power in an American City*, Yale U.P., 1961, and F. Hunter, *Community Power Structure: A Study of Decision Makers*, University of North Carolina Press, 1953. Political power is here used in the sense defined in the text.

18. See the quotation from Arnold-Baker (note 23 of Chapter 2) in Chapter 3.

19. See D. C. Thorns, The Changing System of Rural Stratification, *Sociologia Ruralis*, **8**, 1968, pp. 161–77 for a discussion of a number of issues dealt with in this chapter following the study of a group of villages in south Nottinghamshire.

Chapter 6

1. See Ashworth (note 32 of Chapter 1).
2. See Chapter 13 for a brief review of the planning process.
3. For the south-east region, see M.H.L.G., *The South-East Study*, 1964, S.E. Economic Planning Council, *Strategy for the South-East*, 1967 and M.H.L.G., *Strategic Plan for the South-East*, 1970 (The 'Burns Plan'), all published by H.M.S.O.
4. *Report of the Royal Commission on the Distribution of the Industrial Population*, H.M.S.O., 1940 (The 'Barlow Report').
5. P. Abercrombie, *County of London Plan*, 1943, and *Greater London Plan*, 1944, H.M.S.O.
6. See note 3.
7. See D. E. Keeble, Planning and South-East England, *Area*, 3 (2), 1971, 69–74, for a useful review of the three plans.
8. See note 3; the plan will subsequently be referred to in these notes as 'Burns'.
9. Burns, Studies I, Table 1.6.
10. *ibid.*, Studies I, Table 1.4.
11. *ibid.*, Plan, 2.51.
12. *ibid.*, Plan, 2.7.
13. *ibid.*, Plan, 2.9.
14. *ibid.*, Plan, 2.18.
15. *ibid.*, Plan, 2.12.
16. *ibid.*, Studies I, 2.49.
17. *ibid.*, Studies II, 4.13.
18. *ibid.*, Studies I, Table 1.21.
19. *ibid.*, Plan, 3.13.
20. *ibid.*, Studies II, 1.93.
21. *ibid.*, Plan, 3.14.
22. *ibid.*, Studies II, 1.65, and following paragraphs.
23. *ibid.*, Studies II, 1.22.
24. *ibid.*, Studies II, Figure 1.1.
25. *ibid.*, Studies II, 1.5.
26. *ibid.*, Studies II, 1.16.
27. *ibid.*, Plan, 3.17.
28. *ibid.*, Plan, 3.25.
29. *ibid.*, Studies II, 2.72.
30. *ibid.*, Plan, 3.22.
31. *ibid.*, Studies II, 2.107.
32. *ibid.*, Plan, 2.20.
33. *ibid.*, Plan, 2.23.
34. *ibid.*, Plan, Table 2.5.
35. *ibid.*, Plan, Table 7.1.
36. *ibid.*, Plan, 2.57.

37. *ibid.*, Studies I, 1.82.

38. *ibid.*, Plan, 4.3.

39. *ibid.*, Plan, 4.9.

40. *ibid.*, Plan, 6.36.

41. *ibid.*, Plan, 4.13.

42. *ibid.*, Plan, 10.19.

43. *ibid.*, Studies I, Figure 2.7.

44. *ibid.*, Studies I, Figure 4.5(a).

45. *ibid.*, Studies II, 2.76.

46. *ibid.*, Studies I, Figure 2.6(a).

47. *ibid.*, Studies I, Figure 6.8.

Chapter 7

1. For a selection of these, see R. E. Pahl, *Whose City?*, Longmans, 1970; also the same author's *Urbs in Rure*, L.S.E., 1965.

2. Hants C.C., *Village Life in Hampshire*, 1966.

3. Kent C.C., *Kent Development Plan, Quinquennial Review*, 1963.

4. Cambs. C.C., *Development Plan Review, Report of Survey*, 1968.

5. Suffolk Rural Community Council, *Suffolk–Some Social Trends*, 1969.

6. R. Crichton, *Commuters' Village*, David and Charles, 1964.

7. E. Radford, *The New Villagers*, Cass, 1970.

8. J. Connell, The Metropolitan Village: Spatial and Social Processes in Discontinuous Suburbs, in J. H. Johnson, *The Geography of Suburban Growth*, Wiley, 1974.

9. L. S. Jay *et al.*, Village Planning in East Sussex, *University of Pennsylvania Law Review*, 114.1, 1965, pp. 106–26.

10. See the discussion of this concept in R. E. Pahl, *Readings in Urban Sociology*, Pergamon, 1968, pp. 263–305.

11. This is not to decry the very real insights contained in several classic papers by L. Wirth, for example, Urbanism as a Way of Life, *American Journal of Sociology*, **44**, 1938, pp. 1–24.

12. See note 5.

13. See note 2.

14. See note 12 of Chapter 6.

15. This substantiates the general thesis developed by Pahl and others that 'choice' is becoming more significant than ever before as a basis for location – àt least for the more affluent or 'middle class'.

16. I am indebted to Libby Higgin, previously a Sussex University undergraduate, for this idea.

17. See any of a range of monographs as such communities, for example, W. M. Williams, *The Sociology of an English Village: Gosforth*, Routledge, 1956; I. Littlejohn, *The Sociology of a Cheviot Parish*, Routledge, 1963, and many others.

18. See J. W. B. Douglas, *The Home and the School*, Panther edition, 1967, p. 99.

19. From an analysis of the 1971 Ringmer Household Survey.

20. See R. E. Pahl, Education and Social Class in Commuter Villages, *Sociological Review*, **11** (2), 1963, pp. 241–6.

21. There has been a great deal of discussion in the relevant professional circles concerning whether or not a 'middle-class takeover' has occurred in villages like Ringmer. This book does not add to the discussion since I find the terminology scientifically meaningless (see the second argument of Chapter 14).

22. See note 19.

23. See R. E. Pahl, Class and Community in English Commuter Villages, *Sociologia Ruralis*, **5** (1), 1965, pp. 5–23.

24. See the periodically published Housing Statistics, H.M.S.O.

25. See note 19.

26. See R. E. Pahl. Is the Mobile Society a Myth?, *New Society*, 11th January 1968.

27. 1961 Census, Migration, Table 4.

28. See Radford (note 7), p. 28.

29. See Hants C.C. (note 2), p. 24, and Suffolk R.C.C. (note 5), p. 27.

30. See W. Watson, Social Mobility and Social Class in Industrial Communities, in M. Gluckman (ed.), *Closed Minds and Open Systems*, Oliver and Boyd, 1964.

Chapter 8

1. See *Research Study 9*, Royal Commission on Local Government in England, H.M.S.O., 1969.

2. See Crichton (note 6 of Chapter 7), Chapter 7.

3. See note 1, p. 146.

4. The original thesis propounded in E. Bott, *Family and Social Network*, Tavistock, 1957, has been worked over by a host of subsequent researchers.

5. See the useful review in W. H. Michelson, *Man and his Urban Environment*, Addison-Wesley, 1970, Chapter 8, and especially the work by Gans and by Festinger *et al.* referred to in that chapter.

6. See E. Still, The Middle Class Takes Over, *New Society*, 7th April 1966.

7. See R. E. Pahl, *Whose City?*, (note 1 of Chapter 7), p. 92.

Chapter 9

1. See Suffolk R.C.C. (note 5 of Chapter 7), p. 44.

2. From 1971 Ringmer Survey.

3. Survey carried out in the autumn of 1971 by students of the Brighton Polytechnic.

4. See Suffolk R.C.C. (note 5 of Chapter 7), pp. 36–7.

5. See Hants C.C. (note 2 of Chapter 7), p. 27.

6. See, for example, G. Popplestone, Conflict and Mediating Roles in Expanding Settlements, *Sociological Review*, **15** (3), 1967, pp. 339–55. Popplestone saw his 'established newcomers' as mediators. In Ringmer they appear to be the group most ready to see social divisions and tensions.

7. See Suffolk R.C.C. (note 5 of Chapter 7), p. 41.

Chapter 10

1. Derek Denyer, to whom all thanks for help and co-operation at all stages of the children's project.
2. For an interesting study of children's play facilities and activities in a variety of urban contexts, see A. Holme and P. Massie, *Children's Play: A Study of Needs and Opportunities*, Michael Joseph, 1970.
3. See, for example, Buchanan (note 28 of Chapter 1).
4. See, for example, the designs for the South Hampshire City, Runcorn, Cumbernauld and Hook (which was never built).

Chapter 11

1. C. Bell and H. Newby, *Community Studies*, Allen and Unwin, 1971, p. 27.
2. G. A. Hillery, Definitions of Community: Areas of Agreement, *Rural Sociology*, **20**, 1955.
3. M. Stacey, The Myth of Community Studies, *British Journal of Sociology*, **20**, 1969, pp. 134–47.
4. See Pahl (note 4 of Chapter 4), Chapter 7.
5. See note 1.
6. In relation to both these observations, see the Pahl paper on 'Dormersdell' (note 23 of Chapter 7) and J. Connell, Green Belt County, *New Society*, 25th February 1971.
7. See R. M. MacIver and C. H. Page, *Society: an Introductory Analysis*, Macmillan, 1961, p. 9.
8. See note 2.
9. R. Frankenberg, *Communities in Britain*, Pelican, 1966, p. 16.
10. See note 4, p. 101.
11. Figure given by a professional social security worker.
12. J. Bensman and A. J. Vidich, *Small Town in Mass Society*, Princeton, 1968.
13. R. Warren, *The Community in America*, Rand, 1963.
14. M. Stein, *The Eclipse of Community*, Harper Row, 1964.
15. See a recent edition of his work, *Community and Society*, Harper Torchbook, 1957.

Chapter 12

1. See J. C. Mitchell (ed.), *Social Networks in Urban Situations*, Manchester U.P., 1969, for a useful general discussion and a number of empirical studies.
2. See Pahl (note 4 of Chapter 4), p. 104.
3. See any number of mathematical textbooks, for example, F. Harary *et al.*, *Structural Models: An Introduction to the Theory of Directed Graphs*, Wiley, 1965.
4. J. A. Barnes, Class and Community in a Norwegian Island Parish, *Human Relations*, **7**, 1954, pp. 39–58.
5. J. A. Barnes, Graph Theory and Social Networks: a technical comment on connectedness and connectivity, *Sociology*, **3**, 1969, pp. 215–32.

6. E. Bott, *Family and Social Network*, Tavistock, 1957.
7. J. R. Udry and M. Hall, Marital Role Segregation and Social Networks in Middle-Class, Middle-Aged Couples, *Journal of Marriage and the Family*, **27**, 1965, pp. 392–5.
8. C. Turner, Conjugal Roles and Social Networks: A Re-examination of a Hypothesis, *Human Relations*, **20**, 1967, pp. 121–30.
9. W. L. Garrison, Connectivity of the Interstate Highway System, *Regional Science Association Papers and Proceedings*, **6**, 1960, pp. 121–37.
10. K. J. Kansky, *Structure of Transport Networks*, University of Chicago, Department of Geography, Research Papers, **84**, 1963.
11. See note 1.
12. P. Haggett and R. J. Chorley, *Network Analysis in Geography*, Arnold, 1969.
13. F. R. Pitts, A Graph Theoretic Approach to Historical Geography, *Professional Geographer*, **17**, 1965, pp. 15–20.
14. See note 5.
15. Made frequently in conversations with long-standing residents.
16. The symbol Σ denotes 'the sum of'; in this case the sum of all the distances from i to each of the n distant points.
17. A Southall, An Operational Theory of Role, *Human Relations*, **12**, 1959, pp. 17–34.
18. See, for example, W. M. Williams, *A West Country Village, Ashworthy*, Routledge, 1963.
19. See various papers by M. Gluckman referred to in Mitchell (see note 1).
20. See the discussion in R. Frankenberg, *Communities in Britain*, Pelican, 1966, Chapter 9.
21. See note 9.
22. See H. J. Gans, *The Urban Villagers*, Free Press of Glencoe, 1962.
23. M. Young and P. Willmott, *Family and Kinship in East London*, Routledge, 1957.
24. See Mitchell (note 1), p. 24.
25. See Frankenberg (note 20), p. 290.
26. For a fuller characterisation of 'rural' and 'urban' in less specifically network terms, see Frankenberg (note 20), pp. 286–92.

Chapter 13

1. See Ashworth (note 32 of Chapter 1).
2. R. J. Green, *Country Planning: the Future of the Rural Regions*, Manchester U.P., 1971.
3. See Pahl (note 1 of Chapter 7), p. 155.
4. See, for example, J. Tetlow and A. Goss, *Homes, Towns and Traffic*, Faber, 1965, Chapter 5.
5. *People and Planning*, H.M.S.O., 1969.
6. See note 3, p. 150.
7. *ibid.*, p. 166 (chapter by E. Craven).
8. *ibid.*, p. 165.

9. *ibid.*, p. 167.

10. *ibid.*, p. 168.

11. *ibid.*, p. 173, Table 1.

12. *ibid.*, p. 175, Table 2.

13. *ibid.*, p. 176.

14. See *Private Housing in London*, a study by Shankland Cox and Associates produced for Wates Housing Division.

15. Information given by a director of the company.

16. See M. E. H. Smith, *A Guide to Housing*, Housing Centre Trust, 1971, p. 18. Much of the information in the next few paragraphs is gained from this very useful source.

17. *ibid.*, p. 13.

18. M.H.L.G., *Homes for Today and Tomorrow*, H.M.S.O., 1961.

19. See note 16, p. 49.

20. *ibid.*, p. 50.

21. *ibid.*, p. 21.

22. *ibid.*, p. 61.

23. Information given by an official of the council.

24. See M.H.L.G., *Council Housing, Purposes, Procedures and Priorities*, H.M.S.O., 1969.

25. It was discussed as long ago as 1942 in the *Final Report of the Expert Committee on Compensation and Betterment*, H.M.S.O. (Cmd. 6386).

26. See Smith (note 16), p. 47.

27. K. Coates and R. Silburn, *Poverty: the Forgotten Englishmen*, Penguin, 1970.

28. See J. Connell, Green Belt County, *New Society*, 25th February 1971.

29. A recent survey of house purchasers' preferences, *New Housing in South East England*, Housing Research Foundation, 1970, found that the majority of new purchasers disliked open-plan arrangements, see p. 20.

30. L. S. Jay *et al.* (see note 9 of Chapter 7).

31. It is very difficult to demonstrate relationships between residential design and social pathologies. See W. Michelson, *Man and His Urban Environment*, Addison-Wesley, 1970, Chapter 7.

32. This opinion was given by a professionally qualified botanist consulted by the Ringmer Evening W.I.

33. See *Sussex Express* and *County Herald*, 21st December 1972.

34. R. J. Green (see note 2), p. 56.

35. See L. S. Jay *et al.* (note 9 of Chapter 7).

36. A useful review of the very sparse literature is contained in J. and R. Darke, *Health and Environment in High Flats*, Centre for Environmental Studies, 1970. See also A. E. Martin, Environment, Housing and Health, *Urban Studies*, 4, 1967, pp. 1–21.

37. See note 14.

38. Michael Wates; opinion given in a conversation.

39. *Town and Country Planning*, Cmnd. 3333, H.M.S.O., 1967, p. 1.

40. See Pahl (note 1 of Chapter 7), p. 151.

41. *ibid.*, p. 148.

42. There has been some recent discussion of private/public co-operation in new development, see Department of the Environment, *Report of the Working Party on Local Authority/Private Enterprise Partnership Schemes*, H.M.S.O., 1972.

43. See Department of the Environment, *The Estate Outside the Dwelling*, H.M.S.O., 1972, for some useful findings and a short bibliography.

Chapter 14

1. See, for example, the discussion of Scandinavian systems in C. Buchanan and Partners, *The Prospect for Housing*, Nationwide Building Society, 1971, pp. 55–61. Also *Der Spiegel*, 3rd February 1969, for a review of housing in Germany.

2. See Chapter 13 for a brief review of thinking on the 'betterment' levy idea.

3. P. Collison, *The Cutteslowe Wall*, Faber, 1963.

4. See Pahl, *Whose City?* (note 1 of Chapter 7), p. 115.

5. See H. J. Gans, *People and Plans*, Pelican, 1972 (Chapter 9), for a useful discussion on the question of social homogeneity or heterogeneity in residential areas. Various other essays in this book are of clear relevance to Parts III and IV of the present work. The relationship between, on the one hand, the degree to which people of widely differing socio-economic status are intermixed in residential areas and, on the other, the level of local conflict is simply not known with any certainty. There is often short-term conflict (see note 3 above). This may conceivably work to reduce the eventual effects of more fundamental conflicts based on the structural inequalities in society. The subject is much too complex to pursue here. See R. Dahrendorf, *Class and Class Conflict in Industrial Society*, Routledge, 1959, for a useful review of the views of, especially, Marx and Talcott Parsons on the relationship between conflict and social change.

6. See K. Coates and R. Silburn (note 27 of Chapter 13).

7. *ibid.*, p. 79.

8. A. Schorr, The Non-Culture of Poverty, *American Journal of Orthopsychiatry*, 34, October 1964.

9. J. W. B. Douglas, *The Home and the School*, Panther edition, 1969, p. 67.

10. T. B. Bottomore, *Classes in Modern Society*, Allen and Unwin, 1965.

11. See, for example, the very superficial comments on 'social change' in *The Times* leader of 9th December 1972.

12. K. Marx, *Capital*, Vol. III (1864–5), p. 1031.

13. See Bottomore (note 10), p. 18.

14. This has been a research issue in sociology during the last two decades. See the discussion in E. O. Laumann, *Prestige and Association in an Urban Community*, Bobbs-Merrill, 1966, Chapter 7. See also G. Lenski, Status Crystallisation: A Non-vertical Dimension of Social Status, *American Sociological Review*, 19, 1954, pp. 405–13; W. F. Kenkel, The Relationship Between Status Consistency and Politico-economic Activities, *ibid.*, 21, 1956, pp. 365–8 (which uses housing as a variable); D. J. Treiman, Status Discrepancy and Prejudice, *American Journal of Sociology*, 71, 1965–6, pp. 651–64; and various other papers.

15. See successive issues of the General Register Office's *Classification of Occupations*, H.M.S.O.

16. Housing Research Foundation, *Home Ownership in England and Wales*, p. 47.

17. *ibid.*, Part II.

18. B. Abel-Smith and P. Townsend, *The Poor and The Poorest*, Bell, 1965.

19. *ibid.*, Chapter 5.

20. See Titmuss (note 16 of Chapter 5), Chapter 8.

21. *ibid.*, p. 199.

22. See Bottomore (note 10), p. 37.

23. *A National Minimum Wage*, H.M.S.O., 1969.

24. Identified by members of the Child Poverty Action Group, among others.

25. See D. Jackson *et al.*, *Do Trade Unions Cause Inflation?*, Cambridge U.P., 1972.

26. The national rate of appreciation is naturally less striking, about 75% over the six years. See various issues of *Building Society Affairs*.

27. See J. Willis, *The Social Consequences of House Price Inflation*, Shelter (mimeographed), 1972, Exhibit I.

28. *ibid.*

29. R. Harrington, *Some Fundamental Economics of the Housing Problem*, Shelter (mimeographed), 1972, p. 5.

30. B. A. Corry, *Economists and the Housing Problem*, Shelter (mimeographed), 1972, p. 5.

31. *ibid.*, p. 6.

32. See Willis (note 27), Exhibit II.

33. P. Pearson and A. Henney, *Home Improvement–People or Profit?*, Shelter Paper 4, 1972.

34. See note 16, Part II (by R. L. Wishlade).

35. Information from a council official.

36. Information from G. Rump, the union's area organiser.

37. Information from a local councillor.

38. Figures from Buchanan (see note 1), p. 27.

39. *ibid.*, p. 27.

40. Quotations taken from *Reprieve for Slums*, Shelter, 1972.

41. *Face the Facts*, Shelter (undated).

42. A situation carefully documented in the *Grief Report*, Shelter, 1972.

43. See note 41, p. 3.

44. See Smith (note 16 of Chapter 13), p. 58.

45. E. G. Howes, *Housing in Britain, France and Western Germany*, P.E.P., **31**, 490, Planning, 1965, p. 264.

46. J. Hutton, *Building Society Finance in the 1970s*, Shelter, 1972, p. 12.

47. *ibid.*, p. 13.

48. See note 1, p. 27.

49. See Bruce (note 17 of Chapter 3), p. 156.

50. See M. Wicks, *Rented Housing and Public Ownership*, Fabian Society, 1973.

51. D. Jay, *Financial Times*, 12th September 1972.

52. *The Guardian*, 15th December 1972.

Epilogue

1. From a letter written to recipients by a trustee of the Hays Charity, dated 5th February 1958.

Index

238

Date Due
